# Transforming
# the Urban University

THE CITY IN THE TWENTY-FIRST CENTURY

Eugenie L. Birch and Susan M. Wachter, Series Editors

A complete list of books in the series
is available from the publisher.

# Transforming
# the Urban University

## Northeastern,
## 1996–2006

Richard M. Freeland

UNIVERSITY OF PENNSYLVANIA PRESS

PHILADELPHIA

Published by University of Pennsylvania Press
Philadelphia, Pennsylvania 19104-4112
www.upenn.edu/pennpress

Printed in the United States of America
on acid-free paper
1  3  5  7  9  10  8  6  4  2

*Library of Congress Control Number:* 2018050998
ISBN 978-0-8122-5121-0

*For Elsa Maria Nuñez, my wife and my partner in this work,*
*and for the people of Northeastern University between 1996 and 2006*

A University which will adapt itself to urban influence, which will undertake to serve as an expression of urban civilization, and which is compelled to meet the demands of an urban environment will in the end become something essentially different from a university located in a village or small city. It will gradually take on new characteristics both outward and inward, and it will ultimately form a new type of university.

—William Rainey Harper

# CONTENTS

This is a book about Northeastern University in Boston, Massachusetts. It is also about urban universities generally, especially private ones, a distinctive and socially valuable type of academic institution of which Northeastern has long been a leading example. In addition, this book is about the competitive context for national universities in the United States at the turn of the twenty-first century and how the imperatives of that context, especially pressures to adopt the priorities of the modern research university, devalued long-standing and still useful characteristics of urban institutions. The book tells the story of Northeastern's effort to develop an alternative to the conventional model of the modern research university that would allow the school to flourish while remaining true to its urban character. Finally, this is a personal story, an account of what my colleagues and I at Northeastern were attempting to accomplish during the years that I served as the institution's president, from 1996 to 2006.

*   *   *

My love affair with urban universities long preceded my election to the Northeastern presidency and had deep roots in my personal experience as well as in the social and political history of my generation of Americans. As a graduate student in Philadelphia and New York in the mid-1960s, and in my youthful travels in Europe, I had come to see metropolitan centers as the most impressive social and physical expressions of a modern society. But these were also years when the chronic challenges of urban America erupted in crisis, as, each summer, city after city experienced racially charged and violently destructive riots. Indeed, as I worked on my doctoral dissertation in a small apartment on the Upper West Side of Manhattan, one such episode broke out on the street below, triggered by the murder of Martin Luther King Jr. For young Americans of that era the problems of our nation's cities expressed with particular urgency the long-frustrated yearnings of Black people for social justice as well as the distressing persistence of poverty in the midst of affluence. More broadly, the "crisis of the cities" reflected the failure of the United States to fulfill its promises to all our citizens even as we trumpeted the superiority of capitalism and democracy at the height of the Cold War. Inspired, like many young people, by President Kennedy's call to public service, I decided my focus after finishing my education would be the issues facing urban America.

The Model Cities Program of Trenton, New Jersey, provided the vehicle for my aspirations. Model Cities was one of several federal initiatives of the late 1960s that addressed the struggles of inner-city neighborhoods, and Trenton, the capital of my home state, was experiencing the slow decline characteristic of many old industrial centers in an age of suburbanization. As one of several program developers in the Trenton project, I worked with residents from the mostly Black "model neighborhood" to design new approaches to education, health care, economic development, social services, housing, and public safety. The experience provided an overview of the institutional structures available to address urban problems—schools, hospitals, city agencies, nonprofit organizations, philanthropies—and led me to conclude that urban universities— with their capacity to educate low-income residents and to deploy faculty expertise and institutional resources to help their host cities—offered the most promising setting for my work. In such an institution I could stay connected with the world of scholarship and learning I had come to love while working on social challenges I felt called to address. With my pathway now clear, I moved to Boston, where my family had roots and where state government was creating a new urban campus of the University of Massachusetts, to become known as UMass Boston.

The president of UMass in those days was Robert C. Wood, only recently appointed. Wood had been Undersecretary of Housing and Urban Development in the Johnson administration and was a founding champion of Model Cities. He accepted my appeal to join his young administration and assigned me to the chancellor of the Boston campus, a charismatic former Peace Corps official named Francis Broderick, to help shape the new school's relationship to the city and metropolitan region. The job was a perfect fit, and I immersed myself in it joyously, convinced I was on the front lines of the battle for social justice and national progress. I remained at UMass Boston for twenty-two rewarding years, first as a junior staffer, then as Director of Educational Planning, then as founding Dean of the College of Professional Studies, and finally as Dean of Arts and Sciences. When I left in 1992 to become Vice Chancellor for Academic Affairs at the City University of New York (CUNY), I was more convinced than ever that urban universities held the key to addressing the most urgent domestic issues our country faced.

But Boston, with its center of gravity in higher education and its origins in the aspirational culture of the founding Puritans, had become my emotional home. When, four years after I moved to New York, the Northeastern presidency became vacant, it seemed the perfect next step. I was well acquainted with the school through years of working in the same city and from a short stint there as a history instructor right after graduate school. I had also studied Northeastern's history while writing a book on the post–World War II development of universities in Massachusetts, published in 1992 as *Academia's Golden Age*. All of this had left me with a deep admiration for the University's long history of service to the Boston metropolitan region, combined with an awareness of the challenges it faced as a private institution competing with the state's growing public system, represented most notably by my former employer. I did not realize until after I assumed my presidential duties, however, how deeply the growth of public higher education had eroded Northeastern's local role as an educational destination for young people from modest backgrounds or the extent to which the University was struggling with issues that faced private schools with similar missions in many other cities. What I saw in the Northeastern presidency in the mid-1990s was an opportunity to advance the high academic values of a private university while also addressing the chronic challenges of urban America. I could not imagine a more inspiring administrative assignment. As I have worked on this volume, twenty years after coming to Northeastern, I still can't.

\*   \*   \*

I am indebted to many individuals who assisted me in this project, beginning, of course, with the Trustees who elected me to be Northeastern's sixth president, and especially to the two men who chaired the Board during my years, George Matthews and Neal Finnegan. The Trustees with whom I worked were a highly engaged group of men and women, and many of them gave generously of their "time and treasure" to guide and improve the school. At the end of my presidency, the Board encouraged me to write this account and provided support to help me begin. I am also indebted to the faculty and staff who served with me, including those who held positions of responsibility in campus governance and in the academic and administrative departments. Collectively these individuals constituted the most loyal, engaged, and constructive institutional community with which I worked during my forty-five years in academic administration. I was honored to be their president and thankful for their help. I am especially grateful to the women and men I refer to in these pages as my "leadership team." These were the senior members of my administration, who oversaw most of the work reviewed in this volume; they were largely responsible for the progress of Northeastern during my presidential years. I hope this book appropriately recognizes their talents, their dedication, and their contributions to the university we all loved.

Many current and former members of the Northeastern community assisted me in preparing this account either by reviewing sections in draft form or by responding to my questions about specific episodes. Included in this group are Linda Allen, Michael Baer, Melvin Bernstein, Barry Bluestone, Robert Cunningham, Anthony Erwin, Anna Fravel, Lawrence Finkelstein, Neal Finnegan, Seamus Harreys, David Hall, Ronald Hedlund, Daryl Hellman, Barry Karger, Thomas Keady, Brian Kenny, Edward Klotzbier, William Kneeland, Vincent Lembo, Robert Lowndes, Philomena Mantella, Nancy May, Stephen McKnight, Richard Meyer, Steven Morrison, Kay Onan, Anthony Penna, Dennis Piccard, Richard Porter, Eugene Reppucci, Jane Scarborough, Sam Solomon, Allen Soyster, Denis Sullivan, and Ronne Patrick Turner. I also express gratitude to a number of non-Northeastern colleagues and friends who provided assistance along the way. These include Scott Bass, Steven Diner, Paul Lingenfelter, Daniel Meyer, William Rawn, Virginia Sapiro, Andy Snider, and John Thelin.

Several individuals deserve special mention for the extensive help they rendered. Mark Putnam repeatedly responded with care to questions about the accuracy of my memory and the substantive quality of my drafts. Six colleagues read the entire manuscript and offered helpful comments: Philip Altbach, Lawrence Bacow, Nancy Budwig, Patricia Crosson, William Fowler, and Allen Guttmann. I am particularly indebted to Dr. Crosson, who provided painstaking comments on every chapter as the writing progressed and then reread them all when the first draft was completed; she played a large role in convincing me that the book could have value for the higher education community beyond Northeastern. I owe special thanks to Michelle Romero of the Northeastern University Archives, who responded promptly and professionally to my requests to find key documents or to check important facts. My two research assistants, Michaela Thompson and

Colleen McCormack, provided valuable assistance in mining the University's archival record during the early stages of the project. The staff at the University of Pennsylvania Press, especially Editor-in-Chief Peter Agree and the two editors of this series, Eugenie Birch and Susan Wachter, have been terrific to work with throughout the publication process. David Luljak, my indexer, and Sarah Mealey, my proofreader, did excellent work. Finally, I wish to thank my successor, Dr. Joseph Aoun, for granting me the time and support needed to bring this project to completion.

# Introduction

The term "urban university" has a relatively short and confused history in the annals of American higher education. The epigraph from William Rainey Harper, the founding president of the University of Chicago, is from a 1902 speech titled "The Urban University" and probably represents one of the first public uses of this phrase, especially as meaning something more than a university located in a city. In 1914 the term was adopted by a new Association of Urban Universities (AUU), which was open to all city-based institutions that shared a commitment to breaking free of a "slavish subservience to [academic] tradition" and to shaping the "content and methods" of their programs "in the light of modern civilization," which, in the early twentieth century, meant a civilization centered in cities. The new association grew rapidly and was remarkably eclectic. By 1930 its membership included a fascinating potpourri of thirty-nine colleges and universities, including elite private schools like Harvard University, the University of Pennsylvania (Penn), the University of Chicago, and Johns Hopkins University; the municipal universities of Akron, Toledo and Louisville, and the City College of New York (CCNY); the city-based state universities of Washington, Minnesota, and Ohio; and a range of other private institutions, large and small, secular and sectarian, Protestant and Catholic. The organization continued to grow as the century wore on and numbered over eighty schools by the time Northeastern joined in 1959.

The AUU sponsored important work during its early years in identifying the special possibilities of city-based higher education, including the first systematic study of how to incorporate off-campus practical experience into the curriculum. Unfortunately, however, the organization's history over the course of the twentieth century was more notable for conflicts about what it meant to be an urban university than for identifying the unique educational and scholarly opportunities offered by cities. The years following World War II were particularly problematic. Beginning in the late 1940s, the nation's urban centers, especially those in the Northeast and Midwest, began a prolonged downward spiral driven by white flight to the suburbs, the outmigration of industry to lower-cost locations, and the arrival of African Americans from the segregated South, as well as Hispanics from Puerto Rico and Mexico. By the 1960s, for many Americans, the term "urban" was associated with impoverished Black and Hispanic enclaves; tension between established white neighborhoods and growing communities of color; high rates of crime; boarded-up storefronts; and deteriorating physical infrastructure. In this context there developed a gap between the kinds of educational services most needed by cities and the academic activities most valued by institutions of higher education.[1]

The most obvious disconnect between cities and their universities involved enrollment policy, which represents the primary way an academic institution relates to its service community. Educating the large numbers of young people growing up in low-income urban communities and attending struggling city high schools was a vital social mission; yet, in orienting its admissions policy toward such students, a city-based university rendered itself marginal in an industry where status derived from selectivity, while also making itself dependent on communities in which college attendance was low, capacity to afford tuition was limited, and philanthropic prospects were slim. Similarly, if a city-based university placed a priority on educational programs that equipped students for entry-level jobs in a modern economy—offerings like business, engineering, nursing, and education, which were helpful to local employers and attractive to young people from modest backgrounds—it associated itself with practical educational traditions that mainstream academia considered less rigorous and sophisticated than the arts and sciences. The tension between the needs of cities and the values of higher education was apparent also with respect to the scholarly work of faculties. Struggling city governments, as well as urban communities and the nonprofit organizations and philanthropies that served them, stood to benefit from the insights of scholars focused on issues such as city management, public health, transportation, juvenile delinquency, poverty, and urban education, but academic work in these realms stood well down in academia's prestige hierarchy from research in the basic academic disciplines.

The widening divide between the needs of cities and the ambitions of academia in the 1950s and 1960s produced much confusion and a range of responses among the institutions that, half a century earlier, had come together to form the AAU. At one end of the spectrum were elite schools like Columbia, Penn, Chicago, and Johns Hopkins that, in the post–World War II decades, were increasingly defining their reach as national and international. For these schools identifying closely with their host cities no longer made sense. Indeed their urban settings now represented more a threat than an opportunity, and all four participated in urban-renewal programs during these years focused on improving adjacent neighborhoods by removing low-income and minority residents, practices that generated much resentment and stored up ill will for the future.

Dismay about urban decline was by no means limited to top-tier universities. Even more modestly ranked schools for which urban service was traditionally a central mission, places such as Boston University (BU), New York University (NYU), and the University of Pittsburgh (Pitt), began in the 1950s and 1960s to deemphasize programs for local commuters by shifting admissions efforts toward suburban and regional markets and constructing residential facilities. As alarm about conditions in the nation's cities intensified with the riots of the 1960s, however, leaders at some of these institutions—BU and NYU were prime examples—made concerted efforts to refocus on urban issues, typically through organized research activities rather than through admissions policies, but such initiatives were combined with deep uncertainty about how much a university could or should do to reverse the deterioration of its host city.

At the other end of the spectrum from the elite private schools among AUU members were the municipal universities like CCNY, Louisville, and the two Ohio institutions, along with a new cluster of state-supported urban universities that came into being after World War II specifically to serve inner-city and metropolitan communities, a group that included the University of Wisconsin-Milwaukee, the University of Illinois at Chicago Circle, and the new Boston campus of the University of Massachusetts. These schools were by definition committed to enrolling large numbers of students from their host cities, but their patterns of development often reflected the same ambivalence about being an "urban" university found at more established schools. A 1977 study for the Ford Foundation reported that faculty at UW-Milwaukee actively embraced scholarship focused on urban needs while faculty at UI-Chicago Circle were disdainful of such work. The founding faculty of UMass Boston decided against offering any professional degrees for undergraduates and planned an institution focused at the baccalaureate level exclusively on the arts and sciences.[2]

The varying responses to the problems of their surrounding communities among city-based universities during the post–World War II decades produced a long-running debate within the AUU about the nature of urban higher education and, indeed, whether the term "urban university" had any continuing utility. The most thoughtful voices in this discussion argued that the definition of an urban university should not hinge on admissions policies or programmatic characteristics but rather should reflect philosophical orientation: Did an institution think of itself as simply "in" a city as a matter of location or was it truly "of" its city, committed to taking advantage of the special educational and scholarly opportunities of its setting while also enhancing that community's well-being? Some voices, however, insisted that, whatever else it meant, a true urban university should enroll large numbers of local students. By the 1970s, notwithstanding the continuing debate, it was clear as a practical matter that the term "urban university" had been fatally devalued by the troubles of the nation's cities and had come to mean a university that was primarily local in its interests and focused on students from its host city. These were not characteristics that most members of the AUU were prepared to embrace. The organization voted itself out of existence in 1977.[3]

*   *   *

Northeastern, much like the urban publics, and unlike many of its private urban peers, continued steadfastly to embrace its long-established, city-oriented character during the 1960s, 1970s, and 1980s, emphasizing its commitment to Boston and basing its financial health on enrolling large numbers of commuting students from the city and its urban suburbs. By the time I became the institution's president in 1996, however, demographic and competitive realities had made it clear to the University's leaders that the school's long-standing pattern of operations was no longer viable. For a variety of reasons, it was evident that Northeastern's future depended on redefining itself as far more regional and national in reach, far more selective in admissions, and far more demanding and ambitious in its academic work. But there was also a desire, deeply embedded in the culture of the institution and compelling to me personally, to maintain the school's tradition of engagement with the city. It became my job as president, working with the Trustees, my administrative team, and the campus community, to accomplish this transition. The story of how Northeastern transformed itself into a top-tier national university between 1996 and 2006, and what this change meant for its urban character, is the focus of this book.

    As we began our work my team and I had to address a number of fundamental questions, some of which paralleled the issues that challenged other city-based universities, especially private ones, during the latter years of the twentieth century. Two of these questions related specifically to our urban character: Which of the educational, research, and service practices that linked us closely to Boston continued to make sense and which did not? And, were there new ways to leverage the special educational and scholarly opportunities of our location and to contribute to the well-being of our city that were more compatible with our new academic aspirations? Underneath these general issues were a number of more focused questions, some of which involved us in academic debates that ranged far beyond the world of urban higher education: Was the University's long-standing emphasis on practical programs for undergraduates compatible with the new version of Northeastern we needed to create? Equally important, where did the University's signature program of cooperative education (co-op), a pattern of study that alternated periods of full-time classroom work and full-time paid employment, fit into the new equation? Should we, in fact, shift our focus in the direction of the liberal arts and sciences in order to compete more effectively with traditional schools? Should we also move away from our long-standing emphasis on undergraduate teaching and learning and invest more heavily in the advanced academic functions of graduate education and research, the activities most associated with quality among leading mainstream institutions?

Reflecting the spirit of William Rainey Harper, Northeastern had historically taken pride in basing its priorities on social needs and the dictates of its particular mission rather than on conventional academic ideas or notions of status, and my team and I sought to emulate this perspective as we shaped the new Northeastern. We were also much taken with the advice of one of the consultants with whom we worked in the early days, Robert Zemsky, who counseled that we needed to be not only "mission driven" but also "market smart." My personal goal became to reposition the University as the academically competitive, highly regarded national institution it needed to be while also maintaining its urban character. To this end my team and I embraced a simple formula that framed much of our work during the ten years of my presidency: to seek excellence as a "national research university that is student centered, practice oriented and urban." Members of the campus community soon began referring to this phrase as the "Mantra"; it committed us to being distinctive among national research universities in three ways that ran counter to conventional thinking about how to enhance the stature of an academic institution.

*   *   *

The decision to emphasize Northeastern's character as "student-centered" reflected the conviction that we needed to focus initially on improving our undergraduate programs; assigning secondary priority to improving our research profile; and delaying, though not abandoning, further development in graduate education. In committing ourselves to this course we challenged one of the most widely accepted premises in American higher education in the late twentieth century, not just among urban institutions but among universities of all kinds: that the most effective way for a university to enhance its reputation was to recruit well-known scholars and invest in the advanced academic functions. Our thinking on this matter was informed by the reality that, for as far into the future as we Jcould see, undergraduate tuition was going to be our primary source of revenue. That fact, we felt, imposed an obligation, part practical, part moral, to make sure the undergraduate experience we offered was truly excellent in all its dimensions. In essence, we gambled that we could elevate the University's standing sufficiently to ensure its long-term health by pursuing quality in baccalaureate-level studies. The fact that we succeeded in this effort, transforming Northeastern in ten years into a selective regional and increasingly national university enrolling well-prepared students and boasting a dramatically improved graduation rate, was the proudest achievement of my presidency.

Closely related to our decision to prioritize undergraduate education was our determination to maintain the University's long-standing emphasis on practice through career-oriented programs and cooperative education, two educational patterns closely connected with our urban history. Here, once again, we departed from the conventional wisdom within mainstream higher education, which held that it was strength in the arts and sciences, not in fields like business, engineering, and health sciences, that conferred status, and that co-op, as well as other forms of experiential education, had little or nothing to contribute to the highest form of college-level learning. During my years at urban schools like UMass Boston and CUNY, I had come to doubt the wisdom of both these attitudes.

I was particularly critical of the long-standing tension between champions of liberal education and advocates of professional or occupational studies that had characterized American higher education since the nineteenth century; I believed these attitudes were grounded more in prejudice than reason and that they did a disservice to students and to the country by forcing young people to choose one or the other educational pattern when many, especially those who attended urban schools, would be better served by a combination of the two. I also regarded cooperative education as a powerful but long-neglected educational idea and sensed a trend among well-prepared graduates of top high schools to welcome opportunities to combine classroom study with off-campus, practical experiences during their college years. This attitude—strikingly different from the way my own generation had thought about college—led me to believe that Northeastern's long history of leadership in cooperative education might allow us to catch a wave of change among young people if we could purge co-op of its blue-collar image as a form of financial aid for students unable to afford a traditional undergraduate experience and rebrand it as a powerful enhancement to college-level learning.

The effort to create a distinctive form of undergraduate study based on a reconfiguration of Northeastern's historic strengths became the single most sustained effort of my presidency. We labeled what we were trying to design "practice-oriented education" (or POE, as members of the campus community often called this concept) and elevated Northeastern's practice-oriented character to a place of special prominence among the five elements of our guiding Mantra. The work involved three components that had to be pursued concurrently: first, investing heavily in strengthening our professional majors; second, building our programs in the arts and sciences as equal partners with professional studies in the undergraduate curriculum and emphasizing links between basic and practical disciplines; third, undertaking a complete makeover of our co-op program. Our goal was to foster a three-dimensional learning experience that linked professional studies, the arts and sciences, and cooperative education within programs of study in which each component built on and reinforced the other two. By 2006 we had made significant progress in all three arenas and most students were experiencing some form of this tripartite approach to learning. I regard our effort to provide students with this form of education at a high level of quality as one of the most important contributors to our success in repositioning Northeastern so dramatically in the undergraduate admissions markets.

We also maintained the emphasis on Northeastern's practice-oriented traditions in graduate education and research. Toward the later years of my presidency, after our work on the undergraduate program had gained traction, we began to invest in research activities and doctoral programs where we thought we could achieve genuine excellence, which mostly involved professional and applied fields. In this context, as with our decision to maintain Northeastern's traditional emphasis on undergraduate education of a practical nature, we were working against the tendency of mainstream higher education, which regarded advanced work in the basic disciplines as the surest guarantors of academic status. Our focus was on areas of social or economic

importance to the Boston region and typically to the country as well. A
large part of our growth in graduate education came through our adult-and
continuing-education college, a part of Northeastern that was central to our
history as an urban university but where enrollments were falling in the
early 1990s; this unit was completely transformed under inspired leadership
into an educational and financial powerhouse offering professional master's
degrees in conjunction with our regular academic colleges and departments.

Our decision to highlight Northeastern's urban character was another
feature of our repositioning strategy that challenged conventional academic
wisdom. The negative associations with the term "urban" that had caused
the AUU to fall apart in 1977 remained powerful within American culture
in the 1990s. There were strong indications, however, that young people of
the type we hoped to attract increasingly favored city-based settings for their
college experiences—another significant departure from the thinking of my
own generation. We therefore believed, especially given Boston's reputation
as a college town, that by emphasizing our engagement with the city, and
opportunities for our students to participate in urban life, we could catch this
wave, just as we hoped to catch the wave of student interest in combining
collegiate studies with off-campus experiences. These two patterns were, of
course, closely related, since urban settings offered far more opportunities for
work in the community than did small towns and pastoral landscapes.

Even as we hoped to capitalize on the positive features of our urban
location, however, we understood that we needed to overcome the problematic associations with this word, especially the idea that an urban university
was a locally oriented school that emphasized access rather than selectivity
in admissions and that had limited academic ambitions. The role of providing an affordable college experience to large numbers of young people from
modest backgrounds in the Boston area had been taken over by UMass Boston, which would always be able to provide a less expensive college education than a private, tuition-dependent school like Northeastern. The growth
of UMass Boston was, in fact, a primary reason for Northeastern's decision,
during the difficult years before I was elected to the presidency, that it had to
change course. My years of work at that school had also made me aware that
it possessed an outstanding faculty and offered excellent undergraduate programs, which made it an especially challenging competitor for Northeastern
in attracting the kinds of students we had traditionally enrolled.

Northeastern needed to be a new kind of urban university, one that was
cosmopolitan rather than local, selective rather than accessible, residential

rather than commuter, and associated with high academic standards. Changing Northeastern in these ways became the central purpose of our repositioning effort. But my team and I thought we could still be "of" Boston and not just "in" it, and we regarded the view that only a university oriented toward local students could properly be considered "urban" was overly narrow. Thus, though Northeastern could no longer focus admissions primarily on Boston-area students, we could still make special efforts to recruit, enroll, and support promising graduates of the Boston Public Schools as well as urban students from other cities. We could also partner with Boston's elementary and secondary schools in a host of other ways. In addition, we could make urban-oriented research a priority as we built our scholarly capacity, and we could work with city and state officials to address urban issues. Finally, we could develop our facilities and use our financial resources in ways that helped the city, as we would do when we built affordable housing for our neighbors in Roxbury in conjunction with expanding our residential facilities or when we purchased supplies and services from local vendors. As we sought to contribute to the city, we could simultaneously take maximum advantage of the educational opportunities it offered, not only through co-op placements with private and public employers and community-based organizations but also through new opportunities for community service and service learning and new programs, like architecture and public policy, that benefited from our setting.

Northeastern was not alone in the 1990s in its determination to reinvent the idea of an urban university. Indeed, some of the country's leading schools that had turned away from an urban identity in the 1960s and 1970s were reengaging with their host cities in these years, reflecting a growing realization that the interests of city-based universities and those of their surrounding communities were inextricably intertwined. The University of Pennsylvania was the national exemplar of this new attitude. During the presidency of Judith Rodin, Penn aggressively deepened and celebrated its involvement in the life of Philadelphia, not only with the school's immediate neighborhood but also at the level of civic leadership and municipal government. A similar pattern was evident at the University of Chicago and at Columbia, two institutions that had been aggressive in gentrifying their neighborhoods during the urban-renewal years. Both were now forming partnerships with their neighbors to promote mutually beneficial patterns of development. By the 1990s, it seemed clear that the wheel had come full circle from the early years of the century when the AUU was founded. Top-ranked schools that had been part of that movement and had later distanced themselves from their local communities were now reconnecting, even as the cities themselves, much like Boston, were beginning to recover from the pattern of decline that had dominated urban America from the 1950s to the 1970s. Once again, it now seemed, a university could aspire to be both academically distinguished and explicitly urban. We intended to place Northeastern in the forefront of this movement.[4]

*   *   *

As we pursued a series of unconventional policies regarding education, research, and urban service based on our guiding Mantra, we also departed from the standard academic playbook in nonacademic ways, especially by aggressively broadcasting our progress to prospective students and their families, to high school guidance counselors, to our colleagues in academia, and to the general public. In 1996 marketing was not yet a widely accepted practice in American higher education. Despite a few pioneers, among them the University of Maryland, academia retained a traditional disdain for the kind of direct self-promotion associated with commercial enterprises; what passed for marketing at most universities, Northeastern included, occurred through offices of "university relations" whose job was to place flattering stories about the institution in the media, promote speeches and articles by faculty experts, and keep the president in the public eye. Our view was that this kind of understated self-promotion would not produce the radical change in Northeastern's visibility and reputation that had to occur for the overall repositioning effort to succeed. From the first days of my presidency, therefore, we began planning a major marketing effort that would parallel and support our substantive work. By the time we were done, we had created one of the country's first marketing departments led by a vice president, spent millions of dollars on various forms of advertising, and gained national recognition as an innovator in this previously neglected field.

Our decision to place a priority on the rankings published by *U.S. News and World Report* was even more countercultural than our emphasis on marketing. In the 1990s academia was in revolt against the rankings, including an organized effort among college and university presidents to boycott the magazine's data-collection efforts. We took a different view. We understood the rankings' flaws, but we also knew they had become powerful in fixing the stature of colleges and universities in the minds of young people, and we doubted we could attract the kinds of students we needed to enroll unless we improved

Northeastern's 1995 position of 162 among 228 "national universities." We also believed that dramatic improvements in our standing would validate our efforts to enhance the quality and stature of our programs for our own campus community. In short, the rankings gave us a playing field on which to compete for status and a yardstick by which to demonstrate progress, thus constituting a powerful tool to support our aspirations that had not historically been available to upwardly mobile institutions. We also believed that the indicators on which the rankings were based, despite multiple problems, did a reasonable job of identifying institutional characteristics properly associated with quality, including graduation rates, the academic qualifications of entering students and faculty, and dollars spent on educational programs. Using these metrics not only promoted our reputation but also helped us strengthen ourselves educationally. There is no question in my mind that our success in moving Northeastern into the country's "top 100" universities (we ranked 98th at the end of my presidency) was an indispensable contributor to our success in making Northeastern competitive as a selective, national university.

Aggressive marketing and the use of *U.S. News* rankings were not the only nonacademic arenas that required attention in connection with our repositioning effort. Equally important was strengthening our organization. Here we faced fundamental questions: How could we foster a culture that held itself to the highest professional standards? What additional capacities in what critical areas did we need to build to deliver excellence in undergraduate education as well as in scholarship? What changes in our formal structure were needed to reinforce our programmatic strategies? How could we generate the resources needed to support the operational quality to which we aspired? Addressing all these questions was as important a part of our work as was directly enhancing the student experience. This aspect of repositioning Northeastern forced my colleagues and me to think a great deal about the relationship between organizational change and academic progress and led me to a clear conclusion about one of the most hotly debated questions among students of higher education: Does change occur as a result of rational plans coordinated by campus leaders or does it result from the independent actions of multiple units and individuals operating with a high degree of independence in the highly decentralized world of the university? I believe the Northeastern story demonstrates, and the pages of this book will show, that unplanned, decentralized, "cybernetic" change does, indeed, account for a great deal of innovation in any great university, but that transformational change of the kind needed at Northeastern in the 1990s can only be accomplished through a carefully crafted strategy systematically followed over a sustained period by campus leaders.[5]

*   *   *

For the ten years of my presidency my team and I focused on programs, policies, and organizational arrangements that could propel us forward along the lines defined by our guiding Mantra: excellence as a national research university that was student centered, practice oriented and urban. This framework defined our priorities, informed our decisions about resources, and gave a measure of unity to the work of our dispersed academic organization. We sought national leadership within our distinctive framework, which we did not see as parochial in any way. Rather, we were pursuing the insight that William Rainey Harper had articulated so beautifully in his 1902 address and that was reflected in the participation of leading universities in the early membership of the AUU: A university that embraced its city could be national and even international in scope but could also offer students and faculty enriched opportunities for education and scholarship compared to a school located in a small town or rural setting—or a city-based school that did not actively engage its urban community.

In the pages that follow I describe how the faculty, staff, students, and administrative and Board leadership of Northeastern worked together to reposition our University between 1996 and 2006. I tell this story in the first person to acknowledge that I am hardly an unbiased observer. I have tried, nonetheless, to be accurate and to use my background as a historian to embed our institutional narrative in a larger social and educational context. I have, inevitably, relied on my memory, buttressed by University records and the recollections of colleagues. My goal has not been an exhaustive review of Northeastern during my presidency. That task awaits another book by a more objective author. This volume summarizes my own perspective on the major ways the people of Northeastern worked together to address the challenges we faced.

CHAPTER 1

# Northeastern and the Tradition of Urban Higher Education

Association [of Urban University] . . . members are of most varied origin. . . . [They] include the oldest private university in America and the youngest municipal college. . . . But one thing they all have in common, namely a desire to interpret education in the light of modern civilization, to adapt its content and methods to the life of today. The meetings . . . are therefore refreshingly free of any slavish subservience to tradition. . . . With the increasingly urban type of our population it is only reasonable to suppose that these institutions will, as the years go on, assume an ever growing importance in the American system of higher education.

—Parke R. Kolbe on the formation of the AUU in 1914

Efforts by universities to mitigate the social ills of cities further reinforced the idea that the term "urban university" first and foremost referred to institutions that enrolled large numbers of local commuter students. As a result, "urban university" became a low status label, which many institutions now avoided. . . . The Association voted itself out of existence in 1977, reflecting the resistance of its members to the term "urban university."

—Steven J. Diner on the dissolution of the AUU in 1977

## Early History

Urban universities were a late development in American higher education. Advanced learning in the United States, reflecting English precedents and in contrast to continental Europe, first took root in rural and small-town settings, partly because there were no cities when Harvard, Yale, and Princeton were established but more deeply reflecting what historian Frederick Rudolph has called an "antipathy to towns as college sites" that persisted long after the country developed significant centers of population. The early institutions, sponsored as they typically were by colonial governments to promote religious orthodoxy, were centrally focused on the moral and spiritual development of their students, who were exclusively males. Some version of the classical curriculum, with its focus on ancient languages, mathematics, and moral and physical philosophy—the eighteenth century's version of liberal education— was viewed as the ideal vehicle for shaping adolescent minds. A comparatively isolated location, combined with the residential facilities necessary in such a setting, shielded young men from unwanted influences. Rudolph calls this pattern the "collegiate way": a comprehensive, inwardly focused institutional culture, tightly controlled and closely monitored by college authorities. As always with American higher education there were exceptions to the general rule. Among the colonial colleges, both Columbia and Penn were established in communities that grew into major cities, although both moved multiple times to locations on the urban periphery to limit their exposure to the pressures and distractions of their steadily expanding hometowns.

The small liberal arts colleges that began to dot the American landscape in the years between the Revolutionary War and the Civil War mostly followed the small-town, residential model, in part because of its attractiveness as an educational idea and in part to serve students from areas of the country that lacked an urban center. Most of the early state universities represented a similar pattern, reflecting a parallel aversion to city life. The preference for small-town settings was also evident among the land-grant institutions that were created during the second half of the nineteenth century under the Morrill Act of 1862. Along the way, the country produced a number of additional city-based institutions, mostly through private sponsorship—including Pitt (1787), George Washington University (1821), NYU (1831), Western Reserve University (1862), and the Jesuit schools—as well as the country's first municipal institutions, the College of Charleston (1770) and CCNY (1847). But collectively urban institutions represented a minor theme in the American educational landscape through the middle years of the nineteenth century, and these schools often worked hard to replicate the collegiate atmosphere of their small-town, residential predecessors, even as they celebrated serving residents of their host cities.[1]

Urban institutions emerged as a significant dimension of higher education in the United States only in the early years of the twentieth century, a consequence of the industrialization and urbanization that began in the years after the Civil War and in response to the educational needs of the workers and immigrants who flocked to the new centers of economic opportunity. As the twentieth century progressed and the United States became more urban and large-scale enterprises more common, college credentials grew increasingly necessary for entering skilled occupations like accounting, engineering, and teaching. In this context city-based universities proved valuable both as providers of educational services and contributors to regional economic vitality. Because state-sponsored education had largely avoided urban settings and municipal institutions were limited in number, most of the rapidly growing urban institutions were privately sponsored.

Northeastern was a prime example of a new wave of independent, city-based schools that appeared during the last third of the nineteenth and early years of the twentieth centuries. Founded in Boston in 1898 as the Evening Institute of the Young Men's Christian Association (YMCA), Northeastern was dedicated to helping young people and working adults from the less privileged tiers of the metropolitan community obtain skills to support themselves and their families. The new institution grew steadily in the years before World War II, initiating baccalaureate-level programs in 1916 under the name Northeastern College, renaming itself again as Northeastern University in 1922, and achieving independence from the YMCA and full degree-granting authority from the state legislature in 1935. Other private urban universities participating in this surge of institutional development included Johns Hopkins (1867), BU (1869), Syracuse University (1870), Vanderbilt University (1872), the University of Southern California (USC, 1880), Temple University (1884), and Chicago (1890). The few new public urban institutions founded in these years were chiefly sponsored by the cities themselves and included Hunter College in New York (1870), the Universities of Akron (1870) and Toledo (1872), and the Municipal University of Omaha (1908).

By 1924 urban colleges and universities, while representing only 16 percent of the nation's institutions of higher education, enrolled 44 percent of the students. There was considerable variation among them. A few, like the urban

Ivies—including Harvard, Penn, Yale, and Columbia—as well as Chicago and
Johns Hopkins, had ties to local wealth, enrolled academically well-prepared
students, and achieved standing among the country's leading institutions.
But these schools were unusual among city-based universities; indeed, with
the exception of Chicago and Johns Hopkins, they had not been founded as
urban institutions but became urban as their host communities grew around
them. Most urban universities, both private ones like NYU, BU, and Pitt, and
public ones like CCNY, Akron, Toledo, and Omaha, fleshed out the less elevated tiers of the nation's higher education system, enrolling large numbers
of middle- and working-class students seeking both the respectability and
the social mobility that came with a college degree. Northeastern, reflecting
the historic mission of the YMCA, was among those that focused on students
from working-class backgrounds.[2]

## Urban Universities as a Distinctive Type of Institution

Despite the differences among city-based universities during the first third
of the twentieth century, a number of them coalesced around a distinctive
service model that began to differentiate "urban" institutions from peers that
were merely located in cities. In 1914 a group of these schools formed the
Association of Urban Universities, insisting that, despite their differences,
they all rejected the "slavish subservience to tradition" that characterized
much of American higher education and shared a "desire to interpret education in the light of modern civilization, to adapt its content and methods to
the life of today." The initial membership included almost all of the municipal
universities (Akron, CCNY, Hunter, Cincinnati, Louisville, and Toledo) as
well as a strong selection of private schools, including Johns Hopkins, Washington University in St. Louis, NYU, Pitt, BU, the University of Buffalo, Temple, Penn, and Northwestern University. In its second year the Association
added Brown University, Drexel Institute, Chicago, Syracuse, and Harvard, as
well as the three urban state universities, the University of Minnesota, Ohio
State University, and the University of Washington. Columbia did not join
until 1939. The first Catholic school to enlist was Fordham University in 1929.

In its early years the AUU focused on exploring both the special opportunities and the challenges associated with operating in an urban setting.
A guiding principle was that members should look to the needs of their
host communities as they shaped their educational programs rather than

to time honored practices inherited from their antebellum predecessors. Charles Dabney, the president of the University of Cincinnati and one of the two college presidents (along with Parke Kolbe of the University of Akron) who organized the AUU, characterized "urban" universities as city-based schools that were "of" their communities rather than simply "in" them. Urban institutions were not alone in embracing the notion that higher education should reflect contemporary social and economic needs. Similar ideas were also evident among leaders of state universities and land-grant colleges; indeed, public schools often led the way in shaping educational practices to address modern conditions. But because the location of most state-supported schools rendered them inaccessible to city residents of modest means, it was left largely to private urban institutions to "adapt the methods and contents" of their programs to serving these communities.

The most obvious and widespread innovation of institutions claiming the "urban" designation was the development of occupationally oriented programs keyed to the requirements of an industrial society. At the undergraduate level this meant offering degrees in fields like business, engineering, and education that were not traditionally considered appropriate subjects for college-level study and continued to be spurned by the nation's liberal arts colleges, the modern conservators of pre–Civil War traditions. Northeastern, with its center of gravity in baccalaureate programs in business and engineering, its evening law school, and its view of liberal arts subjects as support for the practical disciplines rather than fields of study in themselves, was a prime example of this pattern, although, as the University's link to the YMCA implies, a concern with the socialization and moral development of students was never entirely absent. At the graduate level elite members of the AUU extended their programs beyond the traditional "learned professions" to include fields like business administration, journalism, and education, while continuing to dedicate the undergraduate years to the liberal arts and sciences. Here, however, as always, there was variation. Penn, for example, developed undergraduate degree programs in engineering, business, and nursing.

Another innovation widely present in "urban" universities was the use of practical experience to reinforce classroom studies. The idea that theory and practice were complementary and mutually reinforcing—"learning by doing"—had been celebrated by John Dewey and accepted by educators for many years, as could be seen by the emphasis on laboratory work in the sciences and on practice teaching for future educators. As occupational and professional studies gained importance, however, the question of how to incorporate non-academic experience into the process of learning grew in significance and was a topic of high interest to members of the AUU, which undertook the first systematic study of this subject. The ensuing report noted that "fieldwork" could be introduced into the curriculum in a variety of ways—for example, by assigning students to study real-world problems rather than simply completing textbook exercises. The most powerful version of this idea was "cooperative education" in which students alternated terms of classroom work with periods of employment in jobs related to their studies. First introduced in engineering at the University of Cincinnati in 1906, the idea of "co-op" spread rapidly, especially among urban institutions whose proximity to centers of employment facilitated this pedagogy. Co-op became particularly popular in engineering and also was quite common in business; by the 1920s 137 institutions, Northeastern among them, offered this experience in one or both of these fields. Over time, as we shall see, Northeastern's commitment to co-op proved to be more extensive than that of most institutions; as the twentieth century progressed, cooperative education, applied in an expanding number of fields, would emerge as Northeastern's most prominent and distinctive characteristic.

For private urban universities, without access to taxpayer support, cooperative education could be as important financially as it was educationally; it put money in students' pockets. For many city-based institutions, committed to serving students from families of modest means, the cost of college was a serious concern. For this reason many private urban universities—Northeastern being very much a case in point—tended to be Spartan, no-frills operations. They were typically non-residential, often with more than half and sometimes as many as 80 percent or more of their students commuting from home to avoid paying for room and board. Financial pressures tended also to preclude the kind of campus life generally associated with residential colleges, which was, in any case, not workable for commuters. The amenities widely associated with the self-contained world of the "collegiate way"— athletic and recreational facilities; dining halls; enclosed, grassy quadrangles and libraries—were minimal at Northeastern and at most of its counterpart urban institutions. Within this cost-conscious framework, co-op earnings were often essential in helping students pay for the next academic term.

The focus of urban universities on educating commuting students from metropolitan communities in occupational fields was typically part of a broader emphasis on local service. Here, again, urban universities were different from their collegiate and small-town counterparts, whose leaders often viewed their host communities, although sometimes important sources of students, as incidental to determining the character of their educational programs. Linked as urban schools were with local employers, for whom they were preparing the workforce, and local high schools, whose students they were receiving, these institutions tended to view contributing to the well-being of their cities as part of their mission. This impulse, reflective of Progressive-era values within academia, took many forms: continuing education for older residents (a major focus of the AUU and of Northeastern); technical training programs tailored for local employers; scholarships for needy graduates of area high schools; and participation of faculty and staff in organizations and activities—school committees, city councils, public health authorities—in which academic expertise could be useful in managing municipal affairs. Harper's University of Chicago, though distinctive among urban universities in its wealth and stature, represented a particularly striking example of the last-mentioned phenomenon, especially in the social sciences during the first decades of the twentieth century. Chicago's sociology professors routinely studied local problems like juvenile delinquency, poverty, and labor relations, creating a body of scholarship that was useful to city authorities while also helping to shape their discipline nationally. Analogous work was done by Chicago's political scientists and economists.[3]

Leaders of more typical urban universities like Northeastern were keenly aware that their focus on commuting students, adult education, modest facilities, practical studies, and local service represented points of difference from the traditional model of higher education in the United States. Precisely because of these differences, and because their students were drawn from the middle and lower tiers of society, these institutions generally occupied less elevated positions in higher education's prestige hierarchy than did their older and better established peers. Leaders of the University of Pennsylvania learned this lesson the hard way; when they adopted an emphasis on serving local students in the early twentieth century their stature among Ivy League institutions plummeted. The association of service to a host community with low status fostered considerable variation among leaders of city-based institutions regarding the degree to which they embraced their urban character. Many members of the AUU had no interest in enrolling large numbers of students from the working-class and immigrant communities of their cities. Some schools moved their facilities to suburban locations, or tried to do so. Schools that were committed to serving urban students often sought to enhance their respectability by adopting practices associated with their traditional peers, as when Northeastern established a separate College of Arts and Sciences in the mid-1930s.

Efforts to achieve heightened stature among urban university presidents were often combined with a defiant pride in the importance of their school's distinctive characteristics. Northeastern President Carl Ell put it this way in 1931: "Northeastern was built to meet the needs of men. . . . It has refused to duplicate . . . other institutions. It has kept uppermost the question: 'What are the needs of society?' It has not been swayed by the question: 'What are other educational institutions doing?'" This statement reads like a manifesto for the Association of Urban Universities, although it was only partly true. But pride in the special character of their schools was real among presidents of urban institutions. Their challenge, always, was to maintain their mission while remaining competitive and improving their standing within the country's academic pecking order.[4]

## Urban Universities in Academia's Golden Age

The twenty-five years following World War II are widely characterized as a golden age of growth, financial support, and public admiration for American higher education. Triggered initially by federal scholarships to support college attendance by returning veterans and sustained by the enhanced social and economic importance of a college degree, a steadily expanding percentage of a rapidly growing youth population pursued undergraduate studies in unprecedented numbers. Both federal and state governments provided generous support to help academia respond to the heightened demand. Growth was particularly striking among public institutions as state governments enlarged existing colleges and universities and created new campuses to accommodate the college-going aspirations of the baby boom generation. The rapid increase in the number and size of tax-supported community colleges absorbed a great deal of the new demand, providing access for students of limited academic achievements and financial means and changing the overall landscape of higher education, especially in urban centers. By 1970 public higher education, historically the junior partner in the nation's academic enterprise, enrolled 73 percent of the country's undergraduates.

In parallel with the exploding enrollments of the post–World War II period, there occurred a dramatic reorientation of academic priorities among top-tier institutions in the direction of research, especially in the basic disciplines, and graduate education, especially at the doctoral level. Here, as with enrollment growth, federal funding played a critical role. The new focus on the advanced academic functions had actually been evident at leading universities as early as the 1930s, but supporting this work was costly and universities had been constrained by the country's difficult economic circumstances. The war had proved transformative, however, convincing national leaders that academic science could foster technological development and, by extension, promote national security, economic development, and health care. The new appreciation of academic work led to a continuing pattern of generous federal funding for university-based research, initially in the sciences but over time in the social sciences and humanities as well. Federal support also drove the development of graduate programs that were needed both to support research activities and to train the large number of faculty required by academia's overall expansion.

The twin postwar revolutions in enrollments and financial support produced a new model of academic excellence at the top of the nation's academic pecking order: the modern research university. This new model prized basic research as the highest institutional value and PhD programs in the basic disciplines as the most prestigious form of education. Reflecting historic academic biases, work in applied fields such as business and engineering, while important, continued to have a secondary stature, although the high status fields of medicine and law still contributed significantly to institutional reputations. As the advanced academic functions came to dominate the priorities of elite institutions, undergraduate education, historically their central function, declined in importance. Faculty members were now often valued more for the quality and prominence of their research than for their effectiveness as teachers. There was, of course, considerable variation within this general framework. Some leading institutions—Princeton was notable in this respect—worked harder than others to maintain a balance between advanced work and undergraduate studies. But the overall trend was clear.

As academia flourished between the 1940s and 1970s, urban America experienced conditions more evocative of a dark age than a golden one. The prosperity of the immediate postwar years brought affluence to an expanding middle class that had delayed both marriage and child rearing during the Depression and the war. Now young Americans, led by returning veterans, eager to create families and get on with their lives, drove an exodus from urban centers to the suburbs, attracted by the prospect of a backyard for the kids and assisted by new programs of federal support for mortgages. In these same early postwar years, the flight of African Americans from the segregated South, which had been under way since the early years of the century and was accelerated by war-related employment opportunities, continued to grow, with most migrant families ending up in one of the large cities of the Northeast, upper Midwest, or West Coast. The nation's urban centers also became destinations for a new wave of immigrants, especially Hispanics from Puerto Rico and Mexico, driven northward by limited economic prospects at home.

As Black and Hispanic communities grew in urban America, so too did racial tensions, ultimately producing a pattern of white flight that reinforced the positive attractions of suburban life. Soon businesses of all kinds followed middle-class purchasing power into suburban malls, further depleting municipal tax bases already eroded by population decline just as cities were being called on to provide enhanced social services for their often needy new arrivals. As these forces interacted during the three decades following World War II, northern cities experienced increasing racial animosity, growing crime rates, deepening hostility between white municipal authorities and minority communities, and steadily decaying infrastructure and overburdening of social services. By the mid-1960s, in the context of the civil rights movement, the resentments and frustrations of ghettoized Black communities reached fever pitch. The result was the urban crisis to which I referred in the opening pages of this book, characterized by summer after summer of racially focused riots in many of America's cities.[5]

The conjunction of a golden age of growth and financial support for academia, the emergence of a new model of elite higher education, and the downward spiral of urban America created a complex environment for city-based private universities. Some elite institutions—Harvard, Penn, Columbia, and Chicago, for example—experienced these years as a time of unprecedented opportunity to become far more selective and national than they had previously been and to aggressively pursue the new priorities of research and graduate education. For these long-standing members of the AUU, the whole idea of defining themselves as "urban universities" had become unacceptable both because it implied an excessively local focus and because cities had taken on such negative social associations. Indeed, by the 1960s, many of these schools had come to see their urban settings as threatening to their well-being, triggering partnerships with city governments in urban renewal and "slum clearance" projects through which housing was taken away from low-income urban communities and transferred to the participating universities for their own purposes. In this manner, the University of Chicago was able to redevelop nearby Hyde Park as an attractive residential community for faculty and staff. The University of Pennsylvania, inspired by the Chicago example, organized a similar effort to revitalize West Philadelphia while also building residence halls to support its efforts to become a top-ranked Ivy League institution. Columbia undertook a parallel, federally supported makeover of Morningside Heights. The case of Penn was especially poignant since the school had recently made service to its city and the enrollment of local students a major part of its identity.

Schools that were locally oriented, like NYU in New York, BU in Boston, or Temple and Pitt in Pennsylvania, confronted a more difficult combination of forces than their top-tier counterparts. Most of these schools lacked the stature and resources to aggressively reposition themselves as national research universities; they came into the post-World War II years primarily as undergraduate, teaching institutions of modest standing. Now they found the middle-class urban communities they had historically served abandoning the city and being replaced by residents who represented far less promising constituencies for academic institutions. At the same time they found themselves confronted with a new generation of public-sector competitors as state after state responded to the growing demand for educational services from urban and metropolitan communities by building new public campuses in cities, including the University of Wisconsin–Milwaukee, the University of Illinois at Chicago Circle, and Cleveland State University, as well as the dramatic expansion of the City University of New York.

The combination of a deteriorating urban setting and growing public-sector competition was profoundly threatening for nonelite private urban universities. Some, like NYU, BU, and Pitt, moved aggressively in the 1950s and 1960s to convert themselves into residential institutions and to enroll students from suburban and regional markets. For others, like the University of Buffalo, the University of Houston, and the University of Kansas City, the only answer was to be absorbed into state systems. As a variation on the theme, Temple in Pennsylvania, seeking to preempt the development of a public campus in Philadelphia, opted to become a "state-assisted institution," accepting a degree of dependence on public funding while also maintaining its own charter, board, and endowments. Pitt followed Temple into the public sector shortly thereafter, its efforts to maintain itself as a private school having fallen short. These were also difficult times for municipal universities, which depended on increasingly resource-constrained city governments. A group of these schools, like their private counterparts, were absorbed into state systems during the 1950s and 1960s, including Wayne State University in Michigan, Wichita State University in Kansas, and the two city-sponsored universities in Ohio, Akron and Toledo. At the same time, the state of New York assumed a large part of the financial responsibility for the multiple campuses of the City University.

By the 1970s the overall consequences for urban higher education of the major trends of the post–World War II period were clear. The rise of the modern research university, with its national and increasingly international focus, had created a compelling vision of excellence and stature at the top of the nation's academic pecking order. This model would become the north star for upwardly mobile institutions, public and private, for at least the next fifty years. It was the underlying reality that led to the dissolution of the AUU in 1977. At the same time, the need to educate young people growing up in struggling inner-city neighborhoods and constrained economic circumstances had become a compelling challenge for city and state governments. In 1989 a group of institutions prepared to focus on these issues created the Coalition of Urban and Metropolitan Universities (CUMU) as a successor to the AUU. Unlike the AUU, however, with its striking combination of high status private schools and locally oriented universities, CUMU was composed almost entirely of tax-supported institutions created specifically to serve local residents—a vital goal but one that offered little academic glory. Indeed, by including suburban institutions in the organization and "metropolitan" in their name, the leaders of CUMU implicitly acknowledged the negative associations of a specifically "urban" focus. Campus leaders at individual city-based institutions were left to do what they could to reconcile these conflicting forces in ways that reflected some combination of the missions and ambitions of their schools, the needs of society, their own inclinations, and the opportunities of the academic marketplace.[6]

## Northeastern University: 1959–1996

The story of Northeastern during the second half of the twentieth century provided a dramatic example of both the opportunities and the challenges that confronted private urban higher education in these years. During the 1960s and early 1970s, buoyed by soaring demand for access to college, Northeastern grew rapidly. Indeed, the University's president, former faculty member and Business School Dean Asa Knowles, wanted his school to be the nation's largest private university, a goal he ultimately achieved though at considerable cost to selectivity. To promote growth he expanded existing programs and added new ones, mostly—in the tradition of urban higher education—career-oriented offerings at the undergraduate level: nursing, physical therapy, physical education, pharmacy, criminal justice. He also established feeder campuses at suburban sites and created a new vehicle called University College to promote growth in part-time programs for working adults. At the same time, aspiring to "a place at the head table of academic respectability" and, nodding to the academic fashions of the times, Knowles supported initiatives in graduate education and research, including the school's first doctoral programs. His clear emphases, however—and his highest values—were practical programming in occupational fields, strong partnerships with industry, and cooperative education, in which Knowles claimed national and even international leadership, a position he hoped to consolidate through a leading role in a new National Commission for Cooperative Education (NCCE). Notwithstanding Knowles's ambitions, however, Northeastern remained very much a Boston institution throughout his presidency, enrolling mostly commuting students from the immediate area and joining the AAU shortly after his appointment in 1959. In 1973, toward the end of his presidency, the Carnegie Commission on Higher Education identified Northeastern as one of the country's premier urban universities based on its extensive engagement with its host community.

Under Kenneth Ryder, a historian turned administrator and Knowles's successor in the late 1970s and 1980s, Northeastern gave heightened attention to the social sciences and humanities, fields that had received limited support in earlier years. Recognizing the growing importance of research in promoting institutional status, Ryder also supported faculty scholarship more aggressively than his predecessor, creating a vice presidency to oversee this work and supporting a special fund to seed new faculty projects. Seeking to project his school's reputation more widely, he played a key role in establishing an international organization devoted to Northeastern's signature pedagogy, the World Association of Cooperative Education. President Ryder also took steps to improve the school's relentlessly utilitarian campus, adding attractive landscaping and—most significantly—fulfilling a long-standing University ambition by building a handsome new library. In addition, he sponsored a cluster of activities—an academic journal, a university press, a speaker series—intended to give Northeastern some of the ornamentation of traditional universities.

Despite gestures toward mainstream academic patterns by Knowles and Ryder, the University for which my predecessor, John A. Curry, assumed responsibility in 1989 was, at its core, the traditional urban institution that Northeastern had been for many years. Admissions standards were modest and keyed to the educational needs of middle- and working-class students from the metropolitan community. The emphasis was on access and scale, not quality and selectivity. While there were sufficient residential beds to accommodate a healthy percentage of freshmen who wanted them, many first-year students continued the historic pattern of living at home and driving or riding public transportation to class. All other undergraduate and graduate students commuted or lived off campus. Tuition was low compared to other private schools, and facilities were modest, but large enrollments provided sufficient revenues for Northeastern to flourish. The University also remained deeply and comprehensively involved with the life of its host city. Among the business and civic leadership of Boston, Northeastern was considered an institutional success and a regional asset. In 1992, the mayor named Northeastern the city's best nonprofit institution for its many "financial and personal contributions" to its host community.[7]

Beneath the surface of Northeastern's successes, however, in the years preceding Curry's appointment, the school had begun to encounter difficulties that would ultimately threaten the viability of its long-standing pattern of operations, a constellation of forces similar to those that had previously forced private urban universities in other cities to let themselves be absorbed into state systems. The underlying reality was that, by the 1980s, the school was confronting the full implications of a change in its competitive environment that had been slowly developing since the 1950s. For most of the state's history, Massachusetts had invested very little in public colleges and universities. There was no state university prior to 1947, when Massachusetts State College in Amherst was renamed the University of Massachusetts. The rest of public higher education at the beginning of the post–World War II period was comprised of a modest collection of regionally focused teachers colleges and technical institutes. There were no community colleges. The absence of a well-developed system of public campuses in Massachusetts helped Northeastern maintain its high level of enrollment from local students for longer than had been possible for similar institutions in other states. Indeed, the primary reason for the limited scope of public higher education was the prior existence of the nation's strongest and most diverse collection of private colleges and universities, which had traditionally met the state's educational needs while using political muscle to slow the growth of tax-supported competitors. In metropolitan Boston, for example, Boston College (BC), BU, and

Northeastern were all large, commuting institutions that historically drew the bulk of their students from different parts of the regional population and were more likely to enroll students from families of modest means than the state's public university, which, true to the tradition of state-sponsored higher education, had been built in a small town in central Massachusetts on the foundations of the state's only public college.

The postwar boom in state funding that transformed public higher education nationally also brought change to Massachusetts. As the baby boom generation approached college-going years, it became evident to state leaders that neither the private colleges and universities nor their underdeveloped public counterparts could provide for the educational needs of the ballooning youth population. In the 1950s and 1960s, state government moved quickly to build its long-neglected tax-supported system. The teachers colleges were converted into comprehensive baccalaureate and master's level institutions. A new system of community colleges was created. Two regional universities were established in the northeast and southeast corners of the state on the foundations of a teachers college and three technical institutes. In addition, the University of Massachusetts was expanded from one campus to three, including a medical school in Worcester and an urban campus in Boston. UMass Boston represented the last of the country's new public urban universities of the post–World War II era.

Northeastern's two sister urban institutions, BC and BU, began reacting to the changing competitive environment in the late 1950s and early 1960s. Observing the state's growing investment in the public sector, mindful of the migration of middle-class families out of the city, and conscious that the growing youth population offered opportunities for their own improvement, both schools began to build dormitories and recruit students from wider regional and national pools, while repositioning themselves as selective, residential campuses.

Alone among the three, Northeastern maintained its historic local focus through the 1970s and 1980s. But declining numbers of high school graduates after the mid-1970s combined with growing competition within the local market, including from the rapidly expanding Boston campus of UMass, made it difficult for Northeastern to maintain the scale on which its financial stability depended. Between 1980 and 1989, the size of the freshman class declined gradually but steadily as did overall undergraduate enrollments. During these same years the University's operating budget more than doubled. A 1991 review by a Trustee committee summarized the situation succinctly: "Over the past decade the University's growth in program, budget and employment has been financed through high tuition, increased government support and diligent fundraising, while enrollments have drifted slowly downward."

For a tuition-dependent institution like Northeastern, this pattern of rising costs and declining enrollments was not sustainable. The tipping point came in the fall of 1990, Curry's second year, during an economic downturn that made students and families especially price sensitive when choosing a college, while also causing reductions in government-supported financial aid. The numbers were dramatic. Freshman enrollments dropped by nearly 1,100, to 2,710 from the 1989 total of 3,770, a 28 percent decline and almost 900 students below the budgeted admissions target of 3,600, even though the University had admitted more than 88 percent of those who applied. Curry and his team, aware of the softening admissions markets, had anticipated continuing enrollment declines but nothing of this magnitude and suddenness. The 1991 Trustee committee report called the situation "life threatening to Northeastern." The University had no capacity to make up the $17 million budget gap that school officials projected for the next fiscal year.

In his State of the University speech in September 1990, President Curry shared with the faculty and staff the new reality that had become clear to him and to the Trustees: Northeastern's historic operating model of high volume, low prices, minimal selectivity, and local orientation was no longer viable. It was time, he stated, for a new strategy based on redefining the University as a "smaller, leaner, better place to work and study." During the 1990-91 academic year, the Trustee committee, chaired by banker and alumnus Neal Finnegan, worked closely with Curry in formulating the new strategy. Its April report argued that Northeastern's long-standing emphasis on maintaining its scale at all costs had severely compromised quality and reputation and could not, in any case, be maintained given demographic and competitive realities. The University had to plan for smaller freshman classes and work on improving the quality of both its academic programs and its extracurricular life. Significant reductions in the faculty and staff would be necessary. The immediate reality was grim, but the University's leadership coalesced hopefully behind the call for a new and more competitive model of the school. The guiding philosophy became "smaller but better."[8]

The remainder of Curry's presidency was devoted to implementing the new strategy. One hundred and seventy-five staff were terminated in the spring of 1991. Over the next five years the pattern of personnel reductions continued, with the emphasis shifting from staff to faculty and from terminations to attrition and retirement incentives. By the time it was over the University had eliminated 700 jobs and reduced its workforce by 20 percent. Curry proved to be the ideal president to lead this process. Like his two predecessors, he was a Northeastern insider, an alumnus for whom the University had been the center of his professional life. He knew the institution, was widely liked and trusted, and was able to execute the necessary changes, which must have caused him deep personal pain, with a high degree of acceptance and even support from the campus community. It was a remarkable achievement. He also took the first steps toward the "better" part of the "smaller but better" formula. His provost, Michael Baer, instituted enhanced standards for faculty appointments and promotions and modernized student recruitment by embracing "enrollment management," a practice that integrated admissions and financial aid decisions and used sophisticated analytics to allocate financial aid with maximum efficiency. The Board also authorized Curry's administrative vice president, Robert Culver, to construct new facilities that would make the campus more attractive for student life and faculty work. By 1995, when Curry announced his retirement, admissions targets had been reduced to what looked like sustainable levels and applicant numbers had begun to rise, allowing selectivity to improve. Financial stability, though not yet achieved, seemed within reach.[9]

## The Challenge of Making Northeastern "Smaller but Better"

Despite the impressive progress toward a new version of Northeastern during the Curry years, many questions remained at the time of my election to the presidency in 1996 regarding the full realization of the "smaller but better" formula. Clearly the new strategy meant fewer and better prepared students from a wider geographical area than had historically attended Northeastern; but could the school, with its long history as an access-oriented local institution housed in dull, factory-like buildings, actually attract such a student body? Beyond that basic question, what pattern of undergraduate enrollments from what sources of applicants would ultimately allow the University to flourish, and what room would there be in the new mix, if we did succeed, for students from modest backgrounds in metropolitan Boston? What about Northeastern's long-standing center of gravity in undergraduate professional programs? Should there be a shift of emphasis toward the arts and sciences? Where would cooperative education, so deeply associated with Northeastern's working-class history, fit in the new institutional configuration? What about the school's historic work in evening programs for adults, which, like the day-time programs, had been offsetting declining enrollments with higher prices during the 1980s? How important a role would there be for the University's long-neglected, and mostly weak, graduate programs or for the small cluster of research institutes, uneven in quality, that had sprung up over the years through the entrepreneurial efforts of individual faculty? Finally, of course, how would Northeastern's relationship to the city of Boston change? In the end, could Northeastern survive and still retain essential elements of its historic character as an urban university? Was it important that it do so?

The many fundamental questions about what the new version of Northeastern needed to look like were both urgent and institution-specific; but, as I anticipated my new responsibilities, I could not help thinking about them in relation to the broader context of American higher education in the late twentieth century. Three large issues, about which I had developed strong opinions during my years at UMass Boston and the City University of New York, seemed to me especially germane to the challenges facing Northeastern.

First, I shared the belief of many observers that undergraduate education, historically the central focus of non-elite urban universities, had suffered from neglect in the years following World War II with the rise of the modern research university. As recognition and rewards began flowing most generously toward faculty who carried their institutions' colors in the worlds of academic research and doctoral education, undergraduate teaching and learning received diminished attention. In my view, research was, of course, a critically important contribution of academia to the vitality of the country, and research universities were an essential part of the nation's educational landscape. But I did not think in 1996 that the country needed every major university to place a primary emphasis on research, which was the tendency fostered by the post–World War II competitive context. I also believed that universities were often creating doctoral programs to improve their status, not to meet any evident social need. It was therefore my predisposition as president to preserve a priority on undergraduate teaching and learning within the framework of a larger strategy of institutional change that included a strong role for research and doctoral education.[10]

Second, I believed that educating students in practical and occupational skills was honorable academic work that did credit to urban universities and had been critically important in the lives of millions of students while also contributing to the economic strength of the country. In my view, the widespread prejudice within academia that this form of education was of lesser value than work in the arts and sciences did not do credit to higher education and had the unfortunate tendency of promoting distance between the academic and applied disciplines. I came to the presidency believing that our society needed these two sides of the scholarly enterprise to collaborate much more intensively in the education of young people than had traditionally been the case.

Third, I deeply admired urban higher education's history of engagement with host communities. Believing, as I did, that cities represented the highest cultural, economic, technological, and governmental achievements of a modern society (as well as their greatest shortcomings), I also was drawn to the idea that city-based universities could and should make intentional contributions to the vitality of their metropolitan regions. This perspective felt particularly urgent to me in 1996 since most American cities, Boston among them, continued to struggle with the pattern of neglect and decline that had characterized urban America in the years following World War II, despite significant progress in recovering from the worst troubles of the postwar years. Given all this, I thought Northeastern's recognition by the Carnegie Commission as one of the country's premier urban universities two decades earlier was something of which my new institutional community should be especially proud—and something we should work to preserve.[11]

A new president's role, of course, is not to impose a set of personal values on the university he or she has been asked to lead but to work with the institutional community to determine the best possible courses of action. Accordingly, the perspectives to which I have just referred were not a template for policy as much as an explanation of why the presidency of Northeastern was so attractive to me. I sensed a high degree of compatibility between my own values and those of my new colleagues, and I was excited by the challenge of helping the school preserve what was most valuable in its history while also finding a new way to compete in the educational marketplace.

# CHAPTER 2

———

# A Formula for the New Northeastern

That is how I would describe us: we are a national
research university that is student centered, practice
oriented and urban. Our task now is to translate this
guiding conception, rooted in tradition but fresh with
potential for the future, into concrete actions that will
release within the conditions of a new century the full
educational promise and intellectual excitement and
social contribution latent in these phrases.

—State of the University Address, 1996

## The Nature of Academic Strategy

Before I became Northeastern's president, I had been a student of organizations, particularly universities. I had been influenced by the work of Alfred Chandler, in his time the nation's foremost business historian, on the evolution of the modern corporation. Chandler's *Strategy and Structure* taught me that the foundation of a successful enterprise in an intensely competitive environment is a well-crafted business strategy combined with an organization that reflects and is capable of implementing that strategy. Inspired by Chandler, I had written a book of my own, *Academia's Golden Age*, a study of the modern history of eight universities in Massachusetts, which sought to understand the trajectory of these institutions through the prism of Chandler's insights. That study convinced me that successful universities, like successful businesses, achieve their goals by carefully defining the arena in which they wish to compete; focusing on programs, services, and activities that reflect their comparative strengths in their chosen competitive context;

and creating an organization capable of enacting those programs and services at a high level of effectiveness.

Of course, as is often observed, a university is not a business. It has different and more complex goals. It is only a slight oversimplification to say that the success of a business enterprise can ultimately be measured by a single metric: its effectiveness in making money for its employees and stockholders. The success of a university is much harder to gauge, in part because, within a very broad framework, these institutions have wide discretion as to where to focus their energies and therefore how they define success, and in part because, even with a clearly defined focus, success is frequently difficult to measure. From a business perspective, a university must meet its payroll, live within its budget, and pay attention to its long-term financial security. But these are minimum conditions of the institution's existence, not its reasons for being.

Most universities undertake some combination of three basic functions: education, research and scholarship, and expertise-based advice to communities and organizations. Institutional decisions about who and how many to educate and at what level in what fields, what kind of research to conduct or services to provide, and how much priority to assign to each of the three classic functions all represent strategic choices. Even after the choices are made, determining success remains problematic. What, for example, constitutes a "successful" undergraduate education at a particular moment in time for a particular student constituency? Is the wisdom of the choices made on each of those questions best measured by graduation rates? Or first-job salaries of recent graduates? Or the societal value of those jobs? Or acceptance of graduates for advanced study? Or the value attached to their education by graduates? Or, indeed, the long-term happiness and success of alumni/ae?—to mention only the most obvious possible indicators, some of which are impossible to quantify. Similar problems attend to measuring success with respect to the other activities that universities routinely undertake. In this confusing world of ambiguous goals and uncertain metrics most people, and many institutional leaders, rely essentially on a crude and usually not very well-informed sense of a university's overall reputation to determine its "success."

Assessing the work of a university is also made complex by the fact that these institutions often have roots in particular value systems that their educational, research, and service activities are intended, as least in theory, to advance. Many, for example, have religious origins, and perpetuating the values if not the specific beliefs of their sponsoring faiths is often deeply ingrained in their institutional cultures and can remain important long after they shed their sectarian affiliations. Other universities, particularly public ones, were created to promote the well-being of a specific state or region, so determining the value of their contributions to regional vitality would seem a critical measure of their success. In modern times, many universities and colleges have identified educational niches—for example, technical subjects or the arts—or adopted unusual pedagogies or mixes of programs—unstructured curricula, problem-based education—that reflect their educational and social values. Research universities regard the advancement of knowledge as their core commitment.

Across the varied landscape of American higher education there are thousands of universities reflecting thousands of diverse histories, animating purposes and programmatic mixes, but they have in common the fact that they invariably see themselves as promoting particular, if not always well-defined, sets of values—social, intellectual, even moral. Those who work for a university, those who lead it and support it financially, and parents who send their daughters and sons to study there are often seriously committed to those values. For institutional communities, success involves not just financial soundness, not just well-regarded programs of education or research, and not just overall reputation but effectiveness in representing and nurturing values that are central to their lives.

Against this background, how can one most thoughtfully conceive the elements of a successful competitive strategy for a university? My studies of different institutions with highly diverse histories led me to a simple conclusion: Successful strategies are those that allow the institution to compete for essential resources (students, faculty, and dollars) in a particular segment of the higher education marketplace; that shape their work in education, research, and public service to reflect the values of their institutional and support communities; and that build organizations in which structures and culture are designed to enact their competitive strategy and inspire the best efforts of institutional members. In *Academia's Golden Age* I called a conception of an institution that effectively integrates all these elements a "strategic formula."

Presidents of universities have many roles to play. The most important, however, the foundation on which all other aspects of a presidency must necessarily rest, is articulating a strategic formula for the university they are leading and then using the powers of their office to channel institutional energies and resources toward the realization of that conception. No one else in a university community is positioned to do this work, though many can contribute to it. No one else is ultimately responsible for the institution's success, though achieving success requires the efforts of many. This was the perspective that I brought to the Northeastern presidency.

## Northeastern in 1996

Northeastern was among the universities I had studied while writing *Academia's Golden Age*. It was also a university that I knew—and had come to admire—through my long involvement in higher education in Massachusetts, which included a brief stint as an adjunct faculty member in the school's history department. I understood Northeastern to be a classic urban university: oriented toward local, commuting students from modest backgrounds; focused on keeping costs low and facilities spare; committed to practically oriented programs, especially at the undergraduate level, that would prepare students for employment; ready to adapt its programs to changing societal needs; and deeply engaged with the city and region of Boston as well as the neighborhoods close to campus. I particularly admired Northeastern's distinctive commitment to cooperative education and its pioneering work in evening, part-time programs for working adults. I understood that these institutional priorities had guided the efforts of President Knowles in driving Northeastern to be the largest private university in the United States during the 1960s and early 1970s and had continued to define the institution's center of gravity under Knowles's successors, Kenneth Ryder and John Curry, though Ryder had sought also to strengthen aspects of Northeastern that had historically been neglected.

What I hadn't fully realized at the time I became a candidate for the presidency was the extent to which Northeastern's historic competitive strategy had been undermined by changing conditions during Curry's presidency. This gap in understanding undoubtedly reflected my preoccupation with my duties as a dean at UMass Boston during the initial years of the Curry presidency, and then my departure for New York to serve as vice chancellor of the City University in 1992. The full story of the enrollment crisis of 1990 and of President Curry's heroic efforts to redesign Northeastern as a "smaller but better" institution only became clear to me during the presidential search. I was not surprised, however, to learn of the school's difficulties. To some degree I had anticipated them in my discussion of Northeastern in *Academia's Golden Age*, which I had completed in 1988, just two years before the institution's enrollments had collapsed.

Revelations about the challenges Northeastern faced in 1996 only increased my interest in the presidency. Here, I thought, was a doable job very much worth doing. Helping urban universities grow and thrive had been the central theme of my administrative career. I believed, moreover, that Northeastern had been held back for many years by an unduly modest sense of its value. Surrounded, perhaps intimidated, by the great private universities of Boston, focused not on the country's "best and brightest" but on the sons and daughters of local working-class families, led by a succession of insiders—both Board members and administrators—who loved their school but had internalized its modest standing, Northeastern had never sought to compete with the heavyweight schools that occupied the upper reaches of the academic pecking order. Now it had no choice, as Curry's "smaller but better" formula implied. I wasn't at all clear how to accomplish the transition Northeastern needed to make, but I believed it could be done.

My confidence in Northeastern's potential was reinforced after I assumed my duties in August 1996. I soon came to believe, in fact, that the school's worst days were behind it even though a University-wide "Restructuring Committee" had just concluded that, despite the belt tightening of the Curry years, we still faced a large structural deficit and that further budget cuts were needed. My thinking was influenced by awareness that the decline in high school graduates that had been occurring nationally and regionally since the mid-1970s and had been an underlying cause of Northeastern's problems, was about to end. Indeed, demographic statistics showed that, beginning in the fall of 1995, the numbers of high school graduates would begin to climb and would continue to increase through most of the first decade of the twenty-first century. I was further encouraged when, within a month after my arrival, Vice President Culver reported that fall enrollments were higher than had been anticipated and that we could probably get through the year without further reductions. I decided to shelve the report of the Restructuring Committee and to remain silent on the structural deficit. It was time, I concluded, to focus on what we could become, not the necessities of survival.

Other considerations reinforced my instinct to take an optimistic view of Northeastern's situation. I was convinced that young people entering college in the 1990s had a heightened interest in programs that would help them prepare for the workplace. Although the causes of this trend were far from clear, the trend itself had been widely observed and involved not only the first-generation students whom Northeastern had traditionally served but also Ivy League-bound students from affluent backgrounds. This trend led me to think that Northeastern's traditional emphasis on practical programs and cooperative education could be attractive to well-prepared students if we could establish ourselves as a respectable university in their minds. I was also encouraged by reports that young Americans were increasingly attracted to urban settings for their college experiences and that the historic notion that higher education was best pursued in a small town or pastoral setting was losing its allure. Finally, I was impressed that the economic difficulties of the late 1980s, which had been another source of Northeastern's troubles, were no longer an issue. Both the nation and the region had recovered their economic vitality, and the Boston area appeared to have a bright future as a center of high-tech innovation linked to the city's great universities and teaching hospitals.[1]

## Conceptualizing a New Strategy

By Northeastern tradition each fall the president addresses the campus community on "the state of the university." I viewed this occasion, scheduled within weeks after my arrival, as a perfect moment to signal my intention to think about our future in a new way. The emphasis would be on opportunities, not difficulties. We needed to seize the opening provided by the new demographic context. But we would not seek to grow or to recover our former scale, even though, since the days of President Knowles, growth and scale had been cornerstones of Northeastern's educational identity and financial health. President Curry's "smaller but better" strategy had wisely pointed us in a different direction. We would use the prospect of an enlarged applicant pool to improve our quality, beginning with the academic level of our freshman class. Taking a phrase that James Conant had employed when he became president of Harvard at the bottom of the Great Depression, I said our circumstances called for the "intensification" of our work within our established pattern of activities, not an increase in size or additions to our offerings. We needed to focus on quality in every aspect of university life, especially those functions that were critical to our future success.

Wanting to foster a sense of urgency as well as optimism, I did not call for a broad-based strategic planning exercise to determine new priorities. I worried that such an activity would consume time and organizational energy at a moment when we needed to improve our performance, office by office, department by department. I was also aware that a long-range planning process had been undertaken toward the middle of Curry's presidency and that the effort, representing the work of multiple committees and containing many valuable ideas, did not produce a persuasive strategy to make the University more competitive. In truth, I was confident—based on my reading of the planning reports, my conversations with my new colleagues, and my prior knowledge of Northeastern and its competitive environment—that I could identify where we needed to focus and what we needed to do, at least in general terms. For all these reasons I set aside my long-held belief that a participatory planning process is the best way to achieve organizational commitment to a new direction. The moment called for leadership, not process. I sensed that was what the campus community wanted from its new president.

My first challenge in the State of the University address was to articulate a vision of the new Northeastern for which I was calling that could inspire the best energies of my colleagues. We knew we needed to be "better," but what, exactly, did "better" mean? In the minds of many in higher education—including many within the Northeastern community—the idea of quality in a university was derived largely from Ivy League traditions and was grounded in the model of the modern research university that had dominated the country's academic landscape since the 1960s. Quality meant the liberal arts and sciences. Quality meant doctoral programs and research, especially in the basic disciplines. Quality meant better prepared and therefore more affluent students. Quality was not associated with the things Northeastern had traditionally stood for: practical programs, cooperative education, undergraduate teaching, involvement in the life of the city, students from modest backgrounds. Our two sister institutions, Boston College and Boston University, had both pursued different versions of the Ivy League model as they had repositioned themselves during the 1960s and 1970s. In the process, they had moved away from the local constituencies they had historically served. Was this the right path for Northeastern? Was there, indeed, any alternative way to prosper as a major private university?

I was convinced that any effort to reconstruct Northeastern on the model of traditional universities or the priorities of the major research universities was the wrong course for us, one that at worst could fail altogether and at best would lead us to mediocrity within a conventional framework. The competition in that arena was too well entrenched in our region and the cost of competing on those terms was far beyond our capabilities. I therefore told my audience that our best hope lay in building on our distinctive characteristics but transforming them—and public perceptions of them—in ways that bespoke quality, not a second-class education for students who could not afford the best. In saying this I gambled that most members of our campus community cared about Northeastern's traditional values and would be inspired by the challenge of becoming competitive with the country's leading universities by emphasizing them.

My message was clear: We would continue to be Northeastern. We would maintain our focus on cooperative education but stress its educational power rather than its role in covering costs. We would continue to stress undergraduate programs in professional fields, but we would push them toward the highest quality, and we would make sure that students in professional majors also received a full experience in the liberal arts and sciences. We would embrace and deepen our connection with the city of Boston and use that platform to showcase our research capacities and intellectual strengths. I told my audience:

> The founders of Northeastern sought to offer students something distinctive, and throughout this century we have taken pride in our difference from traditional universities. . . . For me [this] emphasis on being something particular is both prudent and virtuous, and my intention is to sustain and build upon [our] special qualities. . . .
>
> So that is how I would describe us: we are a national research university that is student centered, practice oriented and urban. Our task now is to translate this guiding conception, rooted in tradition but fresh with potential for the future, into concrete actions that will release within the conditions of a new century the full educational promise and intellectual excitement and social contribution latent in these phrases.

I spent some time explaining the significance of each term I had used: national, research, student-centered, practice-oriented, and urban. Each pointed in a specific direction. Together they would help us identify the activities on which we should focus. I expressed confidence that they represented the pathways toward success. I concluded: "I am very ambitious for Northeastern. I believe this is a university with an admirable past and a beckoning future. I believe we can build on the accomplishments of the recent past to shape a university that is truly distinguished among academic institutions of this nation in the quality and character of our work." In the final part of the speech I offered initial thoughts about the areas that needed immediate attention to move us toward the vision I had articulated, with our work in undergraduate admissions topping the list. I knew, however, that it would take us time to understand the full implications of my general conception. I promised to follow up my speech with a consultative process intended to identify immediate actions that we could take across all parts of the University. But, from my perspective, articulating the vision and inviting my colleagues to join me in its pursuit was a foundational step. It was my first effort to articulate a "strategic formula" for the university I had been invited to lead.[2]

## From Strategy to Plan

A month after the State of the University speech I distributed a memo to every academic and administrative department inviting proposals to improve the quality of their work within the framework of the priorities I had identified. This represented the first financial benefit of our improved position with respect to enrollments and offered a perfect opportunity for me to set a new and promising tone for the institutional community, after years when presidential memos about finances had consistently stressed budgetary constraints and the need for everyone to share the burden of reductions. Repeating a word I had employed in the State of the University speech, I called this initiative the Intensification Program and used it to reinforce a sense of urgency about change and improvement. My memo promptly elicited proposals from almost every unit of the University. By January, having reviewed all these ideas with an advisory committee of faculty and staff, I announced a large number of modest-sized grants. Thus, by the beginning of my second semester, we had given many departments a taste of the improved financial circumstances toward which my speech had pointed, and we had engaged many members of our community in starting to construct the new Northeastern.[3]

It was obvious, however, that the Intensification Program constituted only a limited first step toward the transformation we needed to accomplish. Now, having fostered some much needed momentum, we could step back and think more deeply about the road ahead.

By chance Northeastern was due for a decennial visit from the regional accrediting association, the New England Association of Schools and Colleges (NEASC), early in the third year of my presidency. For campus communities, these accreditation visits, though clearly important in terms of quality assurance, are typically dreary exercises requiring the collection of masses of descriptive data compiled in thick and largely unreadable "self-studies" designed to assure the accreditors that standards are being met. Fortunately, NEASC had found a way to make these exercises more useful, at least for well-established campuses that the organization considered basically sound, by allowing the self-study to focus on issues the campus itself deemed important. As my colleagues and I reflected on the upcoming reaccreditation process in the spring of 1997, we concluded that the issue-focused alternative offered us a chance to further develop the vision of the new Northeastern that I had outlined in my State of the University address.

I was emboldened to pursue this course because, in the months following that speech, I came to believe that my characterization of Northeastern as a "national research university that is student centered, practice oriented and urban" had struck a responsive chord within the campus community. In conversations with faculty and staff I consistently heard approving references to this phrase. Indeed, the term "Mantra" had quickly entered the campus vocabulary as a shorthand reference to it. Consultation with the leadership of the faculty senate confirmed for me that the Mantra had captured our most important qualities and pointed us in the right direction. Against this background, the reaccreditation process gave us a way to involve the campus community in the exploration of these priorities, compensating to some degree for the fact that my announcement of them had not been preceded by any consultative process.

Work on the self-study consumed much of my second presidential year. Under the leadership of a respected faculty member, Professor Steven Morrison of the economics department, and Provost Baer, a network of committees structured around the five categories of the Mantra conducted studies, engaged in wide-ranging conversations, deliberated for long hours, and, in the end, identified dimensions of institutional progress implied by the goal of excellence in each of these arenas. In parallel with this reaccreditation work, we initiated within the administrative leadership—a group that included the deans of the colleges, the vice presidents, and the heads of key administrative departments—a similar discussion of the implications of the Mantra for university priorities. By the summer of my second year we had crafted—through a classic broad-based process—a reaccreditation report containing a thoughtful analysis of how we needed to change to claim excellence within the framework by which we were defining ourselves. I was gratified by comments from the NEASC visiting team in the fall of 1998 that they had heard many favorable references to the Mantra from the campus community. The team chair told me privately that we had fostered an unusually high level of understanding and agreement regarding our strategic directions.[4]

The task of turning the broad concepts produced by the reaccreditation exercise into an actionable strategic plan focused the work of my administrative team during the third year of my presidency. Leadership fell to Baer's successor as provost, former law dean David Hall, who worked with the college deans and his own administrative team to create what we ultimately called the Action and Assessment Plan (AAP). This document, reflecting much consultation with faculty and staff but ultimately produced by the administrative leadership, constituted the vehicle through which we translated our general ideas into concrete goals and measurable outcomes for each of the colleges and administrative units. By January 1999 the first iteration of the Action and Assessment Plan was complete and ready to guide operational priorities across the University. In subsequent years, we annually reviewed and revised this document as we tracked our progress, and we produced annual "report cards" for the Board and campus community. The AAP also became the basis for unit-level plans within each academic and administrative department.[5]

I was immensely proud of all this work. As the third year of my presidency came to an end, I felt we had established a well-thought-out vision of the university Northeastern needed to become, had translated that vision into specific goals to which we had attached measurable outcomes wherever we could, and had achieved a high degree of agreement across the University that this plan was an appropriate road map to a better place.

### The Importance of Marketing

As we worked on the initial version of the Action and Assessment Plan, my leadership team and I were mindful that we could not reposition Northeastern in the academic marketplace simply by implementing our operational goals. As important as the quality of the educational experiences we would provide for our students would be the effectiveness with which we told our story to a range of internal and external constituencies. The implications of this reality went well beyond the business truism that marketing is as important as product development. We knew that in Massachusetts and New England, from which most of our students were drawn, Northeastern was well known as a traditional urban university, with both the positives that term implied about the value of our work and the negatives it contained regarding quality and reputation. To succeed in establishing a new version of Northeastern and attracting a different mix of students from our traditional service area, we needed to change those images dramatically. In addition, we had to recruit students from beyond New England where we were largely unknown, which constituted an entirely different kind of challenge.

In the first months of my presidency I had engaged several external consultants to help us understand how to promote Northeastern more effectively and to assess our organizational capability to do that work. In June 1997 I received the first of these assessments, which stressed two observations: First, Northeastern had no coherent marketing strategy; second, our organization did not include a proper marketing function. What we had, like most universities, was a "university relations" division that produced publications and managed our interactions with the media. This was not surprising. In 1997 the whole concept of "marketing" was still somewhat foreign and even distasteful within academia. Remembering Alfred Chandler's observation that structure should reflect strategy, it was clear to me that we could not afford the kind of delicacy about self-promotion that might work for an Ivy League university. Our ambitions required us to broadcast our message aggressively.[6]

Our discussions about marketing quickly began to influence our work on the reaccreditation self-study and the Action and Assessment plan. One of the consultants engaged to help us develop our marketing program led my administrative team through an exercise to focus our message even more sharply than did the Mantra. This effort led us to make some refinements in that formulation, including substituting the word "Aspiration" for "Mantra" since there was significant sentiment within my team that the latter term was not entirely positive. (I reluctantly went along with this change, and dutifully used "Aspiration" for the remainder of my presidency—and will do so for the remainder of this account. But the new term never took hold; members of the faculty and staff continued to refer to the Mantra in—at least to my ear—generally approving terms.)

The most important contribution of the messaging exercise was forcing us to refine our thinking about the characteristics of Northeastern we most wished to emphasize. Our consultant pressed us to craft a "vision statement" articulating what we believed to be the single most important feature of Northeastern. Not surprisingly, this was a difficult discussion. Within our community, as within most academic communities, there was disagreement about the weight to assign to each of the five themes of the Aspiration though most agreed that all five were important. Some particularly wanted to further our development as a national research university, believing that to be the pathway to a stronger academic reputation. Others thought we could never compete with top-tier institutions as a co-op school, since that format was historically associated with institutions for working-class students. This was not, however, a matter I was prepared to settle through consensus. I believed strongly that Northeastern's qualities as a practice-oriented university represented the most powerful theme for differentiating us from traditional institutions while also catching a wave of interest among academically talented students. After much discussion, my colleagues were persuaded to adopt the following "Vision Statement" to guide our work: "We will create the country's premier program of practice-oriented education."[7]

In crafting the Mantra in preparation for my first State of the University speech, I had used the phrase "practice oriented" to refer to Northeastern's long-standing emphasis on occupationally oriented programs as well as our commitment to cooperative education. But I came to realize that co-op, though vital as a distinguishing feature of Northeastern, was simply a program, localized in one administrative unit. It was not an institutional philosophy. Indeed, there was a noticeable gulf between our professional programs, where co-op was generally well accepted, and our College of Arts and Sciences, where attitudes toward this aspect of Northeastern were mixed and where we had individuals and even departments that were disinterested in co-op as a pedagogical idea and that largely ignored it in recruiting new faculty members. I became convinced that the full realization of our potential required us to emphasize the connection between theory and practice much more deeply and across the full range of our activities: in our approach to classroom study at both the undergraduate and graduate levels and in the arts and sciences as well as our professional programs, in our research, and in our connections to Boston. The decision to highlight the special character of Northeastern as "practice oriented" provided therefore not only a basis for our marketing messages but a touchstone for setting priorities within the broad framework of the Action and Assessment Plan.

Even with the refinement in our thinking that came from the adoption of our Vision Statement, the issue of focus turned out to be the largest challenge we faced in implementing the AAP. Our experience in this respect was not unlike that of other universities, or, I suspect, most complex organizations. Despite the fact that the Plan was constructed on the foundational goal of excellence within the five themes of the Aspiration and that the vision statement had defined an emphasis among these five, the AAP did not fully answer questions about priorities for resource allocation. Discussions at our leadership retreats repeatedly drew attention to this matter: How could we link our budgeting decisions more clearly to the priorities of our strategic plan? Happily, in the third year of my presidency, we found a way to address this dilemma that gave us an additional tool for making policy choices while continuing to build Northeastern's strength along all five dimensions of the Aspiration.[8]

## The Value of the *U.S. News* Rankings

In 1983 the *U.S. News and World Report* had hit upon a new idea for selling magazines: an annual ranking of the country's colleges and universities. The initial version focused on the country's "top fifty colleges" and relied heavily on survey data about institutional reputation, but over time the scheme became increasingly complex and sophisticated. By the 1990s the magazine was grouping most of the nation's colleges and universities based on a typology established by the Carnegie Foundation in the 1970s and then ranking institutions within each category using a number of metrics deemed to reflect quality. Thus, for example, Harvard was assigned a numerical rank within the top tier among "national universities"; UMass Boston in the second tier among "regional universities, north"; and Amherst College in the top tier among "national liberal arts colleges." Amazingly, something conceived as little more than a journalistic experiment turned out to fill a vacuum in public information. High school students and their guidance counselors and families, eager for some way to make choices among hundreds of colleges and universities, began turning to the rankings for guidance. As this happened, top-ranked institutions started to showcase their positions while schools in the lower tiers sought ways to improve their numbers. By the time I became president of Northeastern the *U.S. News* rankings had become a significant competitive factor in the academic marketplace.

The reaction of educators to the rankings was largely contemptuous. Many complained that the information on which they were based was problematic. For example, a great deal of weight was placed on a "peer rating." This was nothing more than a particular school's average score on a five-point scale of quality drawn from a survey of senior-level administrators at colleges or universities in the same institutional group. As I knew from filling out these surveys myself, there was no way that any of those asked to complete these ratings could have an informed opinion about more than a handful of the institutions we were asked to assess, yet the form requested opinions on dozens of other places. In addition, apparently objective data about admissions or class size or finances were self-reported by institutions on a questionnaire designed by the magazine, a procedure that invited manipulation by those worried about their standing.

Beyond the technical problems with the *U.S. News* formula, many educators deplored the very idea of ranking colleges and universities. These institutions, it was widely observed, were too different from each other for any ranking system to array them in a linear hierarchy, even one composed of ostensibly similar schools. Indeed, the notion that the quality of a college or university could be captured in a single number seemed to many illusory, even irresponsible. A campus that might be ideal for one student could be terrible for another. Even more fundamentally, different institutions had different definitions of quality based on their distinctive missions and traditions. As the rankings grew in importance, outcries from educators across the country became increasingly strident. By the 1990s there was a movement among presidents to boycott the entire exercise.[9]

My work on *Academia's Golden Age* had led me to a far more favorable view of the rankings than most of my colleagues. The most disappointing pattern I had observed among the universities in my study was the relatively low priority attached to undergraduate teaching and learning. My limited sample of universities reflected national patterns of the 1960s and 1970s in which graduate programs and research strength were typically the major foci for both faculty and campus leaders. This phenomenon had prompted a body of criticism among academic insiders as well as outside observers, who argued that undergraduate education remained a vital function of American higher education. Yet little changed. My study convinced me that the primary reason for this unfortunate situation lay in the competitive dynamics of the higher education industry. Reputation had long been the coin of the realm as universities competed for students, faculty, and dollars, and in the years after World War II programs of research and graduate education had become far more important than undergraduate offerings as determinants of reputation. The reason for this paradoxical situation, I had concluded, was the absence of any practical means to measure the quality of undergraduate programs while indicators of quality in research and doctoral programs, especially the former, were readily available. These considerations had convinced me that universities would never give appropriate attention to their work with undergraduates until there was a way to compete on quality in that arena. The *U.S. News* rankings, for all their flaws, were an attempt to provide just such a metric. They were, I thought, pointing in a critically important direction, and the effort should be pursued, not deplored. I was convinced that, over time, we would develop more responsible measures of undergraduate program quality.

As a new college president charged to improve my institution's standing, I had a second reason for liking the *U.S. News* rankings: they created an arena in which an institution like Northeastern could compete with better-known schools for standing with the public. What, after all, was the basis of a university's reputation prior to the rankings? Everyone knew Harvard was a great university, but how did they know that? In reality, a university's reputation represented the gradually accreted opinions of many persons over many years ultimately distilled into a conventional wisdom that was then reinforced as successive generations of students, faculty, and funders acted upon it. How could an upstart institution compete in that context? Among the institutions I had studied in writing *Academia's Golden Age*, there were examples of universities that had changed their standing dramatically, but the process had typically taken many years to register in broad public consciousness. I knew Northeastern did not have time for that kind of gradual evolution. We were trying to extricate ourselves from a crisis that had threatened our survival. We were acutely aware that the demographic curve that was turning upward in the mid-1990s would turn down again in 2008. If we were going to reposition Northeastern, we had to get the job done in the space of a decade.

My appreciation of the potential importance of the *U.S. News* rankings for Northeastern developed gradually during the first years of my presidency. I first drew the attention of the campus community to our standing in the fall of 1998, when I reported some favorable movement in our numbers in my State of the University speech. As I reflected on this matter, I was impressed by what seemed to me an extraordinarily important fact: Northeastern was among the lowest ranking private universities in the country, standing 162nd among 228 ranked schools with a "peer rating" of 2.2, well down in the third of the four tiers into which the magazine divided "national universities." We were outranked by all the private universities with which we competed for students. We were also outranked by a number of public campuses, including the major public universities with which we shared applicants. Our ranking seemed to me an especially clear indication of our vulnerability. How could we hope to flourish in a world driven by reputation when we were not only the weakest campus among our private-sector competitors but weaker even than

New England's public flagships, whose cost of attendance was much lower than ours? In fact, Northeastern was one of the few private universities not ranked in the first or second tiers, a group that included approximately 120 institutions. By the fall of 1999 I was ready to share this stark analysis with my campus colleagues. "Until our academic reputation is at least as strong as our competitors," I argued in that year's State of the University address, "until our perceived value is commensurate with our price, our future will not be secure." It was essential, I concluded, that Northeastern move into the second tier.

I had initially talked about our standing in the rankings primarily as a means to dramatize the seriousness of our position. In the months after I aired this issue publicly, however, I noticed that the idea of improving our standing had aroused significant interest around campus. It was a way of giving concrete form to an otherwise amorphous notion that we were not as well regarded as we wanted to be and needed to be. Conversations with my colleagues also led me to think that the goal of moving from the third to the second tier was not especially inspiring. These discussions led to a revised formulation, initially suggested by Professor Barry Karger and then reinforced by others. Since becoming a second-tier institution meant joining the top 120 universities in the country and since getting securely into the second tier had to mean a rank at least a bit higher than the bottom of that tier, why not seek to become a "top 100" university—a far more compelling goal than getting into the second tier.

I confess that initially I found Professor Karger's formulation daunting. All experience indicated that significant upward movement in the rankings was difficult. Rising into the second tier would itself be a major achievement. In the end, however, I concluded that we should adopt the "top 100" goal. It had the potential to inspire our efforts and it was, after all, little more than an outcome I regarded as essential to our long-term security. I took the leap at the annual meeting of the Northeastern Corporation in the spring of 2000, formally announcing my commitment to propelling Northeastern into the top-100 institutions in the *U.S. News* category of "national universities" within the first decade of the twenty-first century. "This is where our aspirations should place us," I told my governing board. "This is where our competitive position requires us to be. And this is what we intend to accomplish."[10]

Our Board chairman, George Matthews, later told me that he and other Corporation members had privately laughed at my announcement. To long-standing members of the Northeastern community, the goal seemed beyond the range of possibility. But, in embracing it, my colleagues and I had found an additional way to focus our work to supplement the priorities within the Aspiration that had emerged from our marketing discussions. Now we could review decisions related to the multiple goals of the Action and Assessment Plan, as well as choices about aspects of Northeastern not strongly linked to these goals, through the prism of "top 100" and make sure that as we implemented the AAP we were also attending to matters that would affect our standing.

My team and I fully understood the dangers of focusing on our ranking, the most important of which, beyond the possibility that we might not reach such an explicit and visible goal, was that the effort might divert us from the substantive purposes identified in the Aspiration and the AAP. It was clear, for example, that progress toward enrolling more students of color, or remaining accessible to students from modest backgrounds, or strengthening co-op, or deepening our engagement with the city of Boston counted for nothing in the rankings and might, at some point, conflict with the ranking goal. We were determined not to compromise our purposes in this way. We believed we could do this because most of the things we needed to do to improve our position—increase the selectivity of our entering class, raise our graduation rates, enhance our reputation among academic peers, and strengthen our finances—were imperatives for us anyway. Besides, I was persuaded by Robert Zemsky's injunction to be "market smart" even as we were "mission driven." I was determined to find a way to pursue the top-100 standing and also to preserve Northeastern's most valuable qualities. The former goal was nothing more than a necessity; the latter was incumbent upon us as stewards of an important institution.

### The New Strategic Formula

With the articulation of the top-100 goal, we had finally defined the most important elements of a new strategic formula for Northeastern. The work had taken us three years and many hours of discussion in multiple university forums. The formula itself had gone through successive refinements. Many voices had helped shape the final result. But the framework for our efforts was now set, and it would not change for the remainder of my presidency. To underscore its importance, I printed the words on the cover of folders we used for important administrative meetings:

## Our Aspiration

We will achieve excellence as a national research university that is student centered, practice oriented and urban.

## Our Vision

We will create the country's premier program of practice-oriented education.

## Our Competitive Goal

We will achieve recognition among the top 100 universities in the nation in the first decade of the 21st century.

From 1999 through the end of my presidency in 2006 I repeatedly reminded my colleagues of the importance of this formula. I saw my job as inspiring our collective efforts to achieve these goals, keeping our energies focused on activities most essential to their realization as identified by the Action and Assessment Plan, and celebrating our successes along the way. I used my State of the University addresses each fall and my reports to our governing Corporation each spring to put our year-to-year work in the context of these themes. I devoted large portions of our semi-annual leadership retreats to discussions of our progress. I charged each unit of the University to create plans for their own activities, indicating how they would contribute. Along the way I endured some ribbing—most of it, I thought, good natured—regarding my endless reiteration of these goals. But I was convinced that if we could accomplish them we would all be proud of what we had done.[11]

# CHAPTER 3

## Strategy and Structure

The thesis that different organizational forms result from
different types of growth can be stated more precisely. . . .
Strategy can be defined as the determination of the basic
long-term goals and objectives of an enterprise. . . .
Structure can be defined as the design of organization
through which the enterprise is administered. . . . The
thesis deduced from these several propositions is then
that structure follows strategy.

—Alfred D. Chandler, *Strategy and Structure*

The ambitious goals we defined for Northeastern at the beginning of my presidency raised fundamental questions about our institutional capabilities: Did we have the administrative competence to succeed at the competitive level to which we now aspired? Did we have the faculty to do so? Did our organizational culture promote the intensity of effort that success would demand? Was the quality of our students' experiences in the classroom, on co-op assignments, and in extracurricular life commensurate with the stature we wanted to claim? Were our formal structures appropriate to the plans we had crafted? Had Northeastern made the investments necessary to support our new ambitions? If not, did we have the resources to do so?

My early impressions of the campus community fostered concerns about all these matters. I knew that before we could be credible as a leading university within the distinctive framework of our Aspiration, we needed first to be strong in ways that are fundamental to all top-tier schools. To be distinctive without being clearly first rate is to risk seeming merely odd—and therefore unattractive to outstanding and ambitious high school graduates, who are typically conventional in their thinking about colleges and universities. It became apparent early on that we had work to do in four critical dimensions of organizational life: building a culture that demanded professional excellence of every member of our community; sustaining the alignment of our colleges and administrative units with the University-level strategic goals that we began to establish through the reaccreditation process in 1997–98; adjusting our formal structures to the requirements of our strategy; and acquiring the resources needed to strengthen our organization in key areas. Three of these issues occur in any complex organization, including the business enterprises that Chandler studied so brilliantly. One is especially associated with universities.

## Building a High Performance Organization

Our most fundamental challenge was in the area of organizational culture. The Northeastern that had grown into the country's largest private university was a sprawling, complex, uneven organization. Across the University I met talented individuals with high professional standards and accomplishments. Among our academic units the departments of electrical engineering and psychology had achieved well-deserved reputations for quality, as had our doctoral programs in physics and biology. Our law school was recognized as one of the country's strong programs oriented toward public service. The Barnett Institute, led by Professor Karger, was highly regarded for its work in biochemical analysis. The Center for the Study of Sport in Society, under Richard Lapchick, was a national force linking popular interest in sports to issues of social justice. Two faculty members, Jamie Fox in criminal justice and Jack Levin in sociology, were widely known commentators on matters of law enforcement. On the administrative side, our facilities department had developed a true culture of excellence under the demanding leadership of Vice President Jack Martin, as had our community relations team, led by Tom Keady. We also had deep strength in the area of financial management, including Vice President Culver's administrative team as well as key trustees on our Financial Affairs Committee under Chair Neal Finnegan.

These represented pockets of outstanding work. They did not define the general character of the institution. As I came to know the University I realized that our modest standing in reputational terms, in an intimidating local context dominated by Harvard and the Massachusetts Institute of

Technology (MIT), had fostered a "good enough for Northeastern" mental-
ity in too many of our departments. A number of units, including our two
most important colleges, Business and Engineering, seemed solid but not
distinguished. Our long-neglected programs in the humanities remained
seriously limited by resource constraints. Several administrative areas were
clearly problematic. Highly visible athletic programs, especially football and
men's ice hockey, were perennial losers. Our infrastructure in information
technology was out of date. Our financial aid office was a source of incessant
complaint from students. Two traditional pillars of Northeastern's reputation, our programs of cooperative education and adult education, were tired
and mediocre. Most of our doctoral programs ranked in the bottom two
quartiles of their disciplines nationally.

The University had also developed some bad habits. I was shocked to
discover faculty members canceling classes on days before vacations and
expecting extra stipends for attending commencement. Some of our events
struck me as poorly organized and badly executed. Fall convocation my first
year was an embarrassment of weak attendance and sloppy planning, as was
our homecoming celebration, at which the undergraduate king and queen
were too drunk to appear. University officers were treating themselves to
junkets to athletic events on institutional dollars. A few faculty and staff who
were active in campus politics were receiving stipends with few apparent
responsibilities attached. There were financial conflicts of interest within the
University's leadership. Alumni/ae programming was weak, and expectations regarding philanthropic support from Board members were between
low and nonexistent. I recall a get-acquainted visit by one of our most
prominent alums who had distanced himself from his alma mater. When
I described my ambitions for Northeastern, he made it clear that success
would require a major shakeup.[1]

When I spoke to the campus community in my first State of the University address about the need for an "intensification" of our efforts, I was
expressing in diplomatic terms my concern that the culture of "good enough
for Northeastern" was far too prevalent. The Intensification grants that we
awarded in the months after that speech were intended as a signal that I was
prepared to invest in individuals and units ready to raise their sights. I also
felt it necessary to make a public display of refusing to tolerate mediocrity or
impropriety. The very nice woman responsible for our homecoming program
in my first year got an angry call from me that Saturday evening, making clear
my distress at the way the University had presented itself to our graduates.

On three occasions I terminated long-term and very popular Northeastern employees, one of them a tenured faculty member, who were using university funds for personal benefit. I also undertook intensive evaluations of units that I regarded as particularly critical, such as admissions, or units where I believed we had significant problems, such as financial aid, co-op, adult and continuing education, and graduate programming.

The goal of transforming ourselves into a "high performance organization" became a central a theme of discussions within the administrative leadership. We devoted time at our regular retreats to this concept. We reviewed essays and books on the characteristics of highly successful organizations. We were particularly impressed by one of the popular management books of those years, *Built to Last* by Jim Collins and Jerry Porras, which argued that successful business organizations were driven by a passion for excellence rather than a quest for profits. We discussed efforts under way within Northeastern to improve the performance of individual units, and we celebrated examples of exceptional work by our colleagues, including a program of annual Excellence Awards that provided budget increments to departments for impressive results within their areas of responsibility. We also established a program of Aspiration Awards that gave cash prizes to individuals who made exceptional contributions to our work in one of the five areas of our Aspiration. Finally, we identified performance metrics for units all across the organization and set annual goals for improved numbers. I reviewed this data with senior members of my administrative team at the end of each academic year and explicitly linked these outcomes to annual salary adjustments.[2]

It was even more important to celebrate excellence on the academic side than on the administrative side, and I seized every opportunity to dramatize to our faculty and students that Northeastern was capable of competing at a high level. A few striking early successes helped make this case. Inspired by a newly appointed and ambitious dean, Allen Soyster, a team from our College of Engineering, led by Professor Michael Silevitch, won funding from the National Science Foundation to create an Engineering Research Center, a prestigious multimillion-dollar award made to a limited number of highly regarded schools. Our innovative High Tech MBA, designed by Professors Marc Meyer and Dan McCarthy, was ranked first in the country by a leading trade magazine. A team of undergraduates from our College of Business, coached by Ray Kinnunen, were perennial winners in an annual case competition against students from top business schools in the region. In all these cases we celebrated loudly and publicly. More quietly we tightened the standards for hiring and promotion to be commensurate with the expectations of the schools with which we intended to compete.

In the end, of course, we were not going to succeed without exceptional academic and administrative talent. Getting the right people into the right positions was an essential part of creating and sustaining a culture of excellence. One early initiative was a program of endowed Trustee Professorships designed to recruit at least one nationally distinguished scholar to each of our colleges. In the first few years of this program, we attracted three exceptional individuals who immediately became models of high achievement in their disciplines both within the campus and to external observers: Barry Bluestone in political science, Harry Lane in business, and Matthias Felleisen in computer and information science. On the administrative side, I was forced to replace a few senior officers who were not going to take us where we needed to go, and voluntary departures allowed me to make additional appointments. With these changes, supplemented by a number of current employees who adapted impressively to heightened expectations, I was surrounded by a team of talented and ambitious individuals who would drive the University's progress over the course of my presidential years, as subsequent chapters will make clear. Four members of my senior team went on in later years to become college or university presidents, several others moved to top-level appointments in their functional specialties at other institutions, and some remained at Northeastern where they continued to do excellent work.[3]

It is difficult to assess the impact of all the steps we took to build a high performance organization, and especially hazardous for a former president to do so. I had some actual data in the form of radically reduced complaints about financial aid or information technology services and dramatically improved numbers in admissions, adult and continuing education, and undergraduate retention. Some improvements I could see with my own eyes, as in the quality of our events and publications. But there were also departments that did not achieve the level to which we aspired and individuals who did not fulfill our hopes when we recruited them. All I can say with confidence is that, from my perspective, raising the bar of expectations for the quality of our work was indispensable to our long-term goal of repositioning Northeastern, and our ultimate success in achieving that result is evidence that, however incomplete our efforts, we made progress.

## Fostering Alignment with University Goals

Deepening and sustaining the shared understanding of what we wanted to become, which we began to establish during the reaccreditation process of 1997–98, posed a particular kind of challenge, not specific to Northeastern but embedded in the character of academic institutions. Management textbooks talk about this matter in terms of "alignment," and it makes sense that any organized human endeavor is more likely to succeed if its different parts and participants are working toward common ends. Within the culture of the academy, however, the goal of alignment bumps up against the more deeply ingrained value of autonomy. Universities insist, rightly, that independence from external control is essential to the quality and integrity of their work. Faculty culture, with reason, insists that individual professors must be free of administrative domination and, in practice, academic freedom is often expansively interpreted as independence from any kind of administrative oversight. The freedom of action generally granted to faculty members and academic units can easily spill over into an expectation within administrative departments as well.

The emphasis that academic culture places on autonomy has a profound impact on the governance of academic institutions and renders the challenge of alignment in universities different from that in the corporations Chandler studied. Any notion of top-down decision making, even on major questions of institutional strategy and direction, is suspect; any expectation by senior officers of compliance with their decisions on the basis of hierarchical authority is likely to be frustrated. In universities, individual schools and academic departments tend to operate almost as independent units, free to pursue the directions and priorities that seem to them most important with only modest attention to broader institutional concerns. In this sense universities are, as Karl Weick has described them, "loosely coupled" systems. Getting the different parts of the institution to agree on a common set of goals and to guide their own efforts in those directions is in some basic ways inconsistent with the character of academic organizations.[4]

Some universities have thrived by embracing the centrifugal forces embedded in university communities. Among Boston-area institutions, Harvard provides the best example. Harvard "University" is little more than a collection of schools run by their deans as largely independent fiefdoms. These units are undoubtedly tied together by a shared sense that Harvard should be outstanding in any field it enters, but beyond that there is minimal coordinating logic to the institution's purposes, as presidents who try to achieve some

measure of alignment among Harvard's component parts quickly discover.
The Harvard model, while an extreme case, is widely accepted among American universities, although some institutions have attempted to foster a more tightly bounded culture and sense of shared strategic direction. MIT was historically the best Boston-area example of this pattern, although as MIT grew larger, more complex, and more committed to basic research, its traditional emphasis on central control diminished dramatically.

From an organizational perspective, Northeastern's traditions were more like those of MIT than Harvard. Northeastern had developed as a niche institution centered on engineering, business, and cooperative education, quite different in character from a comprehensive and diversified institution like Boston University. Consistent with this history, Northeastern had a tradition of being administered much like a business, with a centralized pattern of decision making that was maintained well into the 1970s, even as the University began to develop strengths in the basic disciplines. Within this framework the academic side of the organization—the faculty, deans, even the provost—played far less significant roles in decision making than did their counterparts at more established institutions. This approach to administration had begun to shift during the Knowles era, in part encouraged by him as he sought to bring Northeastern into the academic mainstream with innovations like a faculty senate, but also in part resisted by him as a strong president with definite ideas about how the University should evolve. By the end of Knowles's term the tension between central control and the expectations of an increasingly professionalized faculty were severe enough to foster a movement toward unionization, an effort that might well have succeeded if Knowles had not stepped down and if his successor, Kenneth Ryder, had not adopted a far more collegial approach to leadership.

My predecessor, John Curry, understood that his "smaller but better" strategy for Northeastern implied significant changes in the University's administrative culture. Academic quality and centralized administrative control are inconsistent values in the modern American university, and Curry took steps to empower both the academic administrators and the faculty in ways more consistent with mainstream practices. He made it clear, for example, that his provost would occupy the number-two position in the administrative hierarchy, and he adopted a far more participatory approach to strategic planning than had his predecessors.[5]

From my perspective the pattern of organizational change initiated by Ryder and continued by Curry had moved Northeastern in the right direction and needed to be continued, especially by further empowering the provost and college deans, whom I regarded as the keys to enhancing our academic strength. But the residual institutional tradition of respect for central leadership also had advantages, especially with regard to achieving alignment with University-wide goals. For example, my belief that the faculty and staff would not have an instinctively negative reaction to a strong statement of strategic directions by a new president was an important consideration in crafting my first State of the University address. It also influenced the way my team and I approached the reaccreditation self-study as well as the first iteration of the Action and Assessment Plan within the Office of the Provost, both of which were carried out with a comparatively high level of administrative control. The degree of approval within the campus community of the Aspiration as a framework for our future development that was observed by the reaccreditation visiting committee indicated to me that this way of proceeding had been acceptable to the campus community, at least as a way of establishing an initial trajectory for my presidency.

The challenge of persuading the faculty and staff to fully embrace the goals my team and I had articulated for the University and to work actively to achieve them was an entirely different matter than gaining preliminary acceptance. My years in academic administration prior to Northeastern had taught me that there were only two ways to foster the kind of alignment we needed. First and most important were persuasion and inspiration: faculty and staff, especially the former, need to believe in and care about the priorities a president has articulated. Second was participation: community members need to feel involved in the process of shaping goals they are expected to pursue. Over the years that followed the initial formulation of our long-range plans, my leadership team and I took a number of steps to compensate for the somewhat top-down approach we had initially taken in order to deepen the engagement of the faculty and staff with University-wide priorities.

Our first emphasis addressed the challenge of persuasion and inspiration and lay in the area of communications. I typically devoted the major part of my published annual reports as well as State of the University addresses and speeches to the annual meeting of the Corporation to some aspect of the Aspiration. We used the annual "report cards" summarizing our progress with respect to the five dimensions of the Aspiration and the top-100 goal as a regular agenda item at the semi-annual retreats of the senior leadership. To reach beyond the top tier of University leaders, we instituted twice-yearly gatherings of chairs and directors from all 160 academic and administrative departments to hear briefings on our progress, and I reinforced these messages during regular visits to the individual colleges, academic departments, and administrative units. Our fine Vice President for Human Resources, Kater Pendergast, developed an orientation program for new faculty and staff that emphasized the Aspiration as the distinctive focus for our work. The annual Excellence Awards were always linked to one of the themes of the Aspiration.[6]

In parallel with our relentless reiteration of the value and importance of our strategic directions, we also took steps to institutionalize these goals through the active engagement of faculty and staff across the University. There were two primary vehicles for this: Unit Planning and the University Planning Council (UPC).

As previously noted, a central theme of the Action and Assessment Plan was the development of detailed plans by each academic and administrative unit stating how it would contribute to the overall goals of the University. The Unit Planning process was initiated in the spring of 1999 and continued for the next three and a half years. During this period every academic and administrative department, guided by the appropriate dean, vice president, or senior vice president, worked on these documents, which were required to include metrics by which we could monitor progress. Once accepted by a dean or senior vice president, a proposed plan was reviewed by my senior leadership team. Many plans required multiple reviews before being approved. The Excellence Awards, which could be as large as $100,000, became a vehicle for linking these plans to the budget. The first round of awards to units that had made exceptional progress were announced in the spring of 2000 from a fund of $1 million, a pattern that was repeated annually for the remainder of my presidency.

Despite producing much good work, the Unit Planning process was only partially successful. It did contribute to the overall goal of aligning the work of individual departments with University-wide goals and, in most instances, it yielded useful—in a few cases, even superb—frameworks to guide departmental activities. The quality of the plans was highly variable, however, and a few departments had so much difficulty producing satisfactory proposals that it seemed pointless to push further. I came to believe that to be fully successful an initiative like Unit Planning needed far more professional support than we had been able to provide.

While the Unit Planning process was an effort to embed work on University-wide goals in the activities of individual academic and administrative departments, the role of the University Planning Council involved the ongoing review of the goals themselves. Thus, in the fall of 2000, I charged this group, a broadly representative body originally created to work on enrollment issues, to assume responsibility for overseeing the continued implementation of the AAP. From that time forward this group of faculty, staff, students, and senior members of the administration, convened by our very capable Director of Planning and Research, Mark Putnam, conducted annual reviews of our progress and issued reports recommending where adjustments were needed. This shift from a centrally controlled implementation process to a more broadly participatory one occurred quite seamlessly and was, I believe, an appropriate acknowledgment of the fundamental principle of shared governance in the modern American university.[7]

It is difficult to gauge our success in aligning the work of leaders at all levels of our organization as well as the broader campus community with the long-range goals my team and I articulated at the beginning of my presidency. There was plenty of grumbling about too many goals and too much pressure to improve. At the midpoint of my presidency organizational fatigue became a major concern, and we distributed packets of trail mix at that year's State of the University event, during which I urged my colleagues to stay the course. A presidential review by a committee of Trustees in 2001 expressed serious concern about lack of support for our priorities. However, as time went on and we began to achieve some successes, the campus community responded with enthusiasm. One example occurred in 2002 when *U.S. News* ranked Northeastern number one in the country among universities encouraging students to combine academic study with real-world experience. A survey of faculty and staff toward the end of my presidency indicated a high degree of awareness and support regarding University-wide goals. When we ultimately succeeded, as we did the month I stepped down, in achieving the top-100 goal, there was a palpable sense of shared accomplishment on the part of the University community.[8]

## Adapting Structure to Strategy

When Alfred Chandler wrote that "structure follows strategy," he was referring primarily to the formal organization of the corporations he had studied, matters—like the distribution of authority and responsibility—that would be reflected on an organization chart. He observed that, as his sample enterprises became larger and more complex, they redesigned their bureaucratic structures in fundamental ways. That insight was particularly striking to me as I studied the evolution of universities in writing *Academia's Golden Age* because, with the impressive exception of MIT, I found little evidence of systematic thought about how to relate strategy and structure. Indeed, there appeared to be a fairly standard model of formal organization that was utilized by universities with widely varying missions and strategies and that changed very little over time: a common set of functional divisions—academics, finance, student services, fund-raising, external affairs—headed by vice presidents; an academic structure of colleges or schools composed of discipline-based departments and headed by deans and coordinated by a vice president or provost; possibly, in highly developed universities with a strong set of interdisciplinary research institutes, a separate division of research. The most notable exception to this pattern—a phenomenon of the 1960s and 1970s—was the formation of interdisciplinary units in place of departments, which occurred at a limited number of colleges (rarely at universities) and represented an effort to promote dialogue across lines of professorial specialization and diminish the grip of narrow academic interests on the curriculum.

As I thought about how Northeastern needed to evolve as an organization to achieve our long-range goals, I always began with Chandler's insights. This led me to several decisions that made individual administrators or faculty groups unhappy but that seemed to me likely to improve our chances for success. The most important expressions of this pattern occurred within the academic side of our organization. At the time I was appointed, a cluster of functions directly concerned with students—admissions, financial aid, student affairs, and residential life—all reported to the provost and senior vice president for academic affairs, a common arrangement among American universities. As I observed the workings of this structure, however, it became clear that the first claim on the provost's attention was (and had to be) from the academic deans and the faculty. Student issues inevitably received secondary focus. Yet it was glaringly clear that our commitment to being a "student-centered" university and our goal of attracting more academically qualified applicants were top-tier challenges requiring sustained attention and uncompromised advocacy at the highest level of the organization. Thus, in a series of steps, I created a new senior vice presidency responsible for overseeing all these student-oriented functions. There was considerable criticism of this change, especially from the leadership of the faculty, who argued that admissions, in particular, was traditionally part of the academic structure. But in my mind Chandler's principle trumped administrative tradition. We created the new position and appointed a remarkably skillful enrollment management professional named Philomena Mantella to the post; over the remaining years of my presidency, the work of this division was a primary contributor to our progress.

An even more controversial change involved cooperative education, the centerpiece of Northeastern's claim to distinctiveness among our institutional peers. In the structure I inherited, "co-op" was organized as a centralized division headed by a vice president. Individual co-op "coordinators," who were responsible for helping students find job placements and advising them in connection with off-campus work, were assigned to the various academic departments, but they were administratively responsible to the vice president for co-op, not to the deans of the colleges or chairs of the academic departments, and they were physically housed together in a central location. These arrangements reflected Northeastern's traditional emphasis on the financial benefits of co-op as distinct from its academic value. The centralized structure and isolated location maximized attention to placing students in paying jobs rather than promoting work experiences that complemented classroom study. Indeed, the Co-op Division thought of itself as an independent academic unit, with its own pedagogy and educational goals, rather than as a service department that supported teaching and learning in the colleges. As I observed this structure in operation, I realized that it worked at cross purposes with our goal of positioning co-op in the academic marketplace primarily as a potent enhancement of campus-based learning. Accordingly, Provost Hall and I moved to decentralize the co-op division, assigning the various coordinators to the academic units they served, giving them offices in those units, and charging the faculties to fully integrate the coordinators into their work and to focus on leveraging the interaction between co-op and classroom in structuring their courses of study. This change earned a loud protest from the co-op coordinators and a formal request to the Trustees that the decision be reversed. The provost and I, however, had worked closely both with the Board and the University's faculty leaders on this matter and, with decisive support of our decisions from Trustees Neal Finnegan and Michael Cronin, the protest went nowhere.

A third structural change in the academic arena was almost unanimously welcomed by the faculty, with business being the only major exception: conversion from a quarter to a semester calendar. This was a change in the direction of mainstream academic patterns that many faculty members had advocated for years, arguing, with good reason, that the rapid pace of the quarter calendar—which had initially been adopted because of its perceived compatibility with the co-op program—diminished the quality of student learning in individual courses. When this proposal was first presented to me, I agreed to give it careful consideration, though I worried that such a change would be an enormous drain on organizational energies and possibly a distraction from our long-range goals. As Provost Hall and I looked at this matter, however, we gradually realized that converting to a semester calendar could promote rather than retard the changes we were trying to make. For one thing, we agreed with faculty advocates that the semester calendar had advantages in terms of student learning. We also realized that it had benefits for admissions, since the quarter calendar was unusual and therefore suspect in the minds of some potential students. Moreover, when we consulted our co-op employers we learned that most would actually prefer having students for a longer period of time. So the arguments to make the change began to seem quite powerful. In the end, however, what was decisive for us was the realization that converting to a semester calendar would require every academic department to redesign every academic course and program. This would create a fluid and creative environment in which we could work with faculty not only to modernize and strengthen programs that had grown stale but also to build a much higher level of integration between co-op and classroom. So we made the change. As predicted, the process was long, complicated, and laborious, but it was managed superbly by a University-wide team led by Vice Provost Coleen Pantalone, and, in the end, it fostered exactly the context for rejuvenating our academic program for which we had hoped.[9]

We made a number of other structural changes in our academic organization during my presidential years. Some of these—like combining our colleges of Nursing, Pharmacy, and Physical Education into an integrated College of Health Sciences under a single dean or creating a new School of Social Science, Public Policy, and Urban Affairs within the College of Arts and Sciences—proved immensely helpful in advancing our broader University-wide goals. Others, like creating a School of Technological Entrepreneurship as a freestanding unit, drawing faculty from both Business and Engineering, or adopting a more centrally controlled structure for admissions to graduate programs, were less successful. On balance, however, I believe that the modifications of our academic structures that I have described played important roles in advancing our progress. Having Chandler's work clearly in mind as we managed these processes gave me the intellectual conviction to resist some serious unhappiness within the University community.

Structural changes on the administrative side of our organization were less difficult politically than on the academic side, but they were no less important to our long-term success. Among the most important of these was the creation of a new Office of University Planning and Research (OUPR), reporting directly to the president and charged to provide the analytic capability needed to inform policy development. This step reflected my long-held belief that institutional research was a severely underutilized function in most universities, where staff typically spent their time compiling "fact books" and statistical reports to meet various regulatory requirements. Northeastern had a department that did this kind of work as part of the academic administration at the time of my appointment. What we needed—and got—under the leadership first of Edna Seaman and then Mark Putnam—was an office that conducted sophisticated analytic studies of policy problems and helped us isolate and dissect the issues and target appropriate interventions. Over the years of my presidency the work of this office proved to be indispensable in guiding our work.

Equally important was the creation of a Division of Marketing and Communications headed by a vice president and reporting directly to the president. As I mentioned previously in discussing our early work on marketing, I was convinced from the beginning of my presidency that Northeastern needed to move beyond a traditional "university relations" function and build a modern, aggressive, and highly professional marketing capability, even though such a step was still unusual within higher education. But we did it and were able to recruit talented people to its leadership, initially Sandra King and later Brian Kenny and Fred McGrail. Their work contributed greatly to our efforts to increase Northeastern's visibility both within academia and with the general public. Two new functions were designed to strengthen our ties with business and industry and reinforce our identity as a "practice-oriented" university. The Office of Technology Transfer, led by Anthony Pirri, was charged to manage interactions between our researchers and potential industry partners who could provide financial support and possibly become linked to Northeastern through licensing arrangements or the acquisition of patents, a function that had previously been handled by the academic departments and individual scholars. The Office of Corporate Partnerships under Marian Stanley was charged to promote and coordinate relationships with business partners that often connected with us through different parts of our organization, including co-op, research, fund-raising, and job placement for graduates.

I was particularly proud of the way we organized our relationships with the neighborhoods surrounding the campus, the broader metropolitan community, and the government agencies with which we interacted. In many universities, these activities are viewed as part of the broad external relations arena and are supervised by a vice president who also handles marketing and media relations. There is logic to that structural pattern, but, from my perspective, such an organization was antithetical to our goal of excellence as an urban university. For Northeastern, promoting active, constructive relationships and interactions with our urban community was not centrally about keeping our neighbors and local politicians happy so that we could pursue our autonomous purposes—though maintaining good relationships was obviously important. Our deeper purpose was to organize our activities and manage our development in ways that both advanced the goals of the University and contributed to the well-being of the city. For me there was no better example of Chandler's principle that structure should follow strategy than our decision to treat community relations and marketing as entirely distinct administrative functions.[10]

## Acquiring Needed Resources

Our efforts to attract talented faculty and staff, deploy these individuals within structures that reflected our strategy, set high standards of performance, and inspire the energized pursuit of shared goals were all essential to strengthening Northeastern's capacities. But there were limits to how far initiatives like these could take us. In the end, financial resources were going to make a critical difference. A quick review of the rankings of colleges and universities in any institutional category will quickly validate this point; those at the top are almost invariably the wealthiest. The ability to maintain a faculty of appropriate size and quality, pay competitive salaries, create attractive working conditions, provide faculty with adequate staff assistance, support the various administrative functions appropriately, and offer competitive levels of financial aid all matter a great deal and all are fundamentally a matter of money. My years at UMass Boston and CUNY had made me painfully aware how hard it is for dedicated, talented people to achieve the results of which they are capable when resources are constrained. In pushing Northeastern to compete within the top tier of the country's universities, we implicitly raised a question about our finances: Could we provide the necessary support for our faculty, staff, and students?

Northeastern's revenue, like that of most universities, came from four principal sources: student payments, private donations, endowment income, and government assistance. Among these, for Northeastern, as for most private universities—particularly urban institutions—the first was overwhelmingly the most important, with government-sponsored financial aid, which mostly went to students rather than to institutions, a close second. But the others mattered, and during my presidential years we did a number of things to increase our support from nontuition revenues, especially philanthropy and grants from both private and public sources, to carry out specific research projects and educational or service programs.

Fund-raising from private donors historically posed challenges for non-elite urban institutions. The social and economic backgrounds of the students they served, together with the Spartan, commuting experience they typically provided, tended to work against the development of philanthropic sentiments among alumni/ae, who are typically the primary sources of gifts. Northeastern's fund-raising record amply demonstrated this pattern. Over its early history the University's limited activities in this area had focused narrowly on a few major prospects and had produced modest results. The endowment of $153 million at the time President Curry was appointed was strikingly small for an institution claiming recognition as the country's largest private university, and a significant percentage of these funds reflected transfers from operating surpluses rather than gifts. Curry recognized, however, that the "smaller but better" strategy implied a major effort to improve fund-raising, and he took important steps in this direction, doubling the budget of the advancement office and increasing its staff even as he imposed cuts on the rest of the institution. With these investments Curry was able to substantially raise the bar for fund-raising at Northeastern, launching and nearly completing the Centennial Campaign, which, under the inspirational leadership of Trustee Robert Marini, ultimately raised a record $118 million in donations from private sources.[11]

I shared the belief that Northeastern could not sustain itself as a top-tier university without far more robust philanthropic support than we had historically achieved, and I decided to mount a new effort shortly after completing the Centennial Campaign in the first two years of my presidency. In retrospect, this decision reflected my lack of fund-raising experience combined with an overestimation of the depth and breadth of commitment to

Northeastern among our alumni/ae and of the speed with which my vision for the University would gain traction among potential donors. My Senior Vice President for Advancement, Richard Meyer, after making clear his reservations, gamely went along with my wishes and endorsed a target for private gifts of $200 million, a big jump from the outcome of the Centennial Campaign. Chairman Matthews and the Board of Trustees also supported this plan, though I came over time to believe I should have tested the depth of the Board's commitment much more carefully before deciding to go forward.

Over the course of my presidency, with dedicated efforts from a set of volunteer committees composed of Trustees and members of the Corporation and led by Trustee Ronald Rossetti, plus hard work by an Advancement staff led by Meyer and later Robert Cunningham, we diligently pursued a twofold effort: broadening the base of support through the annual fund while obtaining larger gifts from a constituency of graduates and friends that included, in fact, a significant number of financially successful individuals, some of them extraordinarily wealthy. In the end we achieved our goals, and I shall be forever grateful for the generosity of those who participated in this effort, including George Behrakis, Robert Shillman, Jean Tempel, and George Kostas, who made the outsized contributions that put us over the top, and the larger number who made very significant gifts, including sixteen of $1 million or more. The campaign allowed us to support more scholarships, create faculty chairs, and add important new programs. In private conversations within the campaign leadership and among Board members, however, we acknowledged that the effort was proving difficult. My own limitations as a fund-raiser undoubtedly played a role here. But we also probably hoped for too much too soon. Many potential donors still had difficulty thinking of Northeastern as a candidate for the large gifts that were routine among well-established, top-ranked private universities. In fact, the largest contribution received during my presidency—$20 million—came from non-alum Bernard Gordon, who had no prior ties to Northeastern but who admired our approach to education as well as the work Michael Silevitch and his team were doing in digital imaging.[12]

Given modest contributions to the University's annual budget from donations and endowment income, and limited government support, primarily in the form of state and federal scholarships, Northeastern continued during my years to depend heavily on student payments for operating revenues. The only major exception to this pattern involved federal grants for research, which will be discussed in Chapter 6, but these were focused on particular projects and were not available to support the general development of the University. In a typical year student payments of all kinds provided more than 80 percent of our general operating revenues. Happily, however, we achieved some significant growth in two of these sources: undergraduate tuition and fees, and revenues from continuing education.

Northeastern's history of dependence on payments from undergraduates represented an interesting dilemma. From a financial perspective, President Curry's "smaller but better" strategy was paradoxical: "Smaller" meant less money while "better" implied more expenditures. In this context the question of how small we could become and still support the repositioning strategy required urgent attention. Early in my presidency I charged Edna Seaman's new Office of University Planning and Research to work with a committee of experienced faculty and staff to develop a comprehensive enrollment and resource plan that would address this foundational issue. The group's March 1998 report concluded that a freshman class of 2,800 was the minimum number that would allow us to finance our operations while also improving selectivity and that, even with that number, additional budget reductions might well be needed. Fortunately, this initial plan underestimated the success we would have in retaining the students we admitted, a matter that also represented an early and continuing focus of my presidency. Beginning in the fall of 1998 and for every year thereafter we rigidly adhered to the 2,800 freshman admissions goal while also steadily increasing overall undergraduate enrollments through rising rates of persistence. This phenomenon allowed us not only to avoid the reductions that the enrollment planning committee had anticipated but also to acquire significant new revenue.[13]

Our success in adult and continuing education was a long time coming. Part-time programs for working adults had been a major component of Northeastern's offerings from the University's earliest years and, incorporated into a new unit called University College during the Knowles presidency, these programs had grown rapidly to become major contributors to Northeastern's fiscal health. By the 1980s, however, University College's emphasis on undergraduate work for older students was increasingly out of step with a highly competitive and rapidly changing adult education marketplace; at the time of my election enrollments had been declining for years, prompting steady price increases to maintain a reasonably level revenue stream. It was clear that a new approach was needed. Our initial focus involved the heightened use of technology to support distance education programs, which appeared to be the direction of growth in this field. Unfortunately, the results were disappointing, and by 2001 we were looking for a new strategy. By this time it was also clear that University College, which had continued to offer programs of questionable quality to almost anyone who could pay the fee, was undermining our efforts to rebrand Northeastern as an institution with high academic standards.

In this context I became convinced that the right direction for us was continuing professional education at an advanced level, a field that other universities in our area, most notably Harvard, had developed with impressive results in terms of both program quality and revenue. We had the good fortune to recruit the ideal new leader to move University College in this direction in Christopher Hopey, a creative and entrepreneurial alumnus then working at the University of Pennsylvania. Between 2003 and 2006 Hopey completely revamped this unit, renaming it the School of Professional and Continuing Studies, creating quality programs at the master's level in close collaboration with the faculty and deans from our degree-granting colleges, and extending Northeastern's reach through distance education and international programming. With these changes, enrollments began to grow rapidly, and in the last years of my presidency revenues from this unit made increasing contributions to our annual budget.[14]

Northeastern's continued dependence on student payments as the primary source of new revenue was not the outcome I had hoped for at the beginning of my presidency. What we would ultimately need was a much healthier combination of revenues from multiple sources. Still, in conjunction with aggressive efforts to control costs and collect receivables instituted by our smart, parsimonious Senior Vice President for Administration and Finance, Lawrence Mucciolo, plus the very real contributions of the Leadership Campaign, we experienced sufficient revenue flexibility to support a number of critical investments. Our initial emphasis was on components of our organization that were essential to our progress but were simply not strong enough given our goals. Enrollment Management, Information Technology, and Marketing were three prime examples. For different reasons we also invested heavily in financial aid, to which Northeastern traditionally had devoted limited dollars on the theory that students were earning what they needed through our co-op program. Over time we were able to address other critical issues, especially, toward the end of my presidency, faculty salaries.

In addition to using our strengthened finances to support the broad development of our organization, we were able, for two very different reasons, to support two major investment initiatives that were transformative for the

University. The first of these was possible because our operating revenues were sufficient to allow us to set aside dollars each year during the initial years of my presidency to build an investment fund even as we increased the general operating budget. In discussions with Board Chair Neal Finnegan, who succeeded George Matthews in 1998, I became convinced that our financially conservative Board would support a major initiative if I could make a compelling case. In 2004, after months of planning led by Mark Putnam, Sam Solomon, and Patricia Meservey and an endorsement by the Trustees, we launched the Academic Investment Plan, a multiyear, $75 million program to hire 100 new full-time faculty, a number that would allow us to achieve a competitive ratio of students to full-time faculty, reduce our excessive dependence on part-time instructors, strengthen our capacities in specified areas of scholarship, and improve our ranking. The second transformative set of investments involved a program of facilities development: Eleven new buildings plus two acquisitions—over the course of my ten years. We financed this $450 million effort with income from the structures themselves (the residence halls were revenue producing) and with borrowed dollars, which were available to us because Northeastern possessed a large pool of funds for collateral within our endowment, which had been acquired not as dedicated gifts but as transfers from operating surpluses.[15]

## Strategy and Structure

Over the course of my presidency, through the multiple steps we took to strengthen the capacities and align the efforts of the campus community and to acquire resources to support our work, my team and I endeavored to build the organization that Alfred Chandler taught us was needed to implement our strategy. Such work, of course, is never truly finished. For us it was also, though vitally important, ultimately a means to an end. Our central focus, always, was to serve our current students as well as we could while repositioning Northeastern as a top-tier national research university that was student centered, practice oriented, and urban. The next four chapters tell the story of that work.

## CHAPTER 4

# Shaping a Student-Centered Research University

What will a student-centered university look like in the twenty-first century? This question has guided us over the past five years. Our investment in information technology has grown. . . . We have initiated new construction that will add modern residences. . . . We have kept college affordable . . . by investing . . . in new financial aid. . . . We have enriched our academic offerings and attracted nationally renowned scholars . . . we have concentrated the attention of our faculty on making Northeastern's practice-oriented education a learning model of national significance. These commitments reflect our central strategic imperative: Even as we grow as a national university, our students are the center of everything we do.

—Annual Report 2000–2001

## The Initial Priority: Undergraduate Education

One thing was completely clear to me as I thought about implementing our strategic formula. Job one was delivering excellence in every aspect of the undergraduate experience: in the classroom, on co-op assignments, in extracurricular life, in student services. Our repositioning plan depended on attracting, retaining, and graduating highly capable students who, while they were enrolled and as alumni/ae, would sing the praises of a Northeastern education to their families, friends, high school advisers, and employers.

But how could we attract such students in the first place? Strong applicants would be drawn by a reputation for quality, and Northeastern had
surrendered any serious claim on that score by becoming essentially an open-
admissions institution during the recent enrollment crisis, a claim already
weakened in the 1960s and 1970s by the University's determination to be the
largest private university in the country—and to base its financial health on
maintaining that scale. Conventional wisdom among college presidents in the
late twentieth century held that the way to build the reputation of a university
was to pursue the model of the modern research university: hire well-known
professors, invest in research centers and doctoral programs, and leave much
of the responsibility for teaching undergraduates to graduate students and
part-time instructors. Some of my colleague presidents at urban universities
were pursuing versions of this strategy, most notably George Mason University in Virginia, which was putting itself on the map by recruiting Nobel lau-
reates. Voices within the Northeastern community were advocating a similar
approach for us.

I saw several problems with seeking recognition as a top-tier university by
stressing the advanced academic functions. One concern, though not for me
the most important one, was that such a strategy would be expensive, and we
were struggling to pay our bills. In addition, building a reputation for quality
by investing in research and graduate education would take a long time to
bear fruit, especially if pursued in a series of small steps, which would be the
only feasible way for us to do it, and we were in a hurry. More fundamentally,
I did not think such a policy was the best way to improve undergraduate
teaching and learning. While I understood and partially accepted the argument that research-active faculty are often the most engaging teachers, I had
seen (and studied with) wonderful teachers who were fine and committed
scholars but not productive researchers—as well as excellent researchers who
were mediocre in the classroom. Moreover, my work in academic administration over many years had convinced me that a dominant emphasis on
the advanced functions could well divert attention from undergraduates and
actually weaken their educational experiences.

In thinking about how best to balance our attention between the undergraduate program and research and graduate education, I was also influenced
by the perception I summarized in Chapter 1: The dominance of research
productivity as the primary determinant of elite status among the nation's
universities during the late twentieth century had been a mixed blessing for
academia and for the country. On the positive side, the flowering of great

centers of academic research had brought multiple benefits to American society and largely accounted for the country's newly acquired status as the world's leader in higher education. At the same time, this phenomenon had devalued undergraduate teaching and led too many institutions to focus on research during years when academia needed also to address the challenge of educating an expanding and increasingly diverse undergraduate constituency. Against this background, and aware that the Boston area was already richly endowed with research-oriented institutions, I wanted Northeastern to demonstrate that a university could achieve a reputation for excellence by placing a primary emphasis on baccalaureate-level studies, while also, as a secondary and complementary priority, enhancing research and graduate work. This seemed to me a way for us to do what was best for our students while also doing something important for higher education nationally.

The key organizing concept that my team and I adopted to reflect our emphasis on undergraduate teaching and learning was the "student-centered research university." I had first encountered this idea through the work of another of my urban university presidential colleagues, Chancellor Ken Shaw of Syracuse. Though Shaw's university was not unique in embracing this idea—the University of Virginia and Arizona State University also did so—Shaw was an especially forceful advocate and had translated this concept into a range of initiatives to enhance the undergraduate experience. I liked Shaw's phrase because it implied the integration of two institutional tendencies that pulled in different directions, placing a priority on the undergraduate experience while recognizing the importance, both substantive and strategic, of graduate education and research. I recognized, of course, that achieving the right balance between these two dimensions of academic work would not be easy; that it would take sustained, committed leadership at the highest level of the institution; and that there would always be the potential to succumb to the seductions of the research-focused model. However, if the proper mix of emphases could be maintained, Shaw's concept offered the prospect of a superb undergraduate experience while leaving significant though circumscribed room for the advanced academic functions.[1]

Embracing the concept of the student-centered research university helped my team and me focus our work at the beginning of my presidency. We would seek first to achieve excellence with respect to all dimensions of the undergraduate experience. Later, we would address improving our posture in graduate education and research with the goal of achieving genuine excellence in a limited number of fields while stressing the synergies between the advanced functions and undergraduate studies. In anticipation of this later phase—and to postpone discussion of new doctoral programs—during the first months of my presidency I charged our Vice Provost for Research and Graduate Education, Ronald Hedlund, to initiate the comprehensive review of our graduate programs that had been recommended by a University committee shortly before my election. The remainder of this chapter and the chapters that follow reflect the sequencing of our work. Our efforts to improve the undergraduate experience—admissions, graduation rates, classroom study, student support, and extracurricular life—provide the focus for the remainder of this chapter. Our work on cooperative education and practice-oriented education—the distinguishing characteristics of our undergraduate program and the center-piece of our strategic formula—are reviewed in Chapter 5. Graduate education and research are the subject of Chapter 6.

### The Central Issue: Student Success

Although President Curry did not use the phrase "student-centered research university" to describe his goals for Northeastern, he understood that improving our undergraduate program had to be part of the "smaller but better" strategy. There was a lot to overcome in this respect given Northeastern's history as a large, commuter school often characterized by students as "the factory on Huntington Avenue." During his seven-year presidency Curry took a number of important steps: enhancing facilities, most notably a new recreation complex, a new research building, and a major renovation of the student center; making student services more efficient through stronger staff training and improved use of technology; supporting students of color and diverse sexual identities; enhancing financial aid; and strengthening the role of teaching evaluations by students in faculty personnel decisions. Beyond these concrete initiatives, Curry went to great lengths to be visible on campus, meeting with student leaders regularly and consulting with them on key policy decisions. All of this made him immensely popular and earned him the informal title "the students' president." The phrase I used in the epigraph at the beginning of this chapter—"our students are the center of everything we do"—was borrowed from Curry's first State of the University address. Surveys of student opinion at the time I became president reported generally positive feelings about their experiences at Northeastern.

Curry's accomplishments gave us a great deal to build on, but it also quickly became clear that much work remained to be done to make the reality of Northeastern commensurate with our claim of "student centeredness." Our financial aid program was woefully inadequate given the needs of our students. Our residential facilities were tired and insufficient. Our instructional program was far too dependent on poorly paid part-timers. Extracurricular life was thin, a reality partially attributable to the fact that co-op removed half the students from campus for extended periods. Student affairs staff reported a high level of apathy among undergraduates. There were chronic complaints about our support services, often characterized by students as the "NU shuffle." Benchmarked surveys of overall student satisfaction with the Northeastern experience placed us well below our peer, four-year private universities.

The most powerful indicator of problems was our abysmal graduation rate. For many years Northeastern had been a revolving door for undergraduates, with more dropping out than finishing. In 1996, the year I was elected, the University reported a six-year graduation rate of 40 percent, a number more typical of a low-cost, unselective, public urban university than of the high quality, private institution Northeastern needed to become. We were losing a quarter of our new students after their freshman year. This phenomenon reflected a number of issues. At the top of the list was the unpleasant truth that, under the banner of providing "access," Northeastern had been admitting many students whose academic backgrounds were so weak, and whose financial resources were so limited, that they had little chance of completing a degree. This fundamental reality inevitably fostered distance between students and the faculty and staff, creating a disincentive to invest in relationships with young people who might be gone next semester or next year. All of this had to change. We needed to be a place where every student we admitted had a reasonable chance of finishing, where every member of our faculty and staff was committed to helping every student achieve that goal, and where the quality of the student experience and the value of our degree inspired a determination to persist. We set our sights on a six-year graduation rate of 70 percent, the average among private institutions broadly comparable to Northeastern ranked by *U.S. News* among the top 100 national universities.

Improving our graduation rate became the primary metric by which we measured progress toward excellence as a student-centered institution. I was not naïve about the difficulty of change in this realm, especially at an institution that served urban students. I had struggled with poor graduation rates for many years as Dean of Arts and Sciences at UMass Boston and as Vice

Chancellor for Academic Affairs at CUNY. Those experiences had taught me that even incremental progress was a major achievement. Against that background, moving from 40 percent to 70 percent seemed almost unimaginable. But this was a challenge we had to accept. We could not hope to attract the kinds of students we needed without a respectable profile with regard to completion. Dramatic change was also essential to our goal of becoming a top-100 institution given the weight attached to this metric in the *U.S. News* formula.

We knew success would take time and had to be part of a broad pattern of institutional change. Over the ten years of my presidency, the drive to improve our graduation rate remained a central focus for my leadership team. In 2006, the year I stepped down, we reported a six-year rate of 64 percent, and we knew from retention statistics for our lower division students that we would soon be at 70 percent. The progress remained steady after my departure. The six-year graduation rate for the class admitted in my final year jumped to 79 percent, almost double the rate we reported in 1996. Of all the changes that occurred during my presidency, this is among those of which I am most proud.[2]

## Student Success and Cultural Change

The difficult thing about improving graduation rates is that so many factors can influence this number. Some students drop out for reasons that have nothing to do with their college experience, for example financial constraints. Some leave because the school does not offer the program they want or because they find the work too hard or too easy. Some are influenced by unhappy social experiences or unpleasant interactions with university officers. Some don't like the housing or the food. Awareness of this complexity led us to pursue two different lines of attack. The first was to involve the whole campus—every department, both academic and administrative, and every member of the faculty and staff—in what over the course of my presidency we came to call our "Student Success Initiative." The second was to determine with as much precision as we could what factors were having the greatest impact on our dropout rate.

The importance of student success became a standard theme in my annual State of the University addresses. My message was simple: For us to significantly improve our graduation rate, the attitude of "good enough for Northeastern," meaning mediocre, was no longer good enough in any aspect of our work. Every member of our faculty and staff needed to understand that every interaction of every student with an individual or office representing the University was going to have an impact on that student's attitude toward Northeastern and hence on the student's decision to persist or to leave. Improving our completion rate was not the responsibility of a single office or senior administrator; the whole campus community needed to be committed to it. Given widespread worries about our finances (recent layoffs were on everyone's mind), I pointed out that every 1 percent increase in our graduation rate was worth $1 million in our annual budget.

In conjunction with this rhetorical campaign, we created a series of structures designed to involve all parts of the University in the Student Success Initiative in quite specific ways. The first of these was a University-wide task force appointed by Provost Hall in 1998 and chaired by Dean Larry Finkelstein of the College of Computer Science (later the College of Computer and Information Science, CCIS) and Enrollment Management Vice President Jean Eddy. This group was given two assignments: first, to recommend practical steps we could take at once to improve retention; second, to undertake an in-depth analysis of the whole problem of persistence. The Task Force proposed an initial focus on student services, an arena of chronic student complaint reflected in the phrase "NU shuffle." The most important contribution of the Finkelstein/Eddy group, however, was initiating a research program by Mark Putnam's Office of University Planning and Research. Over the next several years the OUPR completed a series of analyses, several of which were done by our fine statistical analyst, Neal Fogg, which played a significant role in guiding work on our graduation rate.

A successor initiative to the Finkelstein/Eddy Task Force was centered in the provost's office and involved setting retention goals for each college and, within each college, for each department. We also made improving persistence and graduation rates a major focus of the Unit Planning process between 1999 and 2002, thereby requiring every academic and administrative department to develop a specific plan stating how it would address this issue. Yet another broad-based initiative was launched in early 2001, a cross-functional working group charged to promote coordination among every part of the University in increasing retention. As a result of all this sustained activity over the ten years of my presidency, it is unlikely that any academic or administrative department, or any member of the University's middle-level leadership, was not directly involved one way or another in the Student Success Initiative.[3]

There is no need to review all the innovations that flowed from this work. A few examples will convey the diversity of initiatives. With respect to our students' classroom experiences, we charged every department (in conjunction with semester conversion) to review and update its offerings; placed a major emphasis on teaching in academic personnel decisions; established a number of awards to recognize outstanding classroom work; and initiated a program linking cohorts of students in the residence halls with shared courses of study, an arrangement known to improve retention, which subsequent studies showed it did. We struggled, however, to reduce our dependence on part-time instructors even though we steadily expanded the full-time faculty, which grew by nearly 20 percent (from 745 to 884) during my ten years. The problem was that improved retention steadily increased enrollments in ways that offset the added full-timers. We began to make serious progress on this issue only with the advent of the Academic Investment Plan in the final years of my presidency. I was especially impressed by the impact of setting retention goals for each academic department, which inevitably focused the attention of the faculty on an issue they tended to regard as an administrative problem. The Dean of Engineering, Allen Soyster, implemented this initiative in a particularly effective way, creating a formula for evaluating his departments that emphasized graduation rates among their majors. This step revealed that the department generally considered the strongest in our College of Engineering had extremely poor persistence rates, something that no one, including the department itself, had previously realized. The faculty, properly chagrined, took immediate steps to improve its work with undergraduates and achieved striking results in a remarkably short period of time.

An equally high impact change occurred in our approach to academic advising, where, during each freshman class's first semester, we were able to identify students who were at risk of dropping out, mostly because they were struggling in math or English, and get support to them quickly. This "early warning system" rescued dozens of students each year who might otherwise have disappeared without anyone talking to them or trying to help. Also, based on OUPR's discovery that the issues surrounding retention varied significantly among the colleges and that students experiencing difficulties in one might do well in another, we established a new advising function to facilitate the transfer process, a move that saved many students who might otherwise have left the University. Consistent with the recommendations of the Finkelstein/Eddy Task Force, the Student Success Initiative—in some cases aided by funding from the Intensification Program—also resulted in the overhaul of several university functions that were perennial sources of student complaint, most notably Information Technology, which was transformed into a user-friendly operation by a determined new Vice President, Robert Weir, as well as Health Services and Financial Aid. Dramatic improvements in student experiences with these offices became evident through regular, department-specific evaluations that we instituted and monitored for all our service-providing offices as well as through a broader program of annual student opinion surveys called NUPULSE.[4]

As this multifaceted effort was proceeding, the research program undertaken by the OUPR, informed by the published work of Ernest Pascarella and Patrick Terenzini, was drawing our attention to three broad arenas where our policies and programs were especially influential in determining student persistence. These three were admissions, financial aid, and housing. In my view, it was targeted, policy-level, "wholesale" work in each of these areas, complemented by the "retail" impact of dozens of improvements in the experiences of individual students through the initiatives described in the preceding paragraphs, that accounted for the dramatic success we ultimately achieved in improving our graduation rate.

## Increasing Selectivity

Without question, changes in the profile of our entering classes contributed significantly to higher rates of success for our students. During the ten years of my presidency total applications to our undergraduate programs increased by 112 percent, from 12,798 to 27,168, and our acceptance rate (the percentage of applicants whom we admitted) improved from 85 percent to 49 percent. The average SAT score of the entering class at the beginning was 1084; ten years later it was 1230, while the percentage of new students in the top fifth of their high school classes improved from 31 percent to 66 percent. Freshmen from Massachusetts and New England declined steadily (from 47 percent to 35 percent and from 71 percent to 56 percent, respectively), while the percentage of students from beyond the Northeast grew from 5 percent to 12 percent, with the most dramatic increase coming from the West Coast. These changes reflected a number of factors, including our good fortune in embarking on a determined effort to increase selectivity and extend our reach at almost the exact moment that the country's college-age population began to grow. But improvements in our work with respect to

recruitment, including the marketing program, the processing of applications, and coordinating admissions and financial aid awards were important
contributing factors.

Our Division of Enrollment Management was at the top of my list of
departments that needed close scrutiny at the beginning of my presidency.
This was not because I saw this office as problematic; it was merely because
I knew that admissions were our lifeline, and I needed to be sure our work
was commensurate with our aspirations. To this end I met regularly with Vice
President Eddy, carefully reviewed every aspect of the admissions process,
engaged a nationally known enrollment consultant to evaluate our work, and
established detailed annual goals for total applications, applications to each
of our colleges, and the academic qualifications, geographic distribution, and
diversity of our entering classes. I also sought the opinions of high school
guidance counselors with whom we worked. All of this left me with a favorable impression of our admissions programs and our admissions professionals, who seemed to me capable, responsive, and hard working.

My initial positive evaluation of our work in admissions was sustained
for my first three years, during which time we made steady progress. We
increased applications to Business and Engineering, our two foundational
colleges that had recently been losing ground. We reduced enrollments and
tightened standards in Arts and Sciences, which had grown too rapidly and
had become a catchall unit for poorly prepared and aimless students. We
also widened our geographic reach, especially in the Mid-Atlantic states, and
achieved solid overall growth in both the number and quality of applications.
In 1999–2000, however, we experienced a severe and unexpected setback.
Total applications for the fall of 2000 dropped dramatically from the previous
year. Our Enrollment Management team responded with aggressive efforts
to attract the students we accepted, including awarding generous amounts of
financial aid. In September we found ourselves overenrolled and were forced
to mount a University-wide effort to prevent bad outcomes for entering students with respect to housing, course selection, and advising from derailing
our efforts to improve the reputation of our undergraduate experience. In the
midst of these difficulties, Vice President Eddy and her top assistant decided
to leave the University, and I was forced to find interim leadership for Enrollment Management. A subsequent review convinced me that my initial assessment of our admissions effort had been far too positive.

The debacle of 1999–2000, difficult and threatening though it was, proved
to be a watershed in my presidency, prompting a major overhaul of our work

in admissions and financial aid that resulted, over the next several years, in a remarkable success story that became the foundation of our whole effort to reposition Northeastern. With the departure of Vice President Eddy, I asked one of the strongest members of my leadership team, my special assistant, Patricia Meservey, to serve as our Interim Vice Provost for Enrollment Management. Meservey had no experience in admissions, but she was smart and hard working. Her compelling analysis of our deficiencies convinced me to commit significant new resources to this area. At the same time, I focused personally on finding a new vice president, eventually persuading Philomena Mantella, then a vice president at Pace University in New York, to accept our position. This proved to be an excellent appointment. From the moment she arrived in January 2001, Mantella initiated one of the most impressive administrative rebuilding efforts I have ever seen. She recruited superb new leadership for both admissions and financial aid in Ronne Patrick (later Turner) and Seamus Harreys, provided them with the support they needed to build first-rate organizations, and led them through a systematic re-engineering of our activities in both arenas. She also led our cross-functional committee on retention and partnered with our Office of University Planning and Research to conduct nuanced analyses of student outcomes with respect to both matriculation and persistence that drove numerous changes of policy and practice. In addition, she and her team collaborated with our new Division of Marketing and Communications in getting our message to prospective students and to those who influenced them, a story that will be discussed in detail in Chapter 8. By 2006 our enrollment-management operation was widely recognized as one of the most successful units of its kind in the country. In that year, to the amazement of everyone familiar with Northeastern's history, we ranked fourth among all private universities in the United States in total applications and seventy-fifth in admissions selectivity.[5]

## Meeting Students' Financial Needs

Enrolling better prepared students clearly contributed to our success with respect to graduation rates, but there was much more to the story than that. Changes in the financial profile of entering students as well as in the character of our financial aid program were also major factors. Northeastern had historically taken pride in being accessible to applicants from modest backgrounds, but our studies made it clear that we were enrolling a significant number of young people whose circumstances made it highly unlikely that they would be able to persist and graduate. My predecessor, John Curry, had initiated an effort to reduce the percentage of students needing scholarship aid and had made some progress in this regard, but, at the time of my election, the figure was still 80 percent, much higher than we could support. We therefore established the goal of significantly increasing the number of freshmen who could afford the full cost of attendance. Over the course of my presidency this number went from 20 percent to 30 percent.

A dramatic change in the way we structured our financial aid program was even more important than student ability to pay in improving our graduation rates. Analyses completed by OUPR drew attention to our practice of devoting a large percentage of the aid budget to entering students, then reducing support in subsequent years. This was a holdover from an earlier era. It reflected the fact that Northeastern students typically had their first co-op assignments as sophomores and that income from that and successive assignments provided them with the money for their tuition after the first year. I had no reason to doubt that this policy had worked well in the past, but, by the time I became president, its basic premise was no longer valid. Many years of steadily increasing tuition charges, combined with slow rates of growth in co-op salaries, had created a situation in which even our best paying co-ops contributed only partially to covering the cost of attendance, and many of these positions were at best marginal contributors. In essence, the policy of reducing financial aid after the freshman year had become a classic "bait and switch" strategy that was making continued attendance financially impossible for many of our students. We were literally driving them out the door.

Financial aid for upper-level students became one of the first priorities of my presidency. Indeed, in my inaugural address, long before I understood the reasons for our high attrition rates but aware of the problem, I announced a program of endowed Presidential Scholarships to be awarded to sophomores who demonstrated outstanding promise during their first two years. This program proved attractive to donors and was highly successful for the small number of students we were able to help, but it was also, as I soon realized, a drop in the bucket when viewed through the prism of our overall challenges with respect to retention. In that context it was clear that we needed to dramatically expand our financial aid budget and find a way to continue the awards made to freshmen in their upper-class years. The problem was paying for such an effort, given the high percentage of students receiving aid.

Financial aid at Northeastern was mostly funded by reducing tuition charges to recipients, a widespread practice among poorly endowed private institutions called "tuition discounting." The problem with this approach was that every dollar awarded was a dollar lost to the operating budget so that, in principle, an increase in financial aid expenditures produced a decrease in annual revenues—something that Northeastern could not afford. Happily, our financial team saw a potential way around this problem; they thought that increased aid might sufficiently improve persistence to pay for itself, since the aided students would continue to pay tuition that would have been lost had they dropped out. I was, of course, delighted by this argument, though skeptical that it would prove to be true. In the end, however, we decided to proceed on this basis because we had to do something and this was the only means open to us. Besides, as Acting Vice President for Finance William Kneeland put it at a key moment in our deliberations, "It [was] the right thing to do." We therefore promised students accepted for the fall of 1997 that whatever level of aid they received in their freshman year would be sustained throughout their stay at Northeastern, subject to sound continuing academic performance on their part.

Our new approach to financial aid was one of the most important and successful policy initiatives of my presidency. The impact of the change was immediately evident. In the first year of the program our freshman-to-sophomore retention increased by nearly three percentage points, and as students supported in this way progressed through the University our year-to-year retention rates improved at every class level. Remarkably, as had been predicted, the costs of the program were, in fact, recovered as a result of improved persistence even though we increased the aid budget by 268 percent over the course of my presidency. Still, implementation was not without complexities. As part of our review of Enrollment Management following the crisis of 1999-2000, I discovered that the policy was not actually being implemented in a manner consistent with what I had been telling parents and students, and that a large percentage of students were continuing to experience reductions in aid because of arbitrary performance standards that had been instituted, unbeknownst to me, by our financial aid officers. This was one of many aspects of our aid program that Philomena Mantella changed soon after her arrival by persuading me to simplify the policy and firmly commit to a specific level of aid for the four or five years that students were enrolled, provided they remained in good academic standing. Mantella brought numerous other innovations to our financial aid program that contributed to improved admissions selectivity and student persistence. The most striking of these was a practice with which I was previously unfamiliar called "financial aid leveraging." This fancy term simply meant the sophisticated allocation of aid to individual students based on a complex analysis of the amount required to cause an applicant with a particular profile to accept our offer of admission and to persist after enrolling. This kind of analysis led Mantella to recommend that we abandon a long-standing program of generous awards to national merit scholars because the likelihood of their staying at Northeastern if they enrolled was so small. A better use of dollars, she argued, was to support students at the next level down in terms of academic preparation, where the return on investment would be much higher. Over the course of several years I was amazed by the ability of Mantella and her team to tell me, with remarkable accuracy, how much financial aid would be needed to achieve the precisely formulated admissions goals I gave them with respect to geographic distribution, diversity, academic preparation, and likely major. Year after year our Enrollment Management team hit their targets. Their ability to do so was a major factor in the ultimate success of our efforts to improve not only our selectivity and our graduation rates but also, by extension, our rank.[6]

### The Importance of Residence Halls

The third major theme in the Student Success Initiative involved facilities. This was not an arena I had expected to be a focus of my presidency. Board Chair Matthews had told me, shortly after I arrived, that I need not worry much about the physical campus because of the extensive construction undertaken by President Curry. Curry's projects, however, had not included housing, and Northeastern was depending heavily on the ability of students to rent apartments in the surrounding neighborhoods. Within the first months of my presidency, it became clear that this approach was problematic: Even at this early time, well before the dramatic increases in the selectivity and geographic range of our students that lay ahead, demand for beds was outstripping supply. Moreover, in Boston's booming housing market, tension between student renters and local residents was becoming a top-tier political issue for all the city's universities. For both these reasons, we made an early decision to construct additional housing, although at that point we had no clear plan regarding how much we would build or how these facilities would fit into our larger repositioning strategy. Gradually, however, as our admissions effort became more successful, the demand for housing became stronger as did pressure from city authorities to get students out of the neighborhoods and into University housing. We soon came to understand, through the work of the Office of University Planning and Research and the reports of our admissions professionals, the huge impact that new residential facilities were having on both our selectivity and our graduation rate. For all these reasons, the scope and ambition of the building program steadily escalated.[7]

Although I had much to learn as a new president about facilities, I came to this matter with some strong convictions. These were rooted in my history at UMass Boston, which had built an entire new campus on vacant land during my years there. The design, construction, and subsequent maintenance of those facilities had been disastrous in almost every way, and the end result was a cold, colorless, poorly built, and quickly deteriorating facility that conveyed to students and faculty alike a dispiriting message of marginality and neglect. The comparison between that public university setting and what I knew students were experiencing at Boston's selective private universities made me deeply angry. It also taught me the extent to which demoralizing surroundings could drain educational and social energy from an academic community. As a young administrator I promised myself that if I were ever in a position of leadership at an institution that served urban students, I would do everything possible to provide them with a setting that bespoke their importance and their promise. Northeastern gave me that opportunity.

My first—and probably most important—step was to turn to the best architect I knew, a close friend named William Rawn, whose practice included contracts with major universities to create physical master plans and design student housing. I knew Rawn was dedicated to high standards of design and construction, and I knew I could count on him to give me his best effort. One afternoon he and I walked the campus to discuss possibilities. He quickly convinced me to scrap the quick-fix proposal that my own facilities department had advanced to meet our immediate housing need and to undertake a large-scale master planning exercise focused on turning our spare commuter campus into an attractive residential setting commensurate with our ambitions. In deciding to work with Rawn on this matter, I was aware, based on many years of experience in public higher education, that awarding a major contract to a friend is highly problematic; indeed, this was an occasional Northeastern practice of which I had been critical. Thus, while my regard for

Rawn overcame my concerns about contracting proprieties, I made it clear to him that he would get only one job and that subsequent projects, which we were already anticipating, would go out to bid.

We began the building program with three major advantages. First, my two predecessors, Ryder and Curry, had taken important steps to improve Northeastern's dreary, factory-like appearance. Second, there was vacant land to be developed on both our western and southern perimeters. To the west was a large tract devoted almost entirely to parking, though it was designated as a possible site for student housing in a city-approved master plan. To the south were a series of parcels owned by the city and state. One group of three parcels had been cleared for a highway that was never built. A second group of five parcels had been designated for a state-sponsored development project that had failed after the construction of one troubled building, designed as a home for the state's Registry of Motor Vehicles but now vacant. A third advantage, mentioned in Chapter 3, was our ability to undertake a substantial amount of construction with borrowed money and so to proceed quickly, which we did.

During my first year we took aggressive steps to acquire control of the publicly owned parcels on our southern border, a complex process negotiated with great skill by our Director of Government Relations, Tom Keady, and our General Counsel, Vincent Lembo, with an important assist from Trustee William Shea, an officer of the bank that held legal title to the Registry site. Meanwhile Rawn created a master plan for the West Campus—soon to be rechristened West Village—that beautifully combined an openness to the city reflective of our urban mission with semi-enclosed residential quadrangles evocative of a traditional campus. By the spring of 1998 Vice President Mucciolo's facilities team, headed by Jack Martin, Daniel Bourque, and Nancy May, had broken ground on the first of what eventually became seven residential buildings in West Village, six of which were mixed-use structures that included new academic facilities and all but one of which were designed by Rawn and his team. (Despite my intention that Rawn would receive only one no-bid contract, his work proved so impressive to my facilities team and to the Board that I was persuaded to set aside my plan to put all our work out to bid.) In parallel we worked with the city, a neighborhood-based community-development corporation, a minority developer, and an affordable-housing expert to design two new residence halls, to be called Davenport Commons, on the unbuilt highway site to our south, while simultaneously renovating an existing building in the same area as a third new residence. The carefully negotiated Davenport project also included seventy five units of affordable housing for community residents. The final phase of residential construction occurred on one of the Registry parcels and was still in the design stage at the end of my presidency. Over the course of ten years, we erected ten new residence halls, began work on an eleventh, and converted one existing building to residential uses, allowing us to add almost 4,200 beds to our housing inventory, to move the percentage of undergraduates living on campus from 31 percent to 55 percent (including 96 percent of freshmen), and to guarantee on-campus housing for the first three years. As secondary themes of the construction program, we built new homes for two colleges (Health Sciences and Computer and Information Science) and for our African-American Institute, as well as two parking garages and a number of general-use classrooms. Finally, we acquired three existing buildings that gave us additional parking and student performance space.

The West Village complex was especially important not only in helping us achieve our goals with respect to selectivity and retention but also in symbolizing a new chapter in the history of Northeastern to both outside observers and the campus community, while also celebrating our urban character. These buildings won fourteen prizes from the American Institute of Architects and the Boston Society of Architects for both master planning and design. They also proved immensely popular with students. The emphasis on mixing residential, academic, and administrative functions had the effect of keeping the total campus lively on a full-time basis, while grand portals welcomed visitors and passers-by into an attractive, civic-scale quadrangle.

The additional housing on our southern perimeter helped transform a side of the campus historically viewed as somewhat sinister and even dangerous into a lively, well-lit, and inviting urban setting. The total building program, together with the earlier work undertaken by Presidents Curry and Ryder, transformed Northeastern's campus into the most attractive university setting in Boston (Cambridge is another matter), giving us a decided advantage over our crosstown rival, Boston University.[8]

My experience with our building program was the biggest surprise of my presidency. I always knew facilities mattered, as my reaction to the depressing realities of the UMass Boston campus suggests. But before my experience at Northeastern I had an insufficient appreciation of how important they were to the mood and vitality of an academic community. The building program elevated the spirits of our faculty and staff and became a source of institutional pride. It conveyed a message of positive change more powerfully than

any administrative initiative could possibly have done. The impact on recruitment of both faculty and students cannot be overstated. And, of course, it was
a major factor in the success of our effort to improve our graduation rate and,
indeed, our broader effort to create a truly student-centered learning environment. Critics scoff at university presidents who become preoccupied with
buildings. As a young administrator I harbored such feelings myself. These
attitudes could not be more mistaken. The building program is high on the
list of factors that led to the ultimate success of our whole repositioning effort.

## Serving Current Students

As my colleagues and I in Northeastern's senior administration focused on
the long-term, strategic challenge of transforming the University, we were
also mindful that our first responsibility was to current students. Many of
the student-oriented initiatives described in this chapter, of course, had an
immediate impact, and opinion surveys indicated that students understood
and appreciated that fact. Still, there was a danger that our steady and highly
publicized aspiration to reposition the University and achieve a top-100
ranking might be perceived by the student community as inattention to their
own undergraduate experiences. This concern surfaced from time to time
in my meetings with student leaders and in articles in the student paper. I
always did my best to stress the improvements they were actually experiencing, while also pointing out that elevating Northeastern's reputation was very
much in the interest of all Northeastern students, current, future, and former.
For the most part, I found our undergraduates to be both understanding and
supportive of what we were doing. Indeed, one of the most rewarding dimensions of my presidency was their readiness to work with my colleagues and
me to achieve our institutional goals.

There were many dimensions to student involvement in the repositioning
effort. The most important involved extracurricular life. Our student affairs
leaders, first Vice President Karen Rigg, then Philomena Mantella and Rigg's
successor, Edward Klotzbier, talked with students about our transition from
a commuter to a residential campus and the fact that we lacked many of the
social traditions and organizational structures that residential institutions
inevitably build over time. We asked students to help us create these patterns,
and they responded with a host of ideas, including a spring arts festival, a
winter ball, an improved homecoming, and a major rock concert, all of which

occurred. Students and our student affairs staff also participated actively in the design of the new residence halls. They took the lead in creating dozens of new student groups and organizations, which enriched campus life over the course of my presidency. Students also advocated successfully for an alcohol-free social venue that could be open late at night on weekends. Especially impressive to me was their success in establishing an academic honor code, something we did not have that they felt was appropriate at the kind of institution we were becoming.

One of the students' biggest projects was their advocacy for an athletic stadium that would allow our football and soccer teams to play home games on campus rather than at a remote location. This was something I encouraged because I believed it would enhance student life, strengthen our athletic programs, and improve our visibility. When student leaders asked how they might advance this idea, I suggested they support a modest increase in the athletic fee to help finance the project. My hope was that such an effort by students would inspire a commensurate contribution from our alumni/ae, some of whom were outspoken advocates of a stronger emphasis on athletics. The students took this idea to heart, persuaded their colleagues in student government to support it, and won a vote to institute the fee, which we used to fund an expansion of recreational facilities for all students while also building a reserve for the new stadium. To my disappointment, however, I was not able to raise the needed match from our graduates, despite a lead gift from the most generous alumnus of my era, George Behrakis. The students appreciated that I had done my best and were forgiving.[9]

## Keeping Our Promises

As the multiple strands of our effort to strengthen the undergraduate experience produced progressively more selective classes, my colleagues and I began to focus on a challenge we called "keeping our promises." I am not sure precisely when or through whose initiative this notion came into focus. I associate it particularly with our Board Chair, Neal Finnegan, who was concerned about student attitudes and was forever asking those he encountered how they liked the school. I also recall many comments from faculty and admissions officers about how much stronger the students were becoming and how we needed to make sure our programs kept up with their capabilities. Whatever the stimulus, during the final years of my presidency, my colleagues and

I spent many hours thinking about whether we were actually delivering on the promise of excellence in undergraduate education we were making to prospective students and their families. This concern provided a focus for at least two annual retreats of my leadership team, much self-scrutiny by our student-service professionals, and a major initiative on the part of Vice President Klotzbier and his team called the "We Care" campaign, the goal of which was to make sure we had mechanisms in place to respond quickly and effectively to complaints or concerns about any aspect of student life. As noted above, our student surveys regularly probed satisfaction on a wide variety of services and programs and benchmarked our results against our own historic data as well as information from comparable institutions. Those surveys, like our increasing graduation rates—and the random student comments reported by Finnegan—encouraged our belief that we were making steady progress toward our goal of excellence as a student-centered research university. By the end of my presidency our score for overall student satisfaction was higher than that of our benchmarked peers, having been below that average at the time I was elected.[10]

## Two Worries

Almost everything that changed about the University as a result of our repositioning efforts seemed to me positive. I was proud of our rising admission standards, our expanding geographic reach, our improving persistence rates, our attractive new residential facilities, and reports of heightened satisfaction among our students. I was concerned, however, about two implications of our newly achieved selectivity. The first had to do with our history as an urban university that provided educational opportunities for young people of promise from modest backgrounds. I understood that increasing the proportion of freshmen who could afford to attend Northeastern was essential, but I also knew that students from low-income backgrounds were less likely than their more privileged counterparts to have an academic preparation that would make them competitive at a highly selective university. In addition, I understood from my work on *Academia's Golden Age* that upwardly mobile universities without large endowments tend to advance their positions by enrolling progressively more affluent students. I therefore thought it important to make a determined effort to preserve room for high potential students from the communities Northeastern had historically served, not only in Boston and its working-class suburbs but also in urban and minority communities nationally. This issue came into focus as we began to achieve dramatic progress in selectivity after the arrival of Philomena Mantella and will be discussed in detail in Chapter 7. I should report here, however, that in 2002, as part of the five-year unit plan for Enrollment Management, we adopted a goal of enrolling 15 percent of new students annually from Pell-eligible applicants, accepting some decline from prior levels as unavoidable but preventing further erosion; with slight year-to-year variations, we achieved this goal during the remaining years of my presidency.

A second worry about our increased selectivity stemmed from the fact that many of our most successful—and our smartest—alumni/ae had been indifferent students in high school. To me this reflected the reality that academic intelligence is not the same as practical intelligence, or, to state it more broadly, that success in the classroom does not necessarily imply the ability to accomplish important things in the world. It seemed to me a valuable dimension of Northeastern as a practice-oriented institution that we include in our admissions criteria attention to qualities other than traditional academic metrics (like SAT scores and high school grades) suggestive of capacity for high achievement even in the absence of an impressive academic profile. This approach to admissions was also essential to our goal of enrolling promising students from low-income backgrounds. In 2003 Mantella launched a "summer bridge" program to experiment with non-cognitive measures of student ability. On the strength of that experience, with support from alumnus Anthony Manganaro, we developed a program called Torch that provided scholarship support to students from financially limited and often difficult backgrounds from across the country who did not meet normal admissions standards. By looking at a range of factors, such as leadership qualities and impact in their communities, our admissions professionals learned how to identify high-potential candidates who were almost uniformly successful at Northeastern. Under my successor Northeastern extended this approach with the "Foundation Year" program for students from Boston who did not meet traditional admissions criteria.[11]

CHAPTER 5

# Co-op and Practice-Oriented Education

We have the opportunity to move from maverick to leader, not in place of traditional education, but shoulder to shoulder with the great universities of the nation at the head of an important educational movement that I call practice-oriented education.

—Annual Report, 1997–98

## The Idea of Practice-Oriented Education

In delineating a strategic formula for Northeastern at the beginning of my presidency, my team and I identified "practice-oriented education" as the characteristic of our university we most wanted to emphasize. This phrase was a reference to Northeastern's roots in education for the workplace—initially law, engineering, and business, but more recently health-related fields, criminal justice, and education. In stressing practice-oriented studies, Northeastern was following a pattern typical of private urban universities during the early and middle years of the twentieth century. In addition, the school had adopted the model of cooperative education, alternating periods of full-time study and full-time work, a natural complement to occupationally oriented curricula that was also widely embraced by Northeastern's urban peers, though few had built it into all their undergraduate programs as Northeastern had done. Over the years co-op became Northeastern's primary distinguishing feature and a field—though marginal to mainstream higher education—in which the University could legitimately claim national and even international leadership. To the extent that Northeastern was known beyond Boston and New England at the time I became president, it was largely because of the school's pioneering work in this arena.

From my perspective, the decision to make practice-oriented education, and especially co-op, the central elements of our Vision for Northeastern was easy. In addition to being the one thing that extended our profile beyond Boston, co-op had traditionally been the primary reason—after location and cost—for students to enroll. It was the aspect of their college experience that Northeastern alumni/ae tended most to remember and value. Co-op was also the basis of the University's solid reputation among employers and civic leaders in Massachusetts, who appreciated the school's steady production of well-prepared, hardworking, and unentitled young professionals to staff the state's major businesses and industries. (To cite one striking example: In the 1980s 2,300 Northeastern alums held professional positions, six as vice presidents, at the Raytheon Corporation, one of the most important businesses in the state.) When President Bill Clinton told a Northeastern audience in 1993 that their university represented the American Dream, he was acknowledging the way co-op had provided pathways to economic security for thousands of students from modest backgrounds. Against this history, nothing was more obvious than that co-op was a precious asset that needed to play a primary role in our efforts to elevate our status and strengthen our competitive position.[1]

But as a basis for repositioning Northeastern, both practically oriented programs and cooperative education contained negative implications along with the obvious positives. Occupational studies at the undergraduate level had always been relegated to a lower position in the academic pecking order than the liberal arts and sciences, which dominated baccalaureate studies at elite colleges and universities. Professors in the basic disciplines were often quick to label practical coursework as "vocational training," as if studying engineering or management was akin to learning how to install computer modems. Co-op, in particular, was historically associated with low-status, urban institutions serving commuting students from blue-collar backgrounds as well as with narrowly focused technical schools. (A notable exception was Antioch, an experimental liberal arts college that had embraced co-op in the 1930s.) No major, top-tier university or college emphasized this form of education, though it was available in some highly regarded institutions within specified fields—for example, engineering at the Georgia Institute of Technology (Georgia Tech) and Purdue University. Some members of the Northeastern community who were most ambitious for the University—even within our professional schools—had reservations about the value of co-op as we pursued the "smaller but better" strategy, not only because of the field's historic associations but also because they viewed the program itself as mediocre.

As a student of higher education I was well aware of the challenges we faced in basing our efforts to elevate Northeastern on our orientation toward practice. I shared the worry that our reputation as a "co-op school" could burden our repositioning efforts. But I also thought we could turn Northeastern's strengths in professional fields and co-op to our advantage. As I told my campus colleagues in my first State of the University speech, I believed there was a trend among young people, including those from strong academic backgrounds and affluent families, toward fields of study that would prepare them for participation in the workplace right after college. This was a major change from the recent past that struck me as a wave we could catch. I knew, for example, that many colleges and universities that had traditionally emphasized the liberal arts and sciences for undergraduate studies were adding baccalaureate programs in practical fields in response to student interest and that, indeed, the number of institutions devoted exclusively to liberal education for undergraduates was rapidly declining. I was also aware of a strong trend among young people to value experience outside the academic walls as part of their college programs. Internships were becoming common, even at the nation's elite liberal arts colleges. Here, too, was a wave we could ride given our strong reputation in co-op. To turn our commitments to cooperative education and occupationally oriented programs to our strategic purposes, however, required that these programs be perceived as academically rigorous and part of an overall undergraduate experience regarded as first rate. The central challenge for us, I thought, was achieving genuine excellence within the educational traditions we had historically emphasized.

I also believed we needed to update our perspective on what an education that prepared students for work looked like. A major element of that revision had to be a high quality program in the liberal arts and sciences. I did not think the trend in student interest toward studies with practical applications meant that professional studies were going to supplant liberal learning as the most valued approach to undergraduate education for the country's most promising high school graduates. It meant, rather, that there was a hunger among young people to combine the liberal arts with the development of useful skills. I also believed that liberal learning had become essential to the education of fully rounded professionals (as well as individuals and citizens), because of the intellectual qualities associated with these disciplines as well as the breadth of perspective this form of education instilled. The implication of all this for Northeastern was that strengthening our College of Arts and Sciences and celebrating our commitment to liberal education were essential to our overall repositioning. This perspective represented a shift of emphasis for the University, which had initially offered courses in the basic academic disciplines chiefly to support learning in professional subjects, not as important fields of study in themselves, and which, after it did develop a full College of Arts and Sciences, had focused primarily on math and science. This limited perspective had survived into the Knowles years, but President Ryder, Knowles's successor, had worked to elevate the liberal arts and President Curry had continued Ryder's policies. Still, at the time of my election, the legacy of Northeastern's history as a technically oriented school was evident in significant weaknesses in the social sciences and humanities, especially the latter, which had always received limited budgetary support.

I approached the topic of connecting liberal education with the world of practice with more than a touch of missionary zeal. I had spent much of my career, especially at UMass Boston, arguing that academic traditionalists who disparaged occupational studies were doing a disservice to students who would enter the workforce right after college and who needed a means to support themselves. I also felt, as someone who had struggled with computer programming and accounting, that those who insisted the liberal arts had a monopoly on intellectual rigor were speaking from prejudice rather than experience. Indeed, during my years of working in urban institutions I had become convinced that programs of undergraduate study that stressed opportunities to combine liberal with practical studies represented an attractive curricular model for many students, and I had worked hard as a founding dean of a college of management and also as a dean of arts and sciences to achieve that kind of integration. Such programs, I believed, were especially important for students who would not continue their studies right after college (which was most Northeastern graduates) but were also valuable for those headed for graduate school; after all, it made sense for young people, before selecting a professional field for advanced study, to have some actual experience of the occupation to which they planned to devote their lives.

I was equally passionate about the pedagogical power of co-op. Educators had understood at least since the days of John Dewey that learning and experience were deeply connected and that classroom study by itself was less effective in promoting mastery than study combined with practice. The fact that (with some notable exceptions, like laboratory work in the scientific disciplines, clinical work in health care, and practice teaching for future educators) academic leaders had mostly ignored Dewey's insight for the better part of a century seemed to me to reflect bias, organizational convenience, and the propensity to imitate institutions at the top of the reputational pyramid rather than thoughtful reflection. I was therefore excited by the challenge of proving to the academic world that the educational tradition for which Northeastern was most known could be offered at a high level of quality and could be competitive with the best traditional programs in terms of both attracting and educating highly capable undergraduates.

I summarized my thinking on the educational direction Northeastern should pursue in my State of the University address in September 1998 and in that year's annual report, laying out a vision of practice-oriented education based on the integration of three elements: cooperative education, professional studies, and the arts and sciences. Northeastern's goal, I argued, should be the construction of a new model of undergraduate learning in which these three traditions were equally valued and systematically linked so that the synergies among them could be fully exploited. This meant that students majoring in any field, in one of our professional colleges or in the College of Arts and Sciences, needed to have opportunities to take a second major or a minor in a related field from the other side of the liberal/professional divide and that our professional and academic faculties needed to work together to structure these cross-collegiate offerings to maximize the intellectual relationships between them. It also meant that our programs in arts and sciences should pay attention to the practical applications associated with these disciplines, not in place of liberal learning but in conjunction with it. Finally, it meant that co-op needed to be fully integrated into the programs of all our colleges, with job placements and advising support that would help students achieve the full benefit of their classroom studies while also reflecting on how their work experiences deepened or modified what they had learned on campus. If we could do all this, I argued, referring to the trend among young people to favor collegiate programs that combined liberal learning with preparation of the workplace, "we have the opportunity to move from maverick to leader ... at the head of an important educational movement that I call practice-oriented education." I even hoped this phrase might gain acceptance as a way of describing the as-yet-unnamed approach to undergraduate studies that we, like a number of other colleges and universities, were taking. I thought, in the case of Northeastern, this would help us shed some of the negative associations embedded in the phrase "co-op school" that had traditionally been used to characterize us.[2]

## Cooperative Education at Northeastern

In stressing the need for changes in our program of cooperative education I did not mean to disparage the value of co-op over many years for Northeastern students. One needed only to discuss the impact of their workplace experiences with our graduates—as I frequently did—to become not only persuaded but inspired with respect to this point. Yet I was not the first Northeastern president to believe that this historic dimension of Northeastern, important though it was to our work and our reputation, needed a makeover to achieve its full educational potential.

President Curry, in calling for a "smaller but better" University, had stressed the need for co-op to be "refocused and revitalized." In the spring of his first year he had appointed a University-wide committee to review the program and recommend changes. The central issue, in Curry's view and that of his committee, was that co-op had historically focused on making sure students were employed so that they could pay their college bills, an emphasis that produced a high degree of variability in the quality of co-op placements as contributors to student learning. (One especially notorious co-op involved the distribution of towels in the University's locker room.) Indeed, despite the rhetoric about the educational benefits of co-op, students often viewed it chiefly as a jobs program, and the learning associated with it, while real, was more likely to reflect the intrinsic value of work than intentional synergies with classroom studies. As noted previously, however, by the time Curry became president, rising tuition and stagnant co-op salaries had rendered the program a marginal contributor to college costs for most students. What was needed, Curry and his committee agreed, was a reorientation of co-op to emphasize its educational potential by creating far more systematic interactions between students' work experiences and their academic programs.

Over the course of his presidency Curry took a number of steps to strengthen the educational value of co-op. He appointed a well-regarded faculty member from the law school to head the Co-op Division, and he supported her efforts to link the Division's coordinators with the academic departments and to reorient their work from job placement to a broader conception of advising. In recognition of the higher academic standards the University needed to achieve, Curry also ended the practice of placing co-op coordinators on tenure track lines, while seeking to encourage research on co-op by leaving open the possibility of tenure for members of the Division with appropriate scholarly credentials.[3]

Curry's initiatives seemed to me pointed in the right direction, and my initial approach to co-op called for further progress along similar lines, especially with respect to integrating work experience more systematically into our academic programs. As part of the Intensification Program in the spring of my first year I appointed a committee to recommend additional measures to promote co-op/classroom integration, and I set aside funds to support promising initiatives along these lines by either the academic departments or the Co-op Division. With my support, a more comprehensive effort to connect the co-op coordinators with the academic departments was undertaken by the Interim Dean of Co-op in the spring of 1997. I also charged our Office of University Planning and Research to undertake a systematic analysis of the educational benefits of cooperative education to provide a more grounded basis for policy interventions.[4]

Curry's initiatives as well as my own initial steps produced incremental gains, but by the end of my second year I concluded that a gradualist approach was not going to achieve the fundamental refocusing of co-op that our aspirations required. I saw two primary barriers to change. The first was deep resistance within the Co-op Division, especially among its most senior and influential members (all tenured faculty who believed they deserved the same independence with respect to their work as academic faculty), to any significant modification of established work patterns or infringements on the autonomy of individual staff. The second was the disregard of many members of our college faculties for the co-op program and, indeed, for the co-op coordinators.

As a new president I had been surprised by the lack of interest in co-op within our academic departments, an attitude that sometimes came perilously close to contempt. Over time I came to understand that while the external world viewed co-op as the central characteristic of Northeastern, within the campus community the program, though recognized as the University's calling card and favored by the University's leaders, was also isolated, inward-looking, and somewhat beleaguered. In part the isolation was self-imposed. Co-op administrators over the years had viewed the program's separation from the academic side of Northeastern as essential to its well-being. There was also, however, an element of defensiveness in the face of perceived faculty attitudes in the program's insularity. There was variation among our colleges with respect to co-op. Some engineering departments, for example, had strong and mutually respectful relations with their co-op coordinators, but this was more the exception than the rule. Interest in co-op had historically played no role in the hiring of faculty, and faculty were not asked as part of their promotion dossiers to show how being part of a co-op school affected their instructional work. Not surprisingly, given this context, our academic programs looked very much like their counterparts at other universities and did not typically include characteristics that reflected the University's commitment to cooperative education. College deans and academic departments generally played no role in the hiring or evaluation of the co-op coordinators who were assigned to them and who were expected to work closely with their students.

Within the framework of the larger university, the Co-op Division had created an independent organizational culture the strength of which became starkly evident in the antagonistic response of the coordinators to the efforts of the Interim Dean to connect them more closely with the academic departments. The most striking example of co-op's isolation was the response of the co-op coordinators when President Curry and his review committee called upon the Division to move away from an exclusive focus on job placement and become part of the educational process. Rather than seek closer ties with our academic programs, the coordinators created their own curriculum, complete with work-based learning objectives that made no reference to students' majors. This response made it clear that the co-op staff regarded their work as grounded in a separate academic discipline and not as a means to reinforce and deepen students' learning in their chosen fields of study. The coordinators saw teaching courses about the benefits of work experience and conducting co-op-related research as the way to contribute to the University's academic programs.[5]

While I regarded the Co-op Division's insistence on separation and independence as misguided, I was also sympathetic to their stance as self-protective. Given what I was coming to understand about campus culture, I should not have been surprised that calls for greater collaboration between co-op and the colleges, that began with President Curry and that I continued, did not produce much change. The sources of resistance were deep and wide.

## Restructuring Co-op

In the summer of 1998 Provost Hall and I initiated a new and far more aggressive approach to strengthening co-op. With help from colleagues in the senior administration, we jointly produced a blueprint for change titled "A Call to Action on Cooperative Education." This document identified several steps we considered essential to strengthening co-op as an educational experience, with a particular focus on tighter integration of co-op assignments into our academic programs. The Call to Action also addressed the need to strengthen co-op as an employment experience, a reference to our growing concern that the coordinators were not being sufficiently active in building relationships with companies grounded in the new technologies that were beginning to dominate the regional economy. Finally, the Call announced our intention to mount a robust program of research—beyond what the OUPR could undertake—that would establish Northeastern as the nation's leading source of information about this pedagogy.

There were few new ideas in the Call to Action. Mostly the provost and I wanted to make unambiguously clear our determination to accomplish changes that had been widely discussed but never seriously enacted. To this end we did not ask for voluntary proposals or modest experiments as both President Curry and I had previously done. Rather, we announced a series of required actions by the Co-op Division, the colleges, and several administrative departments. We also set deadlines for completing the work we specified, and we created a University-wide Implementation Task Force to oversee follow-up activities and report on progress. To make clear the significance we attached to the Call, we noted that many universities and colleges were establishing co-op-like offerings, mostly based on internships of one kind or another, and we argued that upgrading our own program was essential to maintaining Northeastern' s national leadership in work-based education.

The most challenging step the provost and I took in issuing the Call to Action was terminating the structural independence of the Co-op Division. As discussed briefly in Chapter 3, we had become convinced that this change was essential to achieving the long-sought integration of co-op experiences into our academic programs. Thus the Call announced our intention to place individual co-op coordinators under the joint authority of the vice president for cooperative education and the college deans—a pattern we called "co-supervision," while charging the deans and academic departments to fully incorporate their assigned co-op staff into departmental structures and decision-making processes. To further facilitate integration, we stated that co-op staff would be given offices within their academic departments and would be required to spend a significant portion of their time there—a principle we called "co-location." We did not propose eliminating the central Co-op Division entirely because we believed the coordinators should be part of a professional community for sharing insights about their pedagogical specialty and also because we valued the visibility that having a full division headed by a vice president gave to co-op, both within the University and to the external world.[6]

As Provost Hall and I were drafting the Call to Action we had been well aware that the restructuring we were contemplating was potentially explosive, especially among the co-op staff. Eager to gain as much support as possible, we had engaged in extensive consultation, not only with the Co-op Division but also with the college deans, the leaders of faculty governance, and the Board of Trustees, and we tried to shape our plans to have the greatest likelihood of acceptance consistent with accomplishing the changes we thought necessary. When we finally issued the Call in August 1998 we were guardedly hopeful that our actions would at least be accepted, perhaps grudgingly within co-op but hopefully more positively within the colleges. At the same time, we sought to protect our plans against being derailed by making sure we had strong and informed support from the Trustees. To this end I asked Chair Finnegan to constitute a special Board committee to monitor the implementation process. He selected one of our most influential trustees, Michael Cronin, to lead the Special Committee, and Cronin maintained close contact with Provost Hall and me as work on the Call proceeded.

At first things seemed to go well. The Co-op Division organized committees to implement various parts of the Call to Action as we had instructed them to do. The college deans developed plans detailing how they would organize the integration process. The provost and I sought to encourage this positive atmosphere by appointing a new vice president for co-op, Richard Porter of the Math Department, who was both a vocal champion of cooperative education and a widely respected member of the faculty of arts and sciences. We thought Porter could overcome the fears of the coordinators that they would not be accepted by their academic colleagues and could also persuade the academic faculty to take the goal of integrating co-op and classroom seriously. One of Porter's first actions was to ask the most outspoken early critic of the Call to Action, a tenured, senior member of the Co-op Division and a longtime leader of that unit, Robert Tillman, to join him as dean of cooperative education.

Unfortunately, the positive atmosphere was short-lived. In the fall of 1999, when it was time for the coordinators to move to offices in the academic departments, they protested, claiming they had not understood our intention to move ahead so quickly. When Provost Hall and I persisted, the coordinators asked for a meeting with the Board; Chair Finnegan, with our support, agreed to a session with Trustee Cronin's Committee. We then worked closely with Trustees Cronin and Finnegan to plan the Board's response. When the meeting took place Committee members listened politely to an attack on our policy led by Dean Tillman, then bluntly told the coordinators that the Board fully supported us and that the co-op staff should get on with the work. The coordinators were stunned by the clarity and forcefulness of the Committee's reaction. The next day Tillman resigned as Dean. I realized through this episode that the initial period of cooperation by members of the Co-op Division masked a hope of preventing full implementation of our plan. When it became clear that their strategy would not work, the majority of coordinators, though not all, went into open rebellion.[7]

What followed was among the most difficult periods of my presidency. The co-op coordinators threatened refusing to move into their collegiate offices. In response, my administrative team, working closely with University Counsel Lembo, created a directive specifying in great detail exactly what we expected of each member of the co-op staff. We established a system of accountability requiring the coordinators to report their movements, with particular reference to how much time they spent in their collegiate offices and what they did there and how much time they spent away from campus working with employers to develop new co-op opportunities. These draconian measures produced a tense atmosphere during the spring of 2000, but they ultimately led to grudging compliance, even by the coordinators most opposed to the new policy.[8]

Provost Hall and I were pleased by the forward movement, but our basic goal was to win support among our co-op colleagues, not bludgeon them into submission. Accordingly, Hall initiated a series of private meetings with individual coordinators to seek a resolution. Through patient diplomacy he reached agreement that we would drop the recently installed reporting requirements and seek representation for the coordinators on the faculty Senate in return for cooperation with the Call to Action. We were happy to comply with both requests. By the summer of 2000 we were in a position to move forward with the new policy. As part of this, the college deans made major efforts to create a welcoming environment for the coordinators in the colleges. By June 2001

I was able to inform the Board that co-supervision was fully operational and that, indeed, the coordinators had decided to completely relocate their offices to the colleges by the following fall. As the tide shifted toward compliance with the new arrangements and support for the goals of the Call a number of coordinators elected to leave the University or to retire, giving us the opportunity to appoint nineteen new co-op staff between January 2000 and June 2001.

## Integrated Learning Models

From an educational perspective, the purpose of reassigning co-op staff to the academic departments was to make possible the creation of curricular structures that Provost Hall and I called "integrated learning models" (ILMs). We imagined these as department-level program designs that systematically related students' classroom studies to their co-op experiences. In our minds these new structures would represent the programmatic manifestation of our whole push to strengthen the educational value of co-op. In calling upon the college faculties to create these ILMs, however, we understood we were asking something substantial: our academic departments would need to completely re-engineer their programs, including their majors, and to fully involve their assigned co-op professionals in doing so. We also knew that a significant percentage of faculty members did not share our sense of the importance of integrating classroom and co-op, and we worried about the energy that the departments would bring to this work. Thus, as noted in Chapter 3, one major reason we decided to convert Northeastern to a semester calendar was our realization that this action, which most faculty supported, would also require a redesign of every major (and indeed every course), and we believed this context would be enormously helpful in motivating faculty to create the ILMs. As part of the implementation process for semester conversion, we empowered the University-wide committee overseeing the process to review all departmental plans for semester-based programs. While the committee looked at a number of issues related to program quality, no proposal was approved unless it included a carefully worked out ILM. By the spring of 2003, with full conversion to a semester calendar scheduled for the fall, most departments had developed satisfactory plans.

I was aware, of course, that there could be discrepancies between the language of plans and the reality of courses and programs. Thus I was concerned that the ILMs approved by the oversight committee might look better on paper than they turned out to be in practice. Consequently, when Provost Hall returned to his faculty position in the fall of 2003, I decided to personally supervise the implementation of the new, semester-based curricula, a level of involvement in the academic program that was unorthodox for a university president in the twenty-first century but vital, I thought, to the continuity of our efforts. I requested regular reports from every college and department. I sponsored University-wide meetings of department chairs to talk about their program designs. I met personally with randomly selected groups of chairs to ascertain the status of implementation.

I was impressed by the work of some of our colleges. The College of Business, under Dean Ira Weiss, developed a five-year curriculum in which each of three required co-op placements was designed to play a specified educational role as students moved from the freshman to the senior year and from general to specialized to integrative courses. The College of Computer and Information Science under Dean Finkelstein, mindful that in the fast-moving world of information technology students would encounter next-generation ideas on co-op assignments that had not yet been incorporated into the curriculum, determined which critical skills were best taught in the classroom and which best learned in the workplace, and then designed their major to reflect that analysis. The Dean of Arts and Sciences, James Stellar, sought to build on the experiential education requirement championed by his predecessor and make co-op a central feature of liberal education at Northeastern. He not only pushed his departments to integrate students' work experiences into their majors but, more broadly, urged them to pay attention to the practical applications of their disciplines. There was, however, much variation in the quality of ILMs among our many academic departments and some of the program designs in this first iteration were only approximations of what Provost Hall and I had hoped for. When I left the presidency in the summer of 2006, the creation of ILMs was still a work in progress, but we had taken a quantum leap from where Northeastern had been when we issued the Call to Action in 1998. Co-op was now, truly, part of our undergraduate curriculum, not simply a separate experience that might or might not complement classroom learning.[9]

## Additional Efforts to Strengthen Co-op

Integrating co-op experiences into our academic programs was the most difficult part of implementing the Call to Action and the part that most required my personal attention. But there were other critical components of the plan where accomplishment depended entirely on members of my team, especially Provost Hall, Vice President Porter, and the co-op coordinators. Particularly important were reviewing all co-op positions to cull out those that did not represent valuable educational opportunities—of which there were far too many—and developing new placement opportunities in emerging, mostly technology-based, industries. We also needed to expand the number of co-ops beyond New England and internationally to reflect the growing geographic diversity of our students and their increased interest in global experiences. In addition, we needed to end the antiquated system by which individual coordinators kept descriptions of co-op possibilities in three-ring binders accessible only to their own advisees and make these opportunities widely available in a digitized database. The University made good progress on all these matters over the course of my presidency. A dimension of the Call where the co-op coordinators were particularly helpful was in refining and standardizing expectations for their interactions with individual students during the three phases of the co-op experience: preparation for employment, the work experience itself, and reflection upon what was learned after the return to campus. Finally, through the efforts of our fine Registrar, Linda Allen, we were able to modify our student record system to include performance on co-op assignments along with course grades.

Looking beyond the immediate priorities associated with strengthening co-op, Provost Hall and I had hoped, when we issued the Call to Action, to make progress on several longer-term issues. We sought, for example, to initiate a discussion of moving Northeastern beyond its historic identity as a "co-op school" to embrace other forms of "experiential" or "work-integrated" learning, in recognition of the value of various kinds of non-classroom experiences, including undergraduate research, study abroad, and clinical assignments in the health sciences. I believe we fostered a recognition within the University community that Northeastern needed to expand our reputation (and our programs) in this way, while continuing to emphasize the centrality of co-op, but the work of further developing this broader notion of the University's non-classroom offerings was unfinished business at the time I left the presidency. We identified additional topics for consideration as well. Should we give some academic credit for co-op, a step that seemed to flow logically from our efforts to integrate it into our academic programs? Could we establish and measure clear learning outcomes for our students' work experiences? Could we provide the classroom faculty with better information about the work experiences of the students in their classes? Would our efforts to incorporate noncognitive factors into the admissions process predict high levels of performance on co-op assignments? These were unanswered questions at the end of my presidency.

I probably put more intellectual and administrative energy into enhancing Northeastern's co-op program than into any other aspect of our educational work. I did this chiefly because I believed that integrating co-op experiences into our classroom programs and ensuring that co-op jobs provided powerful learning opportunities would enhance student development. I was encouraged in this view by OURP's studies of the educational benefits of co-op, which showed a majority of students reporting that their co-op experiences strengthened learning in their majors. I also focused on co-op because I believed this program was the foundation of our reputation in the wider world and that our hopes of repositioning Northeastern rested to a significant degree upon maximizing the educational impact of this program and enhancing its image beyond Northeastern. In the end, I was convinced that the steps we had taken, painful though some of them were, represented important contributions to maintaining Northeastern's reputation as the gold standard for experience-based learning.[10]

### Strengthening Core Programs and Promoting Interdisciplinary Work

Excellence in cooperative education was, of course, only one of three dimensions of practice-oriented education that had been summarized in our 1997–98 annual report. Arguably even more important were top-quality classroom programs of professional and liberal education as well as opportunities for students to experience well-structured curricula that bridged the liberal/professional divide.

In Chapter 3, I pointed out that the keys to enhancing Northeastern's academic strength lay with the provost and deans of the colleges. Northeastern is much too large for the president to play more than a general oversight role with respect to individual academic programs, where leadership typically requires specialized expertise across a much wider range of fields than any president is likely to possess. (My involvement in the design of ILMs was, of course, a marked exception to this rule.) The job of the president in the academic arena is to fill leadership positions with accomplished professionals in the relevant fields who possess the necessary mix of intellectual, personal, administrative, and political qualities, and who are ready to develop their colleges within the broad framework of established institutional strategy. After that the president's role is chiefly to help delineate annual priorities for the key officers, and, if they are effective, support and encourage them in every possible way; if individual officers are not effective, of course, it is the job of the president to make the needed changes.

I believe Northeastern was well served by the individuals to whom we entrusted positions of academic leadership during my presidential years. I have already spoken of Provost David Hall, who, among many other things, played an indispensable role in our makeover of co-op. His successor, Ahmed Abdelal, was a seasoned and highly regarded dean from Georgia State University whose scientific background was particularly helpful as we shaped the Academic Investment Plan and built our research and graduate programs during the latter years of my presidency. Among our new deans who served for extended periods, Allen Soyster in engineering from Penn State brought heightened expectations in both education and research to a college that was ready to raise its sights. Steven Zoloth, a biology PhD from Hunter College and the founding dean of our combined College of Health Sciences, established high academic standards in programs that had traditionally emphasized clinical work. Jack Greene from Temple was a hard-driving dean of criminal justice who created a new PhD and terminated a dubious continuing-education program for working police officers. James Stellar in Arts and Sciences, the only new dean from within the Northeastern faculty, played a pivotal role in strengthening his college's engagement with the practice-oriented model of education we were developing. Two deans who were in place when I was appointed and remained well into my presidency, Ira Weiss in business and Larry Finkelstein in computer and information science, welcomed the chance to take their units to a higher academic level and did so effectively. Weiss's successor, Thomas Moore from Babson College, created the country's first fully online MBA program. Our law school maintained its strong reputation in public interest law under Emily Spieler. These individuals, along with colleagues in college and department-level leadership positions, get the lion's share of credit for elevating Northeastern's academic programs, undergraduate and graduate, course by course and major by major, including the development of many new programs that enriched the learning opportunities available to our students.[11]

My own work on Northeastern's core academic programs involved reviewing recommendations for tenure or promotion to a senior rank for individual faculty members, interviewing candidates for appointments at the senior level, participating in periodic evaluations of our offerings by outside experts, and reviewing proposals for new programs. There was, however, one area of educational programming where I involved myself in some depth. This was fostering collaboration across traditional boundaries between academic fields, especially between the professional colleges and the College of Arts and Sciences—a central feature of our model of practice-oriented education

Northeastern had established a solid foundation of interdisciplinary programs prior to my appointment. My goal was to make this pattern widely available across all our colleges and fields of study. I believed every Northeastern student should receive a solid grounding in the basic disciplines of the arts and sciences and also have the opportunity to develop skills that would be useful in the workplace after graduation, and I was eager to deliver on the promise we were making in our admissions materials that all students would have access to a rich variety of well-structured curricula designed to facilitate this kind of opportunity. Thus I constantly encouraged the deans and departments to create cross-college and interdisciplinary double majors, dual majors, and major/minor combinations, and I insisted that progress in this area be part of every college's unit plan.

Over the course of my presidency I was pleased to see steady development of interdisciplinary programming. Three striking examples included a cluster of joint programs between the College of Computer and Information Science and the College of Arts and Sciences; major/minor options working in both directions between the College of Engineering and the College of Business; and a three-way collaboration between Arts and Sciences, Health Sciences, and Computer and Information Science to build our offerings in biotechnology. A different kind of example was a new School of Technological Entrepreneurship, supported by a large gift from Trustee Jean Tempel, which drew on the strengths of both engineering and business. The College of Arts and Sciences created a large number of minors available to students in professional majors as well as interdisciplinary offerings within the boundaries of the college itself. The college also led an effort, toward the end of my presidency, to establish a common general education curriculum for all students, including an experiential education component.

To make it easier for students to take advantage of programs that cut across the colleges, Provost Hall and I required, as part of semester conversion, that all undergraduate programs adopt a common calendar, a major departure from past Northeastern practice. During my presidential years I was impressed by how many students told me they were pursuing a double or dual major or a major/minor combination, but I was also frustrated that by the time I left we had not developed a registration system that allowed us to track these patterns. (Our computer believed that students should have only one major and didn't think minors were worth noticing!) The best we could do was record students' minors on their transcripts after the necessary courses were completed. Overall, I would put the development of boundary-crossing programs as a goal toward which Northeastern made good progress during my presidential years, but this was also an arena that would require sustained administrative encouragement over an extended period.[12]

## Institutionalizing Practice-Oriented Education

As Provost Hall and I worked to strengthen our academic programs and refocus co-op, we also sought to promote the broad concept of practice-oriented education both within the campus community and in the wider world of higher education. We were convinced that the three-dimensional approach to undergraduate studies we advocated—focused work in either a professional or an academic subject with the opportunity to take organized course sequences on the other side of the liberal/professional boundary and to combine classroom studies with work experiences—was a powerful approach to learning that both embodied and validated Northeastern's claim of excellence in undergraduate education. We knew that a number of colleges and universities around the country were working on their own versions of these same ideas, and we hoped that asserting Northeastern's leadership of this trend—not only through our programmatic innovations but also by giving the movement a name—would reinforce our goal of repositioning Northeastern as an academically competitive, nationally significant institution.

Provost Hall took the lead in advocating POE within the Northeastern faculty. He and I both understood that the only way these ideas would have lasting influence was for the faculty to become intellectually convinced of their merit. In the spring of 2000 he formed the Faculty Advisory Group on Practice-Oriented Education to work with him on this challenge, and in the fall this group produced an ambitious document titled "The Institutionalization of Practice-Oriented Education at Northeastern University." This document provided the basis for a series of initiatives. With the help of a generous gift from Trustee Nonnie Burnes, the provost and his committee sponsored a "learning community" that gave interested faculty members released time and financial support to develop their own approaches to implementing POE in their classes and to share their thinking with each other. The Advisory Group also organized the first iteration of a projected biennial conference on POE that brought together educators interested in linking classroom study and work experience from around the United States and from other countries as well. In addition, the Advisory Group produced a thoughtful paper on how Northeastern would need to modify our policies for promotion and tenure if we were serious about encouraging faculty to pursue this educational philosophy. Adopting an idea from the Call to Action, the Group led the establishment of a research center focused on practice-oriented education and used a long-vacant chair devoted to the study of co-op to appoint Professor Joseph Raelin from Boston College as the first director. After Hall returned to the faculty, Provost Abdelal and I created the new position of Special Assistant to the Provost for Practice-Oriented Education to continue this work, and we appointed one of Northeastern' s most thoughtful educators, James Fraser, to this role. For the remainder of my presidency Fraser served as an advocate for POE with the college deans and faculties. Among other things, he instituted a program of annual awards for Northeastern faculty who had demonstrated noteworthy creativity in implementing the principles of practice-oriented education in their courses.[13]

It is difficult for me to determine the long-term impact of our efforts to promote POE as a way of thinking about Northeastern's approach to undergraduate education among the University's faculty. It was clear by the time I stepped down that we had made little headway in promoting the phrase "practice-oriented education" as a way of talking about undergraduate education at Northeastern. We probably should have been more realistic about the difficulty of persuading our colleagues to adopt a new vocabulary to describe their professional work, though we sincerely believed in the value of having a common language to characterize the University's distinctive undergraduate experience. With respect to the substance of POE, however, I was hopeful at the time I left the presidency. Clearly a number of Northeastern faculty shared with Provost Hall and me the conviction that these ideas were educationally valuable. I am sure, in fact, that our advocacy merely provided an opportunity for some faculty to express publicly and put into practice ideas they had developed on their own. It was certainly the case that all the discussions and forums and prizes that we established and programmatic initiatives we sponsored inspired some solid educational work. I have been pleased, morcovcr, as I havc workcd on this book, by obscrvations from long-timc members of the Northeastern community that the ideas that Provost Hall and I were advocating under the banner of practice-oriented education did, indeed, take hold and survive, even though the phrase itself did not.[14]

### Promoting POE Nationally

In parallel with the work of the provost's office in advancing practice-oriented education within Northeastern, I made myself a missionary for this idea in my speaking engagements before external audiences and in opinion pieces in the educational press. We hired a consultant specializing in relationships with the media, who organized meetings for me with writers and editors around the country, including the *New York Times*, the *Washington Post*, and the *Los Angeles Times*, where I pitched Northeastern's program as a new approach to undergraduate education. Not all these sessions produced the coverage for which we hoped, but some did, including two opinion pieces in the *Chronicle of Higher Education* and a feature article in *U.S. News and World Report*. I was particularly proud in 2004 when the *Atlantic* published a long essay titled "The Third Way" in which I argued that numerous colleges and universities around the country were pursuing some version of what we were calling practice-oriented education and that this was something genuinely new in American higher education, a "third way" between a traditional version of the liberal arts and sciences and the narrow professionalism historically associated with career-oriented undergraduate majors.

Looking back on this work ten years after leaving the presidency, it is obvious that I was as unsuccessful in promoting the phrase "practice-oriented education" with my colleagues around the country as Provost Hall and I had been within our own campus community. I believe, however, that we were right that the central elements of POE were becoming increasingly common at leading colleges and universities and that our sustained advocacy for these ideas, combined with the overall success of Northeastern's repositioning effort, played a role in advancing the substance of our ideas. I was particularly struck in 2005 by the decision of the Association of American Colleges and Universities, the national voice of undergraduate liberal arts colleges and universities with 1,350 institutional members, to mount an educational initiative called Liberal Education and America's Promise (LEAP), which had among its central premises the importance of connecting liberal learning with real-world problem solving and building bridges between the arts and sciences and professional fields.[15]

The widespread tendencies across American higher education to combine liberal and practical studies and encourage off-campus experiences represented, of course, the two waves I had hoped to catch in basing our Vision for Northeastern at the beginning of my presidency on our commitment to being practice oriented. My own assessment is that this decision was critically important to the University's rapid reputational ascent. I would argue, indeed, that Northeastern did move from "maverick to leader . . . shoulder to shoulder with the great universities of the nation," although the movement of which we were a part did not yet have a proper name.

CHAPTER 6

## Research and Graduate Education

At Northeastern we stress scholarship that directly
improves human life—through scientific and technical
innovation, and through progress in health care, business,
and social services. . . . Our goal now, as we continue to
shift our institutional emphasis from quantity to quality,
is to enhance those areas of research and graduate
education that promise the highest levels of contribution
and recognition.

—Annual Report, 1996–97

As I noted in Chapter 1, the growth among American universities of research
and doctoral-level education ranks as one of academia's greatest achievements
during the second half of the twentieth century. Stunning progress in these
advanced academic functions catapulted the country's higher education system into international leadership and contributed immensely to the nation's
economic strength, physical health, and military prowess—while also producing the large number of PhDs needed to teach the rapidly expanding population of undergraduates. So compelling was the idea of the modern research
university as represented in the years after World War II by schools like Harvard and MIT, to take two Boston-area examples, that this institutional model
quickly became academia's standard of excellence and pinnacle of status.

Despite the benefits that flowed from academia's emphasis on research and
graduate education, there were, as many observers have noted, some unfortunate
consequences of this development. Two concerns, in particular, have attracted
attention: first, reduced focus on undergraduate teaching and learning; second,
a tendency among universities in the middle and even lower echelons of the

academic pecking order to improve their standing by adopting the priorities of
the new model, which too often resulted in research activities and doctoral programs driven more by the quest for status than by social need. My years at both
UMass Boston and the City University of New York had made me well aware
of the attractiveness of these high-level activities for insecure institutions eager
to elevate their reputations. Less widely noted, but also important, especially in
the context of urban higher education, was the tendency of leading universities
to become progressively more national and international in their orientation,
weakening historic ties to host communities and devaluing the tradition of local
engagement that had long been a defining feature of many city-based institutions. Against this background, I came to the Northeastern presidency, and to
the challenge of improving the school's academic standing, convinced of the
importance of the advanced academic functions in our portfolio of activities
but determined to develop them in ways that served demonstrable societal purposes and reflected our school's special qualities.[1]

I outlined my thinking about research and graduate education in my first
State of the University speech in September 1996 by observing that there were
different kinds of research universities in the United States and that Northeastern had a special character and mission within that broad framework.
Our commitment to being student centered, for example, meant that the
advancement of knowledge through research, though a vital part of our work,
could not be allowed to supplant teaching and learning as our first priority, as
it had done at our renowned sister institutions in Cambridge. I also stressed
the significance of our character as a practice-oriented university, which
implied that we would pay attention, as we built the advanced functions, to
programs that addressed the applications of knowledge to solving significant
social and technological problems. Finally, I noted that being an urban university meant that we would maintain a strong theme of attention to matters
of importance to our metropolitan community. From my perspective, therefore, a review of research and graduate education during my presidency must
consider whether we nurtured these activities in ways consistent with our
guiding Aspiration while also contributing to our repositioning strategy.

## Research and Graduate Education at Northeastern

Among the major universities in the Boston area, Northeastern was late in
developing the advanced academic functions. Prior to 1960 the school was

focused almost entirely on undergraduate education (with the exception of the law school, which was closed in 1953 for financial reasons, and part-time master's programs for working adults), although President Ell recognized the growing importance of research and graduate studies toward the end of his long tenure. He established the graduate school in 1958 and approved the University's first full-time master's program, in engineering, as one of the last acts of his presidency. Ell's successor, Asa Knowles, shared the view that Northeastern was primarily an undergraduate, teaching institution, but, far more than Ell, he understood which way the academic winds were blowing and recognized that achieving a place at "the head table of academic respectability" required development at the advanced level. By the end of Knowles's presidency, Northeastern boasted an array of graduate programs, including nine doctorates in the natural and social sciences and a reopened law school, but the doctorates were an accommodation with trends Knowles felt he could not resist rather than a reflection of his core vision of Northeastern. He kept teaching loads at twelve credit hours per term and limited the research budget to less than 10 percent of total expenditures.

Kenneth Ryder, Knowles's successor and a former faculty member, took a more expansive view of academic research. Unlike Knowles, who worried about dependence on federal funding, Ryder welcomed government support and encouraged the proliferation of research centers and institutes as well as doctoral programs. The University created a dozen new doctorates during his presidency. His memoirs express particular pride in the growth of scholarly activities and his creation of the "Distinguished Professor" title to recognize the University's most productive researchers. It was also clear, however, that the pattern of development under Ryder reflected the initiative of individual deans and faculty members and was not guided by any institutional strategy. As a result, Northeastern's progress at the advanced level during these years was uneven. There were outstanding individuals and programs, but much softness as well.

My predecessor, John Curry, like Ryder and Knowles, believed that research and graduate education were essential to increasing Northeastern's status. It was thus inevitable that expansion at this level would be part of the "smaller but better" strategy. Despite the financial pressures of his years and a limited ability to hire new faculty (most appointments were replacements at the junior level), Curry approved seventeen new graduate programs, including doctorates in English, history, and public affairs. He also signaled the importance of research by winning a naming gift to support the Distinguished Professors Program from Board Chair George Matthews.

By the end of Curry's tenure Northeastern offered ninety graduate programs, including twenty-four doctorates, and was attracting sufficient
research funding to be classified as a "Research II" university by the Carnegie
Foundation. The University's leadership was proud of this designation, but
there was also a growing sense, including among the Trustees, that growth
of graduate programs had been more random than planned. In fact, despite
the new offerings, overall graduate enrollments declined steadily in the early
1990s. Quality and reputation were also problematic. The programs offered
by Northeastern's two most important colleges—Business and Engineering—
were embarrassingly weak. The MBA was experiencing erratic but generally
declining enrollments, and, among the five engineering PhD programs, three
were ranked in the bottom quartile of comparable programs by the National
Research Council in 1995, while a fourth was in the bottom of the third quartile. Only electrical engineering was in the top half. In the College of Arts and
Sciences, most discipline-based departments now offered a doctorate (exceptions were philosophy, music, art, architecture, and the languages), but here,
too, weakness was widespread. Three were in the second quartile nationally,
three in the third, and one in the fourth. The three new programs were too
new and small to be ranked.[2]

The strategic plan completed during Curry's presidency expressed concern about uneven quality and haphazard growth at the graduate level and
called for a comprehensive evaluation of current programs and caution about
creating new ones. The plan also recommended a more focused approach
to research initiatives.[3] These recommendations were pending at the time I
became president and were the basis for the review of graduate education that
I announced during my first year. I did this in part because the assessment
was clearly needed and, in part, as noted in Chapter 4, to postpone discussion
of additional development at the advanced level, especially with respect to
doctoral programs. In truth, I suspected that Northeastern exemplified a university that had built PhD programs primarily to elevate its status and please
its faculty without a great deal of thought or attention to compelling social
or educational needs. The new doctorates of the Curry years were approved
amid an acute depression in the labor market for new PhDs and the departments that would develop these programs, especially English and history,
were among our most historically neglected and resource-starved units. I
was also aware that the Carnegie classification of Northeastern as a "research
university"—while valuable in terms of our institutional image and as a
measure of increased research funding—reflected the scale of our doctoral

development, not the quality of our programs. There was no question that the advanced functions needed both close scrutiny and further development.

## Building the Faculty

I encountered no serious resistance to postponing discussion of new doctoral programs, which probably meant that every department with ambitions along these lines already had one. While Northeastern created a number of master's programs during the early years of my presidency (I believed professional master's degrees, which were often revenue producing, were a natural niche for us), no new doctorates were approved during the first four years of my presidency. This hiatus gave us space to implement the recommendations of both the Curry-era strategic plan and our own Action and Assessment Plan to carefully control further development at the advanced level while strengthening our scholarly capacity. In this context our initial focus with respect to the advanced academic functions was adding faculty strength in appropriate fields, including at the senior level. In support of this effort, I asked one of our most thoughtful faculty members, former Arts and Sciences Dean Robert Lowndes, to identify opportunities to build centers of scholarly strength, which he did in a helpful 1999 report. In the last years of my presidency, when significant new resources became available following Board approval of the Academic Investment Plan (see Chapter 3), the pace of new faculty hires accelerated sharply. During these same years we were also able to reverse the persistent decline of graduate enrollments and mount a small number of new doctoral programs, mostly in professional fields.[4]

The most prominent vehicle for recruiting senior scholars during my presidency was the Trustee Professors program, which I announced in my inaugural address. Wanting to send a clear early signal of heightened academic ambition and to address one of the University's conspicuous weaknesses— there were only thirty-one named professorships at the time of my appointment, some with very modest funding—I promised to raise $25 million over the next three years to endow eight chairs to be distributed across our six colleges. I made it clear that these appointments would be targeted to strengthen a practice-oriented focus in our research: "Northeastern must seek systematically to be a place where current scholarship is brought to bear on contemporary problems. . . . We must view the culmination of research not solely in publication but in applications, and we must create organizational structures to help academic ideas bear practical fruit." The Trustee Professorships would be used to attract individuals "who have achieved national distinction in their fields and whose work is characterized by usefulness and recognition in the professional arenas that correspond to our colleges." My hope was that each appointment would anchor a new center of scholarly strength. This vision reflected both my aspirations for Northeastern and my naiveté as a new president. I didn't realize as I spoke these lines how hard it would be to raise the funding I had projected, and I had neglected to discuss my plan with Chair Matthews, an omission that earned me a sharp and appropriate rebuke and provided an early lesson in the importance of Board-president relationships, especially with respect to fund-raising initiatives.

Raising funds for the Trustee Professorships proceeded more slowly than I had hoped, and in some instances we used operating dollars to support these appointments until the endowments could be raised. Over time, however, we made a series of hires that brought critically needed scholarly distinction to Northeastern. I have already mentioned the first three of these appointments (see Chapter 3). Barry Bluestone, a nationally prominent economist, was appointed the Stearns Trustee Professor of Political Economy in the College of Arts and Sciences in late 1998 based on an uncommitted estate gift. Our goal with this first appointment was to assert a strong role in shaping public policy, especially at the state and local levels, a field identified as an opportunity for Northeastern in the Lowndes report. Over the next several years Bluestone more than fulfilled our hopes, creating the Center for Urban and Regional Policy (CURP), attracting millions of dollars in research funding, building a strong, grant-supported staff, and becoming a major and highly visible source of ideas for public officials in Boston as well as state government, especially with respect to housing and economic development. Later, he was the driving force behind a new School of Social Science, Public Policy and Urban Affairs within the College of Arts and Sciences, and he also mounted a successful campaign to endow CURP and rename it the Kitty and Michael Dukakis Center in honor of a much-admired former governor, who was a member of the Northeastern faculty, and his wife.

The second Trustee Professor was Harry Lane, named the Fred and Darla Brodsky Professor of International Business in the spring of 1999 based on a gift from an alumnus and his wife. Fulfilling a central goal of this appointment, soon after his arrival Professor Lane organized a group of scholars from around the University to plan a research center focused on global innovation, which we supported with modest internal funding until the group was able to win a major, multiyear grant from the National Science Foundation in 2004. The third Trustee Professor was Matthias Felleisen, who joined the College of Computer and Information Science in the spring of 2001. I especially admired Felleisen's unusual combination of interests, which included basic research in programming languages and working with K–12 educators to integrate the teaching of mathematics and computer programming. Though Felleisen was still quite young when we hired him from Rice University, the CCIS faculty had correctly assessed his potential; in later years, he was named a fellow of the Association for Computing Machinery (ACM) and given separate awards from the ACM for distinguished achievements in both research and education.

Growing the Trustee Professors program was a continuing theme of my presidency. By the time I stepped down in 2006, we had made five appointments to these chairs, including, in addition to Bluestone, Lane, and Felleisen, Peter Manning to the Elmer and Eileen Brooks Chair in the College of Criminal Justice and Alexandros Makriyannis to the Behrakis Chair in the School of Pharmacy. Two of these were endowed by alums Elmer Brooks and George Behrakis. In addition, we had obtained gifts for two more professorships, one in engineering funded by Trustee Dennis Piccard, and one in entrepreneurship supported by Trustee Robert Shillman. The appointments to one of these chairs, completed after I left but fulfilling one of my goals, went to a current faculty member, Marc Meyer, an entrepreneur turned professor, who was awarded the Shillman Chair. Meyer's scholarly accomplishments fully justified his elevation, and his appointment served the vital purpose of signaling to current faculty that our highest scholarly recognition was not reserved exclusively for new appointments.[5]

The focus on creating named professorships and hiring accomplished senior scholars extended well beyond the Trustee Professors program. I was also grateful for gifts from alums Alan McKim and Richard D'Amore, Irving and Betty Rudnick, Mort Ruderman, and Jean Tempel, as well as from Board Chair Neal Finnegan and parent Ira Lipman, each of whom provided the basis for a new chair. Several senior leaders of Camp Dresser and McKee, an engineering firm with strong ties to Northeastern, led by Trustee Robert Marini, came together to endow the CDM Professorship in Civil Engineering. We also promoted other deserving current faculty to named chairs, with this distinction going to Michael Silevitch in engineering and Jamie Fox in criminal justice, and we recognized additional outstanding faculty as Distinguished Professors. Over the course of my ten years, we made fifteen new appointments to named chairs and forty-five appointments at the senior level (out of 200 new faculty), not counting individuals promoted from within. Most of the credit for these hires goes to the provosts, deans, and department chairs who identified areas of need and opportunity, found accomplished scholars who fit our frame, and did the hard work of recruitment. My role was to lead the fund-raising (often with critical support and, in some cases, leadership from deans and chairs) and to make sure these appointments fulfilled our university-wide goals and addressed important educational and societal purposes. I believe our batting average was pretty high on all counts.[6]

## Creating Centers of Research Excellence

Consistent with the Action and Assessment Plan, we proceeded cautiously with respect to the further development of organized research activities. An important initial step, accomplished between 1996 and 1998, was delineating new and more demanding criteria for establishing research centers and institutes based on recommendations from the Research Council, a broad-based group of faculty and administrators. A second early initiative was creating an Office of Technology Transfer to address our growing need to nurture and manage relationships with corporate sponsors and consumers of research. With assistance from several Trustees whose companies interacted regularly with academic scientists, the office became operational in the summer of 1999 with the appointment of its first director, Anthony Pirri. During these same early years of my presidency, also consistent with the first iteration of the Action and Assessment Plan as well as with Professor Lowndes's recommendations, we undertook a broad review of our administrative infrastructure for promoting and supporting research, since existing structures were clearly inadequate for current needs and could not possibly sustain the scale of activity to which we aspired. This project, led by Vice Provost for Research and Graduate Education Ronald Hedlund, resulted, in 1998, in the complete reorganization of our Division of Research Management to include specialized offices for research development, sponsored project management, and compliance. The recently created Office of Technology Transfer was folded into this new arrangement as a fourth component. Over the course of my presidency, with these new structures in place, the University's investment in administrative support for research doubled.

By 2000 we were ready to begin investing in new centers of scholarly strength. In May of that year Provost Hall's office invited interested groups of faculty to submit proposals for new, campus-wide research institutes, which we were prepared to launch with seed funding from an allocation in the next year's budget. In June 2001 three proposals—Nanomanufacturing, Molecular Biotechnology, and Race and Justice—were selected for initial support, which included five years of funding, beginning with $250,000 in the first year, and then declining by $50,000 yearly until a final $50,000 grant in year five, by which time the new centers were expected to be self-sustaining. A second competition for funding, in 2002, led to the establishment of three additional centers in Complex Scientific Software, Urban Health, and Professor Lane's Center for Global Innovation. During the course of my presidency, combining the new institutes supported by successive rounds of internal funding, with additional entrepreneurial initiatives of deans and faculty members, Northeastern launched twenty-two new research centers. There was a strong theme of interdisciplinary work in these initiatives, something that had been emphasized in Professor Lowndes's report. Not all of these initiatives achieved the capacity to sustain themselves with external support, but many did. Between 1996 and 2006, Northeastern's research expenditures derived from government and industry support increased by 172 percent, from $17 million to $47 million.[7]

Although the expansion of research during my presidency involved a number of disciplines and reflected the energy and creativity of many individuals, we made a focused effort in four fields in which we had particular faculty strength, that were highly compatible with our practice-oriented character, and where, given patterns of regional economic and social development, we believed we could make a significant contribution. The four were biotechnology and molecular biology, sensing and imaging, nanotechnology, and public policy. All four were targeted for special attention and support when we launched the Academic Investment Plan in 2004. Much credit goes to Provost Abdelal and the college deans for their discipline in shaping the AIP to focus large investments on a few strategic priorities.

I have already spoken of the remarkable achievements of Professor Bluestone and the Center for Urban and Regional Policy in establishing Northeastern's presence in the public policy arena, and our initiatives in Urban Health and Race and Justice added to our visibility and impact in this field. The story of sensing and imaging also dates from the early years of my presidency and actually long predates my election, since our efforts in this discipline built on Professor Michael Silevitch's Center for Electromagnetics Research,

which was established in the 1980s. This was the existing strength that convinced Dean Soyster that we could compete for one of the National Science
Foundation's coveted Engineering Research Center grants (see Chapter 3).
Prodded by Soyster, led by the dogged Silevitch, aided by reinforcements
from the Raytheon Corporation courtesy of Trustee Piccard, and supported
by $500,000 in internal funding, the project team developed their plan over
a multiyear period, formed institutional partnerships with scientists at other
universities and with corporate sponsors, rallied from an initial rejection, and
in 2000 won a five-year, $16.2 million grant from the National Science Foun-
dation. The Center for Subsurface Sensing and Imaging Systems (CenSSIS)
soon developed into one of Northeastern's most notable research power-
houses and earned a second five-year award from NSF in 2004, by which time
it was a clear target for additional support through the Academic Investment
Plan. In the final year of my presidency, led again by Silevitch, we persuaded
Bernard Gordon, a corporate pioneer in the field of subsurface imaging, to
give Northeastern $20 million to take CenSSIS to a higher level of scholarly
productivity and add a master's program to nurture future entrepreneurs.

Like CenSSIS, the Biotech initiative built on significant preexisting scholarly strength and followed a long and complex path to its ultimate success.
The project began as a joint effort of the colleges of Arts and Sciences and
Health Sciences in 1999 focused on molecular biology and pharmaceutical
science. Over the next several years, led by Deans Stellar and Zoloth, the
initiative steadily expanded to include Professor Karger's Barnett Institute,
with its strengths in analytic chemistry and separation science; the College
of Computer and Information Science, which was developing a strong theme
in bioinformatics; a group drawn from physics and pharmaceutical sciences,
which was focused on nanomedicine; and the department of psychology,
which was building capacity in neuropsychology. We provided the necessary
internal funding to support this process, first as a small planning grant, then
as one of the first three research institutes funded through the internal competition for seed money in 2001. In that same year the group won a grant
from the Sloan Foundation to create a master's program in biotechnology.
By 2002, with Provost (and microbiologist) Abdelal in place and the Academic Investment Plan in its formative stage, our commitment accelerated
dramatically with the simultaneous appointment of two nationally distinguished scholars: Alexandros Makriyannis, who became the Behrakis Trustee
Professor of Pharmacy and the director of a new Center for Drug Discovery, and Michail Sitkovsky, who was appointed to the vacant Black Chair in

Immunophysiology and Pharmaceutical Biotechnology as well as Director of the New England Inflammation and Tissue Protection Institute. The start-up costs for these two appointments represented financial commitments on a new scale for us—I recall Chief Financial Officer Mucciolo's horrified expression—but both were strong candidates for attracting external support. By the time I left the presidency the multifaceted Biotech initiative had dramatically elevated Northeastern's scholarly significance in the life sciences.

Our progress in nanotechnology, as in the other fields I have discussed, reflected the persistence and acumen of a few key people and the collaboration of many. The catalyzing force in this case was Professor Ahmed Busnaina, whom Dean Soyster recruited to the College of Engineering to fill the vacant Smith Chair in Mechanical and Industrial Engineering. This was an instance in which our location in Boston, with its dense research community and vibrant, technologically oriented business sector, made a crucial difference. Professor Busnaina had a well-established research program at Clarkson University in upstate New York, but he was somewhat isolated in that setting, especially with respect to corporate partners. We attracted him with the promise of significant support, including an endowed professorship plus seed funding for his Institute for Nanotechnology Research. (This institute was also one of the first recipients of the seed grants awarded in 2001.) By 2003, Dr. Busnaina and his team, having formed a partnership with colleagues at the University of New Hampshire and the University of Massachusetts Lowell and having won a commitment of funds from the Massachusetts state government, competed successfully for a $12.4 million grant from the National Science Foundation to create the Center for High-rate Nanomanufacturing. To further solidify Northeastern's presence in this important field, alumnus George Kostas gave the University $2 million to renovate a floor of the Egan Research Center to house Professor Busnaina's activities.[8]

I could write with enthusiasm and pride about several other research groups that were important contributors to the University's scholarly development during my presidency. I have singled out a limited number for special mention because they represented our commitment to investing in research in a strategic and focused manner and to being faithful to our character as a practice-oriented and urban institution. The aggregate story is, however, equally important in illustrating the University's progress. I have already mentioned that overall research expenditures from external sources increased by 172 percent during my ten years as president, much of it leveraged by a significant growth of institutional support. In 1999, we held the first

annual "research expo" to showcase creativity and innovation at Northeastern; by 2007, the year after I stepped down, this event had grown to include
posters by sixty-eight faculty and ninety-nine graduate students. There
were concentrations of particular strength. In 2005, we ranked first in New
England in funding per faculty member from the Engineering Directorate of
the National Science Foundation. In that same year, we ranked first nationally among private universities for funding per PhD pharmacy faculty member from the National Institutes of Health and eighteenth internationally for
articles published in the *Journal of International Business Studies*. Our efforts
to establish a robust Technology Transfer function, however, proved to be
premature; there was some growth in licensing revenues through the efforts
of this new office, but overall development of commercially viable research
proved to be limited during my years.

One final note on our work to develop Northeastern's research dimension: We never forgot our commitment to being a student-centered research
university. This meant not only that we focused on a limited number of scholarly arenas in which we had a chance to excel but also that we emphasized the
importance of utilizing our scholarly strength to enhance the undergraduate
experience. In this context, the deans routinely urged faculty members submitting proposals for external funding to include opportunities for undergraduate participation, something that federal funders often welcomed.
Undergraduate work was always included in our annual Research Expo;
in 2007, fifty-one students participated. Provost Abdelal was a particularly
strong advocate for undergraduate research and in 2004 established a special
office to promote these opportunities. There were few more exciting experiences for me as president—and few things that made me more hopeful about
the future—than wandering the Expo exhibit hall and talking with students
about their projects.[9]

## The Review of Graduate Programs

The review of graduate programs that had been recommended at the end of
President Curry's years, and which I embraced at the beginning of my presidency, was structured according to recommendations adopted before my
arrival that emanated from the University Graduate Council, a broad-based
body of faculty and students. The group had projected a comprehensive, internal exercise that would not involve outside experts or visiting committees.

The Council had also specified that any changes resulting from the review had to originate in the Faculty Senate. (University bylaws actually required that any graduate program elimination must be preceded by an affirmative vote of the sponsoring college faculty and the Faculty Senate.) In November 1996, consistent with the Council's recommendation, Provost Baer initiated the review process with the appointment of a Graduate Program Evaluation Working Group composed of seven faculty from across the University and Vice Provost Hedlund. This group was charged to review all our master's and doctoral programs based on brief self-studies to be prepared by the sponsoring departments and to recommend to the provost which programs were strong, which needed to be strengthened, and which should be eliminated. The criteria governing the review were compatibility with the University's mission, program quality, and financial viability. The working group gave the departments three months to prepare the self-studies, which were duly received in February 1997.

I was not enthusiastic about the way this badly needed review had been organized. It seemed intended to limit the discretion of the administration in making significant changes. This was not surprising. There was a great deal of apprehension among the faculty about the review, since the process had initially been proposed as part of the broader pattern of budget cutting that dominated the Curry presidency. As the review process was getting under way, Vice Provost Hedlund informed me that he was being inundated with worried inquiries from various department chairs who believed their programs were targeted for elimination. From my perspective, the review process reflected an ambivalence within the faculty about graduate development. There was widespread agreement that our work at this level needed to be reevaluated and that some programs were probably too weak to maintain, but there was also apprehension that particular programs might be vulnerable. Despite my concerns about the whole exercise, I regarded the review as a useful step. I believed there would be ample room for administrative initiative in a successor stage of assessment for programs about which there were serious questions.

The Graduate Program Evaluation Working Group did its work both conscientiously and expeditiously and delivered a report to Provost Baer and me in June 1997. This document contained many thoughtful observations. It noted, for example, that several programs addressed similar needs and recommended that redundant offerings be consolidated into unified, interdisciplinary curricula. The report also stressed the University's limited resources and the need for focused development at the graduate level, stating that Northeastern should not aspire to offer a comprehensive array of doctorates. Finally, the report suggested that savings from program eliminations and consolidations should be reinvested in our most promising programs. Against this sensible background, the Working Group expressed "high concern" about forty-one programs, of which thirteen should be eliminated and the rest required to institute changes intended to make them viable. Two Engineering PhD programs and four Arts and Sciences PhD programs were on the "high concern" list, although only one of these, economics, was proposed for elimination, a step the department itself supported. All three of the new PhD programs established during the Curry years were on the "high concern" list.

In identifying a number of programs requiring additional scrutiny, the Report of the Graduate Program Evaluation Working Group did as much as I could reasonably have expected given its composition and charge, the scale of the task, and the time allotted for the work. In the months after we received their report, Provost Baer and I consulted with the college deans to determine how best to proceed. In the end we followed the Working Group's recommendations with respect to all the "high concern" programs, closing the thirteen identified for discontinuation (after obtaining the required governance approval), consolidating several others, and charging the rest to make the changes that the Working Group had specified. The most difficult decisions for me involved the new PhD programs in Arts and Sciences. I was not persuaded that Northeastern should be in the doctoral business in English and history (alas, my own beloved disciplines) and was aware that retaining these programs was at odds with my stated intention (and that of the Working Group) to concentrate resources at the doctoral level on a limited number of fields. But I also understood that these programs were new, had not been given a fair chance to establish themselves, and were important to the departments that had developed them. Focused as I was at this early stage of my presidency on strengthening Northeastern at the undergraduate level and aware that I would need broad faculty support to advance my agenda, I convinced myself that the Working Group's recommendations represented a useful if modest step toward a more strategic configuration of our graduate programming. The new offerings, as well as the other "high concern" programs, would have a chance to prove their value; we would conduct rigorous external reviews of all these programs in due course; there would be a new round of National Research Council assessments to inform our thinking in a few years; and I would return to this matter—and to the broader question of focusing our work at the advanced level more strategically—at a later date.[10]

## Defining Our Role at the Graduate Level

Although work on particular issues related to graduate education and to specific graduate programs was ongoing throughout my presidency, it was only in the latter years that I focused the attention of my academic team on the postponed broader question of Northeastern's role at this level. Several issues, in particular, required attention: priorities for the development of new programs, the possibility of offering graduate degrees through University College (UC was the unit that offered part-time programs for working adults), the continuing problem of declining enrollments, and the still unaddressed need for a comprehensive graduate strategy.

With respect to encouraging new program development, my primary focus at the doctoral level was on our professional colleges. As I have noted, I was concerned that Northeastern had launched more doctoral programs in the arts and sciences than we could support at levels that would allow genuine excellence, but I felt we were underdeveloped at the advanced level in several of our professional fields. Given our aspiration to be a national leader in practice-oriented education, I thought we should give serious consideration to offering the highest form of training in the major professional disciplines represented by our faculties. I therefore encouraged the deans of our professional colleges to be ambitious with respect to graduate offerings, although I also recognized that in several areas—nursing being a prime example—we needed to build faculty capacity before undertaking programmatic initiatives at the advanced level. This theme of my presidency began to manifest itself in 2000 with the launching of a doctorate in computer engineering, followed between 2002 and 2005 by new doctorates in criminal justice, audiology, physical therapy, and nursing. These same years also saw a renewal of doctoral program development in Arts and Sciences focused on practice-oriented programs. The first two came in 2004 in neuroscience and applied economics. The economics program was pointed toward careers in business and government and represented the return of the economics department to advanced work following the earlier discontinuation of its more traditional program. The neuroscience program was part of our broader effort to build the life sciences. By the end of my presidency I felt Northeastern had made significant progress in establishing a position of leadership in advanced professional education.[11]

The story of graduate education in University College was part of the root and branch makeover of this important unit that occurred after the appointment of Christopher Hopey as dean in 2003 (see Chapter 3). The transformation we hoped for required that UC move into the graduate arena, a change that faculty and deans in the other colleges had adamantly opposed whenever it had been raised. Hopey's task, therefore, involved not only designing new programs that could work in a highly competitive academic marketplace but also overcoming deep political resistance across the University. He carried out both parts of his task brilliantly. He built strong partnerships with the college deans and shared revenues with them; he provided full-time faculty with opportunities to earn extra income; and he and his team designed exciting programs, many of which had a strong online component. With these changes, Hopey rapidly moved Northeastern into an entirely new era in continuing professional education, a transformation reflected in the renaming of University College as the School of Professional and Continuing Studies (SPCS) in 2004. A year later the school launched twelve master's programs in a range of fields. This was the beginning of a steady stream of advanced offerings for working adults that would continue to the end of my presidency and for a number of years thereafter. The result was a dramatic change of fortune for Northeastern in the realm of adult and continuing education as well as online programming. By 2006 SPCS was on a path to becoming one of the most robust engines for new programs and increased revenues at Northeastern.[12]

Like the failings of University College, declining enrollments in the graduate programs of Northeastern's regular colleges were evident at the time of my appointment and were a major source of concern for the Trustees. From the beginning of my presidency, therefore, a charge to the deans and department chairs was to address this matter, but year after year went by without significant progress. By 2000 my team and I had concluded that a more radical approach was needed. The challenge was that graduate admissions, unlike its undergraduate counterpart, was highly decentralized, with each academic department responsible for its own affairs—a typical pattern among American universities. Still, impressed by the remarkable success of Philomena Mantella's Division of Enrollment Management with respect to undergraduate admissions, and convinced that lack of expertise in recruitment and marketing among our departments was a big part of our problem, I took the risk of proposing the centralization of graduate admissions within a special unit of Enrollment Management. Not surprisingly, my plan produced widespread resistance. It also put Provost Abdelal in a difficult position, since he understood my concerns—both the importance of solving the problem and the rationale for my approach—but basically shared the faculty view that departments should have considerable independence in this arena. This difficult dynamic resulted in several false starts and tense moments, but ultimately it led me to acquiesce in leaving graduate admissions largely decentralized (though informally overseen by a senior member of the Enrollment Management staff and supported by centralized services for data collection and marketing) but with the caveat that unless specified levels of growth were accomplished in an agreed-upon period, I would revisit the question of central control for underperforming departments. At least in broad terms, this compromise strategy worked. Beginning in 2002, after ten years of steady decline, graduate enrollments began to trend upward. After 2005 the upward trend became dramatic.[13]

While I was pleased with the progress we made in developing new graduate programs, both in the regular colleges and in the School of Professional and Continuing Studies, and in reversing adverse enrollment trends in both areas, I cannot make the same claim for my efforts to craft a University-wide strategy for graduate studies. Indeed, this issue became the occasion for one of the few serious disagreements with the Trustees that I experienced. As I have noted, the Board had been properly concerned about the uncoordinated development of graduate programs and declines in graduate enrollments at the time of my appointment. They did not feel that either of these issues had been addressed effectively by the review process conducted during the early years of my presidency, an assessment that I shared but which I saw as the consequence of appropriate strategic priorities. At the point that Provost Abdelal and I began to work on a broad review of our graduate programming, Chair Finnegan suggested instead that this work be undertaken by a special committee of the Board, not unlike the committee on enrollments that he had chaired in the early 1990s. I tried to dissuade him from this course, since I felt that it would be more productive (and also more proper) for the campus administration to conduct the needed review and present recommendations to the Board. In the end, however, the Chair was determined to proceed with the special committee, which was duly constituted under the leadership of one of our most thoughtful and respected Board members, Judge Margot Botsford.

The work of the Special Committee inevitably sidetracked the internal review process that I had hoped to initiate through the provost's office. For the next two years—from December 2003 to December 2005—most of the provost's and deans' attention with respect to graduate programs involved supporting and advising the Special Committee. The result, in Judge Bots-ford's capable hands, was a thoughtful, encyclopedic report affirming the importance of graduate programs in the University's repositioning effort, noting that we were not as far along in developing strategies for this level as we were for the undergraduate program, and providing data-rich descriptions of current offerings together with summaries of each college's plans for further development. While pointing out various weaknesses and some redundancies in our graduate activities, the group did not recommend closing any programs, and it expressed support for our emphasis on building interdisciplinary curricula linked to our flourishing research centers and institutes. In essence, the Special Committee arrived at the same place as our internal review in 1997–98, calling for a range of needed improvements while mostly endorsing the current configuration of programs.

Reflecting on the report of the Special Committee ten years after leaving the presidency, I conclude that, despite my frustration with the way the Board proceeded in this matter, the overall outcome was the right one for Northeastern, and the process had the added benefit of vastly increasing the Board's understanding of our work at the advanced level. The most serious shortcoming of the Committee's report was its failure to articulate an overall strategy for development at the graduate level, something I had hoped to accomplish through an internal review. At the same time, the Committee recognized—correctly—that the Academic Investment Plan had become a vehicle through which we were defining priorities for new investments in research and graduate education and was therefore largely accomplishing the work of a strategic plan.[14]

## Assessing Our Progress in Research and Graduate Education

The basic question in evaluating the record of my presidency with respect to research and graduate education is how effectively we enacted the principle that I believed should guide our efforts: that is, building these dimensions of the University in ways that reflected and deepened our character as a student-centered, practice-oriented, and urban institution while also contributing to our repositioning strategy. With respect to the first of these two criteria, as I hope this chapter has demonstrated, I believe we were generally quite faithful to our guiding Aspiration in our decisions about new programs and investments, and I also think the initiatives we took added measurably to Northeastern's scholarly standing. It must quickly be acknowledged, however, that a university is a large, complex organism that moves forward along multiple fronts driven by a diverse set of actors extending far beyond the president's senior team. Institutional change is, therefore, never entirely a complete reflection of a guiding administrative strategy. Nor should it be, and ours clearly was not, as the survival and progress of our PhD programs in history and English clearly demonstrated. Indeed, a good definition of a successful development strategy for a university is one that defines the central themes of progress while also encouraging, within appropriate limits, the creative initiative of the faculty. I hope my colleagues would agree that that was the spirit that guided our work in research and graduate education during my presidential years.

The one thing we clearly did not do, of course, was significantly limit, let alone cut back, the breadth of our programming at the doctoral level. At the end of my presidency, as at the beginning, the major departments in the College of Arts and Sciences offered PhDs and, with my blessing, every professional college except Business now also offered the doctorate. This constituted a wider array of advanced offerings than I thought appropriate at the time I became president, a view that I believe was shared by the Board. I did not, however, see significant negative consequences from this outcome. On the contrary, I believe our progress in graduate education added greatly to Northeastern's intellectual vitality. At the beginning of my presidency, I had had two primary reasons for wanting to constrain doctoral program development: limited resources and potentially adverse impacts on undergraduate education. With respect to our finances, we were in an entirely different place in 2006 than we had been in 1996, and I saw no reason at the end of my presidency to doubt that we could support the programs we had in place at an acceptable level of quality, although some clearly needed continuing investment to reach their potential. This was also the view taken by the Board's Special Committee on Graduate Education.

Similarly, with respect to undergraduate education, I was not seeing in the latter years of my presidency any adverse impact of our growth in research and graduate education. Indeed, I believed—perhaps I should say hoped—that the steady emphasis that my team and I put on the quality of the undergraduate experience had strengthened the University's preexisting commitment to this aspect of our work. In addition, I was persuaded that our progress at the advanced level was enriching rather than diminishing the baccalaureate-level experience, as the growth of undergraduate research opportunities exemplified. My further hope was that the primacy of undergraduate teaching and learning was sufficiently embedded in our organizational culture that this value would be sustained in the context of further development at the advanced level that was anticipated by the Board's Special Committee on Graduate Education.

Finally, how important was our growth in research and graduate education to the success of our repositioning strategy? I believe that it had a positive but limited effect and was far less significant than our work at the undergraduate level. What mostly drove Northeastern's striking ascent in the *U.S. News* rankings was the dramatic increase in our undergraduate selectivity combined with equally striking improvements in graduation rates. Our strengthened financial position also mattered as did, during the second half of my presidency, our investments in faculty salaries and full-time faculty appointments.

The place where advances in research and graduate education were most likely to help our *U.S. News* ranking involved our reputation within academia as reflected in our peer rating on the magazine's annual survey of senior administrators at other national universities. In fact, our score did improve dramatically during my presidency, from 2.2 to 3.1, with the final increment putting us into the top 100 in 2006. An improved reputation was also evident in our increasingly successful efforts to recruit top faculty at both the junior and senior levels. Overall, however, improvements in our peer rating were a secondary contributor to our upward trajectory in the rankings, and one could debate the extent to which our rising reputation reflected our work in research and graduate education or our progress at the undergraduate level or our broader efforts in institutional marketing. My guess would be some of all three. In the end, I would argue that we accomplished a central goal of our repositioning strategy: to significantly enhance Northeastern's status largely by strengthening undergraduate education. Progress in the advanced academic functions, though important, followed and did not lead this change. As I stated in the Introduction to this volume, I thought demonstrating that this could happen would be a positive contribution to higher education in a competitive context where the conventional wisdom was that building the advanced academic functions was the only way to elevate institutional stature.

# CHAPTER 7

## A New Kind of Urban University

Our urban character is . . . a vital distinguishing feature.
The modifier "urban" evokes our history as a commuter
institution. . . . We honor that tradition . . . but we
have also reinterpreted what it means to be an urban
university. . . . We now emphasize policy-oriented
research . . . community service . . . and educational
programs focused on urban life. Above all we aim to be
the Boston area university most conspicuously committed
to promot[ing] regional development. Pursuing this
aspiration powerfully supports our quest for national
recognition.
—Speech to Northeastern Corporation, May 2006

It did not require much thought, once I became Northeastern's president, to realize that my charge to lead the repositioning of the University raised questions about the school's relationship to Boston just as it did about our commitments to cooperative education and to practice-oriented programs for undergraduates. All of these long-standing dimensions of Northeastern were associated with modest academic ambitions and low academic status, so the question about the University's relationship to Boston paralleled the questions about the school's other traditional characteristics: Did it make sense to continue emphasizing urban engagement when we needed to elevate our reputation? The 1991 Report of the Trustee Special Committee on Enrollments provided only limited guidance on this point. It stressed the importance of attracting well-prepared applicants from a wider geographic area and noted that our Boston location should be an asset in that effort; but the

Committee also endorsed the University's "access mission," which referred to Northeastern's role in educating large numbers of disadvantaged students from the Boston area. The strategic planning report produced during the Curry years stressed the University's responsibilities to its host city not only in enrolling local students but also in helping civic leaders address social and economic challenges. Moreover, even as he pursued the "smaller but better" strategy, President Curry deepened the University's involvement with Boston, including promising students at a nearby elementary school full-tuition scholarships if they finished high school and were admitted to Northeastern. In 1992 Boston's mayor named Northeastern the city's best nonprofit institution for its many "financial and personal contributions" to the city. In essence, in the years immediately preceding my election to the presidency, Northeastern's leaders stressed the need to become more selective and geographically extended in admissions and to improve the school's academic standing while also affirming the importance of local service. The task of determining whether and how these competing goals could be reconciled remained to be addressed at the time I assumed my responsibilities.[1]

## The Changing Context of Urban Higher Education

As my colleagues and I undertook the challenge of reshaping Northeastern's role in Boston, major changes were occurring nationally in the relationship between academic institutions and their host cities. A central theme in this new pattern was a growing sense among academic leaders, including at elite universities, that earlier efforts to wall their schools off from deteriorating neighborhoods and to disengage from their communities had been misguided and even counterproductive. The most widely celebrated exemplar of the new attitude was the University of Pennsylvania during the presidency of Judith Rodin between 1994 and 2004. West Philadelphia, where Penn was located, had spiraled downward in the 1950s and 1960s. The University's initial response, mentioned briefly in Chapter 1, reflected the spirit of urban renewal that dominated elite thinking about cities in that era. Penn purchased abandoned or deteriorating sites, relocated low-income residents, built new or renovated facilities for its own purposes on the acquired parcels, and strengthened campus security. Over time, however, the school's leaders realized they could not ignore the social ills that surrounded them. Penn's reputation was linked to Philadelphia's. Perceptions of safety and the overall attractiveness of the city and the neighborhood affected the University's ability to recruit students, faculty, and staff. Moreover, as time passed, community residents, traumatized by urban renewal, became progressively better organized and more able politically to resist land takings and relocation programs.

Penn's reengagement with the community began during the presidency of Sheldon Hackney between 1981 and 1993. Hackney added local residents to the West Philadelphia Corporation, which oversaw area redevelopment, and created an Office of Community Partnerships within the Office of the President to promote community service among Penn's faculty and students. Penn's changing perspective took on heightened urgency shortly after Rodin succeeded Hackney, when the murder of a student close to campus set off alarms about adverse impacts on admissions. In response, Rodin launched an intensified program of neighborhood engagement and restoration that became a defining feature of her presidency. She also intensified interactions between the school and the city, personally cultivating the mayor and seeking positions of civic leadership while assigning other University officials to represent Penn in a range of public activities.

The dynamics that characterized Penn's engagement with Philadelphia between the 1950s and 1990s were repeated with varying details in major urban centers around the country. Columbia University in New York and the University of Chicago, both participants in controversial urban-renewal programs during the early post–World War II decades, now committed resources to building healthy communities in adjacent neighborhoods in collaboration with area residents. Similar patterns occurred at Yale University in New Haven, Trinity College in Hartford, Ohio State University in Columbus, St. Louis University, and the University of Pittsburgh. More broadly, the National Association of State Universities and Land Grant Colleges (later the Association of Public and Land-grant Universities) promoted the idea of universities as "stewards of place" and encouraged its members to engage with their host communities in addressing local issues, priorities also advanced by a new organization of major public institutions located in central cities called the Urban 13, soon to be renamed the Great Cities Universities. Responding to these trends, the federal government, which had turned away from urban issues after the 1960s, began in the 1990s to fund university-community partnerships through the Department of Housing and Urban Development.

Changes at the institutional level fostered and were echoed by a heightened interest in urban research among university-based scholars. In New York, Columbia and the New School faculty collaborated to create the

"Setting Municipal Priorities" project, which issued annual reports on local issues, and NYU created a new Urban Research Center. The University of Chicago sponsored the Urban Family Life and Poverty Project, while the University of Illinois at Chicago Circle established the Great Cities Project to link teaching, research, and service to community needs. "Engaged scholarship," in which faculty members and students undertook research projects on local problems in collaboration with community organizations, became fashionable, as exemplified by the Center for Urban Research and Learning at Loyola University in Chicago.[2]

The pattern of urban reengagement by city-based universities during the 1980s and 1990s coincided with a heightened receptivity among city officials to collaboration with local campuses. This was a change. Historically, notwithstanding traditions of community service by urban universities and allowing for variation among cities, relationships between "town and gown" were more notable for tension than for cooperation. The reasons for this are not hard to understand. The schools needed costly city services but were exempt from the real estate taxes that paid for them. When universities expanded, as they inevitably did, they took revenue-producing land off the tax rolls. Students were a disruptive and often unwelcome presence in the community. In addition, faculty, students, and campus officials tended to exist in their own institutional bubbles, indifferent to the neighborhoods around them, often patronizing about the concerns of local residents, and contributing little to the larger life of the city.

During the last two decades of the twentieth century, however, several forces prompted municipal leaders to focus on the benefits of hosting academic institutions. In cities struggling with high unemployment, especially among individuals with limited skills, a university or a college could provide jobs in maintenance, office work, and security. Students and staff bought things that could support retail enterprises and restaurants, brought life and energy to sometimes deserted streets, and helped sustain the market for residential real estate. The schools themselves could purchase supplies, equipment, fuel, and electric power as well as an array of services from local vendors, boosting urban economies. Moreover, as federal support for cities declined after the 1960s and mergers removed long-standing corporate headquarters and, by extension, corporate philanthropy from traditional urban locations, universities represented rich and powerful institutions that could not easily move away to which city leaders could turn for financial assistance. In addition, the growing importance of academic research as a driver of new business activity was turning universities into engines of economic vitality, something that had not historically been the case. One indicator of the new perspective was the Initiative for a Competitive Inner City led by Michael Porter of the Harvard Business School. Porter's organization promoted the perception that academic institutions, if appropriately managed, could play major roles in strengthening urban economies. A second manifestation of the new attitude was an organization called CEOs for Cities that brought together mayors with business and academic leaders to explore shared strategies for urban revitalization. All of this reflected a heightened appreciation among city officials of shared interests with academic institutions that converged with the evolving perspectives of campus leaders. The notion of universities as "anchor institutions" for the cities in which they were located entered the vocabulary of urban planners. By the time I became Northeastern's president, both academic and city officials around the country were creating new models for how universities, including those with high academic ambitions, could form mutually beneficial partnerships.[3]

## Placing a Priority on Urban Engagement

I made clear the value I attached to Northeastern's history of urban engagement by including the word *urban* in my characterization of the University's distinguishing qualities in my first State of the University speech in 1996. I was pleased, in the months following that occasion, that my campus colleagues embraced this emphasis as we crafted the five-point Aspiration that framed our repositioning strategy. Indeed, a survey revealed that half of our faculty members were influenced by our location in what and how they taught, and almost as many believed we should increase our involvement with the city. That first fall I created an Urban Outreach Council, composed of faculty and staff interested in urban issues, to begin defining what this emphasis should look like in the context of the "smaller but better" strategy. This group, chaired by former Governor Michael Dukakis and co-chaired by then law school dean David Hall, produced a thoughtful report that became the starting point for the committee on the urban dimension of the Aspiration during work on the 1997–98 reaccreditation self-study. The Action and Assessment Plan of 1999 took these discussions one step further, asserting our ambition "to be a national model for ways in which an urban university can organize and utilize its resources to benefit its surrounding community." The AAP identified specific contexts—the public schools, health care institutions, the city's economy—where we should focus our efforts, and it stressed the importance of continuing to enroll at-risk urban students. The Plan also identified ways in which Northeastern could make greater use of the city's resources to enrich our educational programs as well as our scholarly activities.[4]

These were important ideas. They expressed a goal that was close to my heart and resonated with the decision I had made many years earlier to devote my professional life to urban higher education. They pointed the way for Northeastern to combine high academic standards and intensive engagement with our community. They encouraged me to believe that we could remain the leading private urban university in Boston. Neither the Council nor I saw these aspirations as conflicting with the need to raise Northeastern's stature nationally and even internationally. Indeed, as the University of Pennsylvania was demonstrating, and as the University of Chicago had shown a century earlier, it was entirely possible for a great academic institution to be deeply involved in the life of its host city and still be a place of far-reaching educational and scholarly consequence. The question was how to achieve this combination of goals at Northeastern.

### Urban Engagement and Admissions Policy

The most difficult challenge my team and I faced in adapting Northeastern's urban traditions to our repositioning strategy involved admissions policy. As the Report of the Urban Outreach Council emphasized, enrolling students from modest local backgrounds was the centerpiece of our historic identity, as it was at most of our sister urban universities around the country. That pattern clearly had to change—dramatically. The University's survival within the context of intensified competition from low-cost public institutions depended on enrolling significant numbers of well-prepared, middle-income, and affluent students from a wider geographic area. As I noted in Chapter 4, the success of our Enrollment Management team in accomplishing the needed changes in our student body was the foundation for the overall transformation of Northeastern that occurred during my presidency. As we pursued the goal of heightened selectivity, however, we also made room for the kinds of students Northeastern had traditionally enrolled. Paradoxically, both these efforts—becoming more selective and continuing to serve local as well as low-income students—so different from each other and even, to some degree, at odds with each other, involved a celebration of Northeastern's urban character.

The value of our location to our efforts to recruit a stronger and more geographically diverse student body reflected a striking change in college-going patterns among young Americans of the late twentieth century. In 1959, when I graduated from high school, the traditional notion that the most desirable undergraduate colleges were located in isolated settings was still quite prevalent. The leading liberal arts schools were almost all in small towns, and top-ranking universities located in cities rarely touted their locations as major attractions. By the 1990s all this had changed. Students of this latter era were on average more sophisticated and more widely traveled than their counterparts of my undergraduate years. For the generation we needed to attract, attending college in a city with the amenities, cultural opportunities, and social diversity available in such a setting was often an advantage. This was especially true for high school graduates who had grown up in metropolitan centers. In this context, Boston, with its reputation as a leading college town, was particularly appealing, as the Trustees Special Committee on Enrollments had recognized. Our challenge in enrolling a more selective and more national student body lay less in convincing potential applicants that Boston was a great place to go to college than in winning our share of young people who were already inclined to attend one of the city's well-regarded academic institutions.

I should point out, in stressing the advantages of our Boston location in recruiting strong students, that our home city in the 1990s represented a particular version of the nation's long-running urban crisis. By the time I became Northeastern's president, Boston had made a remarkable recovery from the economic doldrums into which it had fallen during the middle years of the twentieth century. Powered especially by the growth of high-tech industries linked to university-based research labs, the city and metropolitan area were en route to becoming one of the most economically vibrant regions in the country. But this did not mean the urban ills of high unemployment, chronic poverty, and associated social phenomena, like crime and broken families, were being eliminated. What was occurring, rather, was the division of the city into two worlds: one, mostly white and increasingly affluent; a second, heavily minority and only marginally benefiting from the city's recovery. This new pattern, which was also evident in other metropolitan centers, explains the paradox that characterized Northeastern's approach to admissions during my presidency. The vibrant, prosperous Boston helped us attract talented students from all over the country—and, indeed, the world; but the city and its struggling urban neighborhoods continued to need the engaged attention of a committed urban university.[5]

To reinforce and highlight the benefits of our Boston setting for well-prepared and intellectually adventurous students, we made a concerted effort to strengthen the urban dimension of Northeastern' s undergraduate experience, just as the Urban Outreach Council had recommended. Co-op played a key role. Combining work experiences with classroom study is particularly well-suited to cities because of the availability of employment opportunities, and an important part of our drive to enrich the educational value of co-op was strengthening ties to Boston's name-brand employers and its emerging high-tech sector. At the same time, we greatly expanded opportunities for students to work with the area's many community-based organizations through a new Center for Community Service, made possible by financial support from Trustee Arnold Hiatt, and also by expanding service-learning opportunities within the curriculum. We also supported new academic programs that took advantage of our setting, including a degree in architecture that emphasized city planning, a new school of education that specialized in preparation for urban classrooms, and a new urban studies minor. Our social science departments, led by Professor Bluestone, highlighted the urban theme by organizing themselves into a School of Social Science, Public Policy and Urban Affairs within the College of Arts and Sciences. Beyond the classroom, we facilitated student access to Boston's cultural riches, taking advantage of our location within walking distance of the Museum of Fine Arts and the city's two premier concert halls, as well as, of course, Fenway Park, home of the Boston Red Sox, and the fashionable shopping district of the Back Bay. Our admissions professionals consistently reported that the promise of experiences linked to Boston was a vital recruiting asset.[6]

An important dimension of our admissions work, and of our broader effort to be a model urban university, involved the racial and socioeconomic diversity of our campus community. The kinds of students we hoped to attract often wanted to be part of a pluralistic student body. We also considered the presence of such diversity essential to our role in preparing students for an increasingly multicultural society and, indeed, a key element of any plausible contemporary claim to "excellence" in undergraduate education. These considerations fostered a sustained focus on student diversity throughout my presidential years—an emphasis that built on President Curry's good work in this area. In terms of socioeconomic diversity, the financial profile of families of entering freshmen clearly shifted upward as we sought more students who could afford our tuition and as we became more selective; but we also continued to seek out students from modest backgrounds, aided by our School of General Studies, which provided a supported freshman-year experience for students who did not meet traditional admissions criteria, as well as several more-focused initiatives, including the Torch Scholarships, which brought us a steady though small stream of exceptional students from unusually difficult circumstances. At the end of my presidency, 70 percent of our admitted students applied for financial aid and, among these, a quarter were from families with annual incomes below \$51,500. We maintained Pell Grant recipients at approximately 15 percent of our undergraduates. With respect to ethnic and racial diversity, we achieved modest percentage increases in students of color: from 7 percent to 8 percent for African Americans, from 3.4 percent to 7 percent for Hispanics, and from 8.1 percent to 10 percent for Asian Americans. These gains were not dramatic, but achieving them as we also increased selectivity and without the help of endowment funds for scholarships seemed to me a genuine accomplishment.

Closely linked to the goal of enrolling a diverse student body was maintaining a campus culture that supported students from all backgrounds. This had been a central theme of the Curry years, and my team and I sought to build on and extend this record. Critically important in this context was the composition of the faculty and staff, and I was pleased that during my ten years as president we improved minority representation on the full-time faculty from 9 percent to 15 percent. To further foster a welcoming atmosphere, we expanded support for the two existing cultural centers: one focused on the African American community; the other on the Latino\a community. We established a third cultural center to support Asian American students. In addition, we changed our Office of Affirmative Action, with its emphasis on compliance with legal and regulatory requirements, to an Office of Diversity and Affirmative Action, with primary responsibilities for promoting a welcoming atmosphere for the different parts of our campus community, a perspective strongly embraced by the office's new director, Donnie Perkins.

It must be acknowledged that, despite our efforts to nurture a diverse campus community, deep and persistent tensions remained between students of color and the broader University population, including the University administration. This became evident in connection with our proposal to build a new home for the African-American Institute, which involved demolishing the dilapidated building in which this unit had been housed since its creation. Many of our Black students simply did not believe we would fulfill our promise to replace their home, and, joined by supporters from the Roxbury community and students from other universities, they protested angrily against the plan to tear it down. Working through this situation was one of the most challenging moments of my presidency. But, knowing we meant what we said and that the end result would be a big improvement, we persisted, and the elegant new facility that we created became a showpiece for the University and a source of pride for our African American students and staff. The most important measure of success with respect to student diversity, however, was the academic progress made by students of color after they enrolled. I was pleased that, as the University's overall persistence rates increased, so too did those for Black and Hispanic students, although there remained a modest but real gap between minority students and the overall student body with respect to this metric.[7]

Our sustained emphasis on diversity was a natural bridge between efforts to attract strong students on a national basis and our continuing attention to enrolling low-income students from Boston and the region's urban suburbs. Over its long history Northeastern had developed a number of scholarship programs for high school graduates from these communities. As the University devolved into an open admissions institution in the late 1980s and early 1990s, we became essentially a school of last resort for large numbers of such students, and for their advocates, including politicians who knew a call to Northeastern on behalf of a marginal applicant was likely to produce a positive result. Against this background, maintaining a strong connection with the schools and communities that reflected our historic urban character as we steadily tightened admissions standards—and dealing with the political fallout from this change among local politicians and guidance counselors— was a significant challenge during my presidential years.

We wanted Northeastern to be the strongest supporter of the Boston Public Schools (BPS) among all private universities in the region. Between 1996 and 2003, however, as our overall admissions program was achieving remarkable success, the number of BPS graduates we admitted declined steadily. By 2003, it was clear that an intensified effort was needed. In that year, at my request, Vice President Mantella crafted a new Boston Public Schools Scholarship Program that included twenty full-cost awards, doubling our previous number. We also dedicated a member of our admissions staff to working with the city's schools as well as with those of the urban suburbs, and we created a new summer bridge program to help graduates with weak high school backgrounds prepare for college-level work. In addition, we strengthened our outreach to Boston's two community colleges, including a formal partnership with Roxbury Community College, which served the city's premier African American neighborhood, and we increased the number of BPS graduates transferring from those institutions. These measures, taken together, allowed us to achieve the hoped-for result. By the end of my presidency Northeastern was enrolling more graduates of the Boston Public Schools (340) and providing more of them with full-cost scholarships (50) than any of our sister institutions, while also leading the way in total institutional financial aid to Boston residents ($3.5 million).

Our work with the Boston Public Schools went far beyond admissions and financial aid. We had much to build on in this respect. At the time of my election, almost all our colleges had outreach programs of one kind or another, totaling dozens of initiatives: professional training for K-12 faculty, research opportunities for students in our science and engineering labs, placement of practice teachers in the city's schools, tutoring programs, after-school and summer-enrichment programs; science fairs, and opportunities to participate in organized sports. One program that I especially admired was the Boston Algebra Project led by associate professor of mathematics Robert Case, who had developed an innovative and highly successful approach to helping urban high school students master a subject that was typically the most daunting barrier to their progress. I was proud toward the end of my presidency to promote Dr. Case to a full professorship based on his contributions to math pedagogy, even though his record of scholarly publication did not meet our normal requirements. Putting all of these efforts together, the aggregate value of our contributions to the Boston Public Schools in both services and scholarship support—$34.5 million in 1999–2000—exceeded that of any other Boston-area university.[8]

## Urban Engagement and Faculty Scholarship

Our Boston location was as powerful an asset in recruiting faculty and building centers of scholarly excellence as it was in recruiting students. To some extent this had been the case for many years, not only for Northeastern but for all the colleges and universities in the metropolitan region. But Northeastern was unusual in the degree to which its faculty members were interested in scholarly work related to urban issues, which was a major reason for the Carnegie Commission's decision in 1973 to identify Northeastern as a leading urban university. At the time I became president examples of this pattern could be found all across the campus: the Center for Labor Market Studies and the Center for Urban Education in the College of Arts and Sciences; the Center for Family Business in the College of Business Administration; the Center for Urban Law and Policy in the Law School; the Center for Health, Education, Research and Service in the Bouvé College of Pharmacy and Health Sciences—in addition to the many science and technology-oriented research centers linked to the region's business enterprises.

Believing that scholarly excellence and urban engagement were complementary values, my team and I sought to strengthen and extend Northeastern's pattern of "engaged scholarship" as part of our effort to enhance the school's academic reputation. The two most obvious manifestations of this perspective were the Dukakis Center for Urban and Regional Policy (see Chapter 6) and the School of Social Science, Public Policy and Urban Affairs, both led by Professor Bluestone. A core idea for the new school was that it would establish relationships with both city and state governments that would inform the scholarly priorities of our social science faculty, just as such links had done for the economists, political scientists, and sociologists at Harper's University of Chicago, not to the exclusion of other research interests but as an important and continuing theme. I was pleased when the mayor of Boston, Thomas Menino, spoke at the school's inaugural celebration and embraced this notion. In the succeeding months, as the new school was getting organized, the mayor's office collaborated with Professor Bluestone to organize meetings between the heads of city departments and members of the Northeastern faculty with a view to identifying research issues of interest to our scholars that could also inform the work of city government. In succeeding years, interactions with both city and state leaders became a standard feature of the school's scholarly activities.

Our efforts to organize our research capacities in ways that strengthened the Boston region and the reciprocal benefits of doing so were evident in many aspects of our scholarly work. The Biotech initiative gained from links with Boston's world-class teaching hospitals and their strong research programs. The same was true for the Center for Subsurface Sensing and Imaging Systems and the Center for High-rate Nanomanufacturing, both of which forged partnerships with area businesses that helped them win federal research support while contributing to the region's innovation economy. New institutes for Urban Health Research and Race and Justice as well as a new Center for Criminal Justice Policy Research represented further examples of scholarly work that elevated the University academically while contributing to the community.

To some extent, of course, the social and economic benefits of scholarship occur as a natural and even incidental consequence of university-based research. Any major university located in a city can legitimately point to the local contributions of its research activities, and many do so by issuing "economic impact reports" designed to justify their exemption from real estate taxes and to maintain good relationships with political leaders. These claims are legitimate, but their validity does not, in my view, make an academic institution an "urban university" in the sense that we defined that term. As I have noted, champions of urban higher education distinguish between schools that are "in" their city and those that are "of" it to differentiate institutions that seek deliberately to contribute to the well-being of their host communities and those that do not. Our aspiration to be a model urban university and the leading such campus in the Boston area implied that we would consciously organize our scholarly resources to contribute simultaneously to the progress of the University and the vitality of the Boston metropolitan area. This was not the only prism through which we established scholarly priorities, but it was an important one.[9]

## Urban Engagement and Facilities

For reasons previously discussed, the expansion and construction of physical facilities are a prominent source of tension between city-based universities and host communities. At the same time, the development and management of buildings and grounds can provide universities and cities with rich opportunities for mutual benefit if there is a will to collaborate on both sides. As my team and I worked to enhance our campus in ways that supported our repositioning strategy, we always sought to improve the physical environment of the community. This was a good thing for our relationships with the city because Mayor Menino was a strong believer that new academic construction should produce "community benefits"; had we been inclined to resist this notion, we would have been in endless conflict with municipal authorities. As it turned out, despite our inclination to be a good neighbor and a responsible corporate citizen, moving physical development projects from conception to completion was often a difficult process.

Our basic policy with respect to expansion was that we would not take financial advantage of the city when we acquired new land; we continued to pay taxes on any tax-producing property that we acquired. We also worked closely with city officials as we designed and developed new buildings, which was pretty much both a political and a regulatory requirement during the Menino years. We asked our architect, William Rawn, to express our urban character in the design of our facilities, a guideline that produced a campus with open borders, no fences or gates, and celebratory archways welcoming the community into our space. In addition, our community-relations staff, led initially by Tom Keady and later by Robert Gittens, worked out policies that invited city residents to use our campus to the maximum extent consistent with the needs of our own students and staff. Neighborhood residents had access to our recreational facilities. Students in the city high schools were welcome in our library and our student center as places to study and hang out. We devoted an entire building to housing a public high school focused on health careers and fostered interactions between this school and our Bouvé College of Health Sciences, including the use of our labs. We gave free space to a nonprofit organization that provided skill training to community residents. We partnered with an organization of young professionals, who used instruction in squash as a vehicle to mentor neighborhood kids toward academic success, to build and operate a first-class squash facility on university land. From time to time, our own students complained that high school kids were being disruptive and wondered why we allowed them such liberal access to our campus. Our answer was always the same: This is part of what it means to be an urban university; if we want to enjoy the benefits of the city, we also need to contribute to its well-being. This was a perspective that, for the most part, our students readily understood and accepted.

Undoubtedly, the most significant examples of our partnership with Boston in the area of facilities were two major projects along Columbus Avenue, which defined the boundary between our campus and Roxbury: Renaissance Park and Davenport Commons, both of which were mentioned briefly in Chapter 4. Renaissance Park involved our acquisition of a vacant building that had been briefly occupied by the Massachusetts Registry of Motor Vehicles but then abandoned due to resistance from workers who claimed there were problems with air quality (although it is possible they never wanted to move there in the first place). After an extended negotiation with both city and state officials as well as with the bank that held the deed, we purchased this building along with three adjacent undeveloped parcels, adding also a fourth parcel, privately held, that had been zoned for a parking garage, something Northeastern desperately needed. As part of the agreement, we promised to devote space in the Registry building to community-oriented uses, including a pharmacy and a health center. We also agreed to dedicate some of the undeveloped parcels to uses that would benefit the neighborhood, especially a much hoped-for hotel. Over the years since we made this agreement, both the building and the undeveloped parcels have proved to be extraordinary assets for Northeastern while also bringing positive new activity to the neighborhood, although we were never able to bring the hotel to fruition.

Davenport Commons provided an even more striking example of a university-city partnership. This project involved our acquisition of three vacant parcels that had been cleared in the 1960s for a controversial highway project that was ultimately abandoned. Subsequent efforts by city and state officials to identify alternate uses for the land also failed, and the three parcels had remained an empty, ugly, and even dangerous tear in the fabric of Roxbury for many years. Our community-relations team saw this as a perfect opportunity for the kind of win-win activity that is the holy grail of university-community partnerships. Northeastern needed land for our program of residential construction, which was just getting under way. The community needed to have these long-vacant parcels put to positive uses. The mayor was pressing universities to build more housing to reduce reliance on off-campus rentals, which were taking housing options away from residents and pushing up prices.

Discussions with city officials and community leaders, led by Keady and General Counsel Lembo, extended over many difficult months and came close to breaking down on multiple occasions. There were suspicions in all directions, especially between community residents and both the University and the city. But all three parties stayed at the table in recognition of the potential benefits. Ultimately, we achieved a plan that divided the land more or less evenly between student residences and affordable, owner-occupied housing, plus limited commercial development. As part of a complex financing package, the University agreed to contribute a subsidy that kept housing prices within reach of neighborhood residents. Once built, Davenport Commons became a popular address for Northeastern students, provided seventy-five units of housing for Roxbury, helped transform Columbus Avenue from a place where people did not walk at night into a vibrant urban thoroughfare, and put a feather in Mayor Menino's cap. The project has been widely recognized as a model for how a university and community can work together on a major development initiative.[10]

## Structural Tensions with City and Community

From the perspective of the University, the commitment to being a constructive contributor to the life of the city and community was a pervasive aspect of Northeastern's culture. Beyond key policy arenas like admissions and facilities, the pattern of seeking ways to benefit the city and community was evident in many areas of institutional life, including: community service activities by students, faculty, and staff; community events, such as an annual Thanksgiving Dinner for senior citizens; hiring and purchasing programs that included systematic attention to helping community residents and small businesses; and partnerships with community organizations like the Police Department and the community health centers. In any given year, the University's many departments mounted more than 100 community-oriented activities. Despite all this, however, and despite the fact that it was often possible to find points of convergence between the city's concerns and the University's needs, it could not be forgotten that, in the end, the interests of institution, city, and community were not identical. Conflicts were bound to arise and some degree of tension was inevitable. Indeed, it is precisely because of this underlying reality that investing in relationships with city and community over an extended period makes political sense for an urban university, quite apart from the other benefits that derive from these connections. When difficulties occur, it helps to have fostered a spirit of collaboration with those who might, under other circumstances, become adversaries.

Undoubtedly the largest irritant in our relationship with both community and city stemmed from the transition we were making from local, commuting university with unselective admission policies to nationally competitive residential institution. As we recruited more and more students from beyond Boston and New England, despite our program of residential construction, students became an increasingly visible presence in the neighborhoods that surrounded the University. As this process continued, both the competition between residents and students for housing and the behaviors associated with student communities everywhere—drinking, loud parties, late nights—became frustrations for our neighbors as well as for city officials. This phenomenon was complicated by the changing character of the neighborhoods themselves, as Boston's prosperity fostered an influx of homeowners living in renovated buildings that had previously housed low-cost rentals managed by absentee landlords. In our work with city officials and in my personal interactions with the mayor, my colleagues and I sought to explain why changes in the character of Northeastern were unavoidable and how the city was benefiting from them. But local political leaders found our transformation difficult to digest, especially since Northeastern had for so long been a place where young people from the families they represented could get a decent education and where their own requests on behalf of particular applicants were likely to be successful. I don't believe I ever persuaded Mayor Menino that Northeastern was not simply abandoning the city in pursuit of our institutional interests—although he may also have concealed any effect I might be having along those lines to keep me off balance.[11]

## The Super Bowl Riot

In February 2004 the tensions arising from our expanding presence in the Fenway neighborhood turned into a major crisis, producing the worst period of my presidency in our relationship with both city and community, and, in my view, threatening our progress toward repositioning Northeastern in public perceptions as a first-class academic institution. Boston's reputation as a fanatic sports community is well earned, and the victory of the New England Patriots in that year's Super Bowl triggered an outpouring of public celebration on the city's streets, especially among young people, that quickly turned violent. All over the city, in student centers like Harvard Square, Allston (BU and BC), and Kenmore Square (BU), fires were lit and cars overturned by rampaging mobs. In Northeastern's Fenway neighborhood this out-of-control behavior led to tragedy. A passing vehicle driven by an immigrant from the Caribbean was surrounded by rowdy students, mostly white, who began rocking the car. Terrified, the driver gunned his engine and roared through the crowd, injuring several bystanders and killing the son of a state trooper. Police and University officials on the scene were overwhelmed. When it was over, the finger pointing began, and city officials, led by the mayor, were quick to blame both the students and University leaders for the outrageous and tragic events of that night. Media coverage was lurid and unrelenting. Although problems had occurred in multiple locations, the focus was on Northeastern because a death had occurred in our neighborhood.

Subsequent investigations would show that the student crowds had been infiltrated and provoked by nonstudent troublemakers who had anticipated the opportunity that the Super Bowl victory provided. These reports would also show that the city's police were woefully underprepared for the kind of violent outbreak that occurred. Still, faced with a drumbeat of criticism from Boston City Hall and the media, my team and I quickly decided not to join the finger pointing but to acknowledge responsibility and move decisively to discipline students whose behavior was clearly unacceptable, make amends for damage to community property, and put in place policies to prevent such an event from happening again. I was personally moved to take this stance by viewing videotapes that convinced me that, whatever else may have been true, some of our students had behaved disgracefully and no fellow student had stepped forward to object. We resisted the mayor's highly questionable demand that we summarily dismiss any student named in a police report, and we instituted procedures to identify those who had actively participated, ultimately expelling seven students, disciplining two others, and cooperating with the police who charged seventeen students with misdemeanors. In addition, we canceled a major and long-planned rock concert that had been scheduled for the next weekend on the grounds that we needed to focus on the problems we had created and on restoring the University's good name, not throwing a party that would remind everyone of what had happened a week earlier. Many students (and parents) were outraged by a decision widely perceived as punishing innocent students for the behavior of a few; but my colleagues and I believed the problems had been more extensive than a small number of troublemakers, and we held our ground.[12]

The Super Bowl riot led to an extended period of tension with City Hall and our neighbors. As a consequence, we were required to enter into agreements with community leaders on a number of issues, including control of student behavior, the use of rental housing by our students, the construction of additional residential facilities, and a physical planning process with heavy community involvement. We did all of these things. At the same time, we worked with student leaders to create policies and programs to prevent a recurrence, including a freshman orientation featuring student speakers and stressing the responsibility of Northeastern students to be respectful of community residents. The mature way in which our student leaders worked with us on this effort was deeply impressive to me and one of the few positive outcomes in an otherwise painful sequence of events. Repairing the damage to relationships with city and community was the work of many months. Only at the end of my presidency, in the summer of 2006, did we finally reach agreement with the city and community regarding an acceptable manner of building the housing to which we had committed our-selves in the spring of 2004.

The Super Bowl riot was a severe setback to our efforts to foster part-nerships with our city and our community and underscored the fragility of these relationships and the structural complexities inherent in them. A long history of sometimes tense interactions between Northeastern and its neighbors was not quickly forgotten, despite the many contributions of the University to the community. City officials, especially the mayor, were leg-atees of a tradition that viewed universities as problems rather than assets, although, at critical moments, Menino acknowledged that Boston benefited from its academic institutions. University officials sometimes resented being asked to contribute to projects favored by politicians, even when we were developing land we already owned. Our Trustees wanted to be sure we were not being asked to do more than our sister universities. In the end, manag-ing these relationships successfully required goodwill and a long view on all sides of the equation. Painful as the events surrounding the Super Bowl riot had been, they also underscored, in the way we were able to work with our neighbors and with the city to repair the damage and move forward in many areas, the value of the work Northeastern had done over many years, including but not limited to my presidency, to be an engaged and responsi-ble corporate citizen of our city.

### Advocating Urban Engagement

I titled this chapter "A New Kind of Urban University" to convey our goal of maintaining Northeastern's tradition of engagement with the city while vigor-ously pursuing the effort to establish Northeastern as a top-tier national uni-versity. The preceding pages provide a reasonably comprehensive accounting of how this effort played out over the course of my ten years. How would a fair-minded observer assess our urban balance sheet? Clearly, we compiled a substantial list of successes both in taking advantage of our Boston location and in contributing to the well-being of the city. It was equally clear that there were continuing challenges, highlighted by an uneven relationship with the mayor's office and the problems associated with the Super Bowl riot, as well as, of course, the city's persistent social and economic challenges. My own view, as I reported in my final address to Northeastern's governing Corpora-tion, quoted at the beginning of this chapter, was twofold: first, our policies

had appropriately honored our history of urban commitment while rein-
terpreting that tradition in a manner required by changed competitive circumstances; second, emphasizing our urban character had been a significant
contributor to our repositioning strategy.

I should not leave the topic of Northeastern's urban policies without
touching on the moral dimension of this work. This chapter has emphasized
that partnerships between urban universities and host cities should be conceived in terms of shared interests. This way of thinking about university-
community interactions is important because universities, like all social
organizations, are fundamentally driven by self-interest, which is therefore
the only reliable basis on which to advocate a particular pattern of institutional behavior. That said, it is also true that the steps we took to strengthen
Boston were never based entirely on close calculations of institutional interests, even when those interests are construed in the most enlightened possible terms. There was also, at least for me, a moral aspect to our work with the
city, and I always believed that this perspective was important to many of my
colleagues in the Northeastern community, indeed was part of what motivated their participation in this work and was therefore a force that helped
bind us together as an organization.

Academic work, at its best, is always about improving the world, and
there are few better ways to do that than educating the young and conducting
scholarship that adds to the world's understanding of itself. Our outreach to
the Boston Public Schools, our determination to continue being a place of
opportunity for young people from difficult backgrounds, our policy research
on the challenges of urban life, all partook of the same impulse to engage the
most important social and economic challenges of American society that led
me to choose a career in urban higher education shortly after I completed my
graduate studies so many years earlier.

In the final years of my presidency, strongly supported by my able communications team, I redoubled my advocacy for partnerships between urban
universities and their host cities. We produced an essay for the *Chronicle of
Higher Education* calling upon leaders of city-based universities and city officials to set aside long-standing suspicions in favor of collaboration. We generated four opinion pieces on this same topic for the *Chronicle*, coauthored with
leaders from politics, health care, banking, and higher education. I became
Boston's academic representative in the national CEOs for Cities organization
and co-chaired a commission created by the Boston Foundation to promote
university-community partnerships across the city. We used my 2004–2005

annual report to explain the significance of urban engagement for Northeastern and were pleased that Mayor Menino provided a statement for this document endorsing our efforts. I devoted major portions of my final State of the University address to this topic. As I left the presidency, I believed Northeastern had helped validate a way of thinking about relationships between universities and their host cities that the country urgently needed.[13]

CHAPTER 8

# Marketing and Rankings

> I am always a little uncomfortable in discussions of the
> rankings. . . . Thoughtful observers invariably regard
> [them] with skepticism. . . . And yet . . . I set aside my
> reservations, and I proclaim the importance of improving
> our standing. Indeed, I go further. I regard . . . getting
> Northeastern onto any reasonable list of the best 100
> universities in the country as an institutional imperative
> toward which we should bend all our energies. . . .
> Achieving this goal, in a manner consistent with our
> values, is the simple central object of our drive for
> institutional transformation.
> —State of the University Speech, Fall 2000

My team and I knew that heightening the quality of the University's work—the education we offered, the scholarship we sponsored, our engagement with the city and region—however intrinsically important and professionally rewarding, was only half our task. The second half, equally vital given the existential crisis the University had experienced in the early 1990s, was repositioning Northeastern in public perceptions as a selective national university—a goal we ultimately defined as breaking into the top 100 "national universities" in the *U.S. News* rankings. The substantive and the reputational challenges were interdependent, of course, because success on the second both depended on and propelled progress on the first. If we did not persuade a variety of publics that Northeastern was a top-tier university rather than a commuter institution of modest academic standing, our future was very much in doubt.

My understanding of the obstacles that colleges and universities face in changing their positions in the nation's academic hierarchy was grounded in my experiences in academic administration and my work on *Academia's Golden Age*. Two decades at UMass Boston had impressed me with the difficulty that universities characterized as "urban" encounter in achieving reputations for quality, especially in a setting like metropolitan Boston with its impressive cluster of traditional institutions. The state's public urban campus was far better than the community realized. The City University of New York, with its roots in the storied City College of New York, had enjoyed a reputation for high academic standards during years when it was a selective institution, but it had lost that position quickly after adopting open admissions in 1969. Selectivity and quality were deeply linked in public perceptions.

Writing *Academia's Golden Age* taught me another fact of life about academic reputations: once established, they are hard to change. Both locally and nationally the academic pecking order in 1900 or 1950 or 1990 looked remarkably similar. Yet some universities had improved their standing. Both Boston College and Boston University, particularly the former, had managed to dramatically enhance their reputations in the four decades after 1960. UMass Amherst had also gained heightened respect during these years. Nationally, Duke, Stanford, and Vanderbilt, generally accepted by the late twentieth century as top quality universities, had been, within recent memory, locally oriented institutions of modest standing. The University of Southern California, long derided as a "University of Second Choice," was transforming itself into an academic powerhouse in the 1980s and 1990s. These success stories, however, had typically occurred over extended periods of time and had been associated with large infusions of money. Neither condition applied to Northeastern. We had no realistic expectation of a financial windfall, and we knew we had to move quickly. The demographers were telling us that the number of young people graduating from high school would decrease after 2008, with especially steep declines in New England, from which we drew most of our students. We had a narrow window of favorable circumstances.

Given all of the above, nothing was more important than mounting an aggressive program of communications and marketing. This effort proved to be among the most sustained, multifaceted, and challenging dimensions of my presidency.

## Building the Foundation

In 1996 my new team and I were complete amateurs with regard to marketing. Moreover, there were few models to learn from. The improved reputations of Boston College, Boston University, and UMass Amherst seemed to have been produced less by sophisticated marketing than by the effects of substantive improvements over extended periods—hiring well-known scholars, building impressive research programs, recruiting stronger students, appointing presidents with star power, sponsoring highly visible athletic teams. In the 1990s marketing and especially advertising, as these activities are understood in business, were underdeveloped functions in higher education, and more than slightly suspect. A few institutions had developed full-blown programs—the University of Maryland was one striking example—and we learned what we could from these pioneers. But most institutions had departments of "university relations" that handled interactions with the media and placed stories about the school in the press. Various subunits—admissions, alumni affairs, individual colleges and schools, athletic teams—managed their own communications to reach their particular constituencies. Northeastern's approach to marketing was typical of this restrained, fragmented, and nonstrategic pattern.

In the early going we benefited from the assistance of two successful marketing professionals among our alumni/ae, Edward Wax and Joseph Cronin, both members of our governing Corporation. We also engaged a series of marketing consultants. The feedback was consistent. At the institutional level Northeastern had no clear message, no common graphic look, no proper marketing organization, and no marketing strategy. It quickly became evident that, before mounting a major campaign to promote the University, we had foundational work to do, beginning with clarifying our thoughts about how to differentiate ourselves in a crowded academic marketplace. One of the consultants, Michael Keeshan, led my leadership team through an extended exercise to address this issue. This process, discussed briefly in Chapter 2, helped us embrace the five-point Aspiration as a statement of our institutional character and adopt the differentiating Vision that Northeastern would provide the country's premier program of practice-oriented education. These would be the self-defining concepts from which we would build our communications program.[1]

I was fascinated to learn, as a neophyte in the world of marketing, that the same process and ideas that were critical in building the University's strategic formula and plan also provided the basis for our marketing and advertising strategies. In retrospect, this should not have been surprising. Of course the values and priorities that guided our substantive development needed also to frame our communications. For an advertising program to work over time, the product needed to validate the claim. It wasn't just about taglines and jingles. Understanding this greatly increased my respect for the whole field of marketing and messaging.

The discussions that led to the third component of our strategic formula—in addition to the Aspiration and the Vision—the competitive goal of becoming a top-100 national university in the *U.S. News* rankings—did not emanate from our marketing discussions but rather represented a way of dramatizing the challenge we faced for the campus community. As we were to learn, however, the progress we were able to make in the rankings became, inevitably, a validator of our improving quality and therefore a major contributor to our marketing effort. Indeed, Robert Zemsky has argued that the rankings are less an indicator of quality than of "market power." That formulation seems to me a powerful and important way to understand the real role of rankings, though it is also somewhat unfair since the *U.S. News* metrics do measure some things generally associated with academic quality, including faculty credentials, graduation rates, selectivity, and dollars spent on academic programs.

Our initial foray into marketing left no doubt that we needed to radically redesign our Office of University Relations and add staff capacity we did not possess. This was one of several arenas in which foundation-building was needed before we could undertake the kind of advertising program we knew we needed. I was not unhappy to proceed step by step. Our first priority had to be improving the quality of our work (our "product"), especially the undergraduate program in all its dimensions, so that the claims we intended to make would be consistent with the experience we offered. As we focused on that work, we also began establishing the organizational arrangements that were prerequisites to mounting a large-scale, university-wide promotional campaign.

We took a critical step in early 2000, following the retirement of our longtime Director of University Relations, by charging that office to develop messaging and graphic standards for all the University's publications (both print and digital) and to oversee the communications programs of all University offices. This was a major change that would take time for the University's departments to digest, accustomed as they were to a high degree of autonomy in this area, but the Interim Director, a well-liked Northeastern veteran named Janet Hookailo, was the perfect person to coax our colleges and departments through this process. The new arrangements forced each part of the University to think systematically about how it wanted to communicate with its constituencies and how it could fit its communications into the broader framework of our guiding Aspiration and Vision.

The foundational work of strengthening the undergraduate program and building the organizational basis for a unified, University-wide communications program took the first four years of my presidency. By 2001 we were ready to begin designing a large-scale advertising program. The first step early in that year was recruiting a marketing professional to lead the Office of University Relations, which we accomplished with the appointment of Sandra King, who had business as well as academic experience. Over the next five years, first under King, then under Brian Kenny, we took our institutional communications to an entirely new level, propelled by a corporate-style "branding campaign" in which we invested more than a million dollars per year. During this same period we elevated the top position in University Relations to a vice presidency and changed the name of the division to "Marketing and Communications." By the time I left the presidency, Northeastern was being cited as a national leader in a new wave of institutional marketing that was sweeping across American higher education.[2]

### Some Tentative First Steps

During the years when we were laying the groundwork for the branding campaign, we did what we could to make our communications more effective. I was especially focused on admissions, since recruiting stronger students in large numbers was our most urgent priority. In this context the responsibility for telling our story rested with our admissions professionals, who represented us to high school students, their families, and their guidance counselors. But we knew we could not focus narrowly on these groups, since they were themselves influenced by their immersion in a larger communications network involving their residential, workplace, and social communities, not to mention the amorphous but significant world of general public opinion. Our graduates were also important since they served as de facto experts on Northeastern in their home communities. What our own faculty, staff, and students said to friends and associates about the University also fed into this web of communications. We had to think about all of these groups. We were also aware of the growing importance of the internet, which was fast becoming the first place that prospective students looked for information about colleges.

As noted in Chapter 4, in the first years of my presidency I involved myself deeply with our admissions activities, including the communications-related dimension of that work. I had an external consultant critique every aspect of those efforts, from the look and messaging of our view books, to our letters to prospective students, to the tours we gave visiting families. I weighed in on all these matters. I met with our admissions professionals to make clear how I wanted them to characterize Northeastern, and I also met directly with high school guidance counselors, both locally and in cities around the country. I made similar efforts with respect to our graduates, appearing regularly at events organized by our alumni office, as often as possible with my wife, Elsa, and working with our publications professionals to focus our alumni magazine more clearly on promoting enthusiastic support of the University. Aware that budget constraints would limit our ability to expand admissions staff, I encouraged the development of a strong program of volunteer alums to meet with interested students in their home communities, something that had not previously been an important component of our recruitment efforts. We also formed a guidebooks committee to monitor descriptions of Northeastern in the large number of publications used by high school students and their families to learn about colleges, and we did what we could to influence that commentary.

Internal marketing was a particular focus. Unless the faculty, staff, and students of Northeastern reinforced the University's presentation of itself, our messages would be fatally undercut. This was especially the case in metropolitan Boston, the heart of our historic service area, and in national networks of academic professionals. With respect to our students, the challenge was less about communications than substance: they needed to actually feel the impact of our efforts to improve their experiences. With the 2,400 members of our faculty and staff, we needed to overcome what we saw as a self-deprecating undercurrent about the educational quality and standing of Northeastern fostered by years of living in the shadow of Boston's more prominent colleges and universities, as well as by institutional practices, especially the emphasis on being the country's largest private university, which tacitly suggested that quality was a secondary consideration. I paid a great deal of attention in my annual addresses to the campus community—as well as in my annual reports, in regular meetings with department chairs and directors, and in discussions with individual academic and administrative departments—to talking about all the ways Northeastern was becoming stronger and to showcasing examples of exceptional work and professional recognition by members of the University community. As we began to achieve real progress—as our admissions became more selective, as new buildings began to appear, as we hired star faculty members or won major grants, and as our position in the annual rankings began to move upward—this work became significantly easier.

We were aware that parts of Northeastern not generally thought of in a marketing context had significant impacts on our reputation. The decisions to create the School of Technological Entrepreneurship and the School of Social Science, Public Policy and Urban Affairs were inspired not only by our belief in the programmatic value these units represented but also by an awareness that their creation would proclaim the University's strength in these academic fields. I was especially eager to assert Northeastern's primacy in entrepreneurship in competition with Babson University, which had made a national reputation for itself in this field despite the far more impressive record of Northeastern alums in creating new businesses. The decision to completely transform University College into the new School of Professional and Continuing Studies stemmed in part from a concern that our notoriously low standards in adult and continuing education were subverting our efforts to reposition Northeastern as a top quality university.[3]

Similar considerations played into our thinking about athletics. We were a Division I school, but our most visible teams were perennial losers, a reality that diluted our efforts to associate Northeastern with the idea of excellence. One of my first decisions was to replace the Director of Athletics with a gifted young sports administrator named Ian McCaw, who initiated a long-overdue professionalization of our athletic administration and brought heightened expectations to our programs, especially football, where we enjoyed a period of unprecedented success. McCaw's successor, David O'Brien, moved us from a weak, regional conference into the Colonial Athletic Association with member campuses in major media markets up and down the East Coast, including such premier athletics programs as the College of William and Mary and the University of Delaware. The construction of new facilities also had a marketing dimension, not just within the campus and for visiting families but for the general public; the decision to locate the first new residential hall on the campus perimeter facing one of Boston's major thoroughfares was a statement to the public that it was a new day at Northeastern University.

I was aware of the extent to which public perceptions of a university are influenced by the visibility and reputation of its president. This had long seemed to me one of the most striking realities about higher education, where the persona of the chief executive plays a larger role than in other fields, such as in health care or business. I am by nature more of a "work-horse" than a "show horse," but I also felt responsible to make myself the visible representative of the University we were trying to become. I produced numerous opinion pieces in the Boston media about topics related to higher education, became a member of important local boards, and urged our Division of University Relations to arrange speaking opportunities for me before significant local audiences. I made similar efforts at the national level, producing essays for the *Chronicle of Higher Education* and the mainstream national media, becoming a director of the American Council on Education and the two leading organizations of cooperative education institutions. Working with a consultant, I met with newspaper and magazine editors around the country trying to inspire stories about Northeastern. This latter effort paid off with a series of articles in the Boston-area media in the spring of 2004, highlighting the dramatic changes at the University. Our biggest success was a front-page article in the *Chronicle of Higher Education* reporting that the University was "no longer a safety school" but had "transformed itself" and was now one of the "hot places to go to college in the Boston area ... along with Harvard and Tufts Universities, Emerson College and the Massachusetts Institute of Technology."[4]

## The Branding Campaign

I had not heard the term "branding campaign" until Sandra King proposed that we do one shortly after her appointment in early 2001. But the basic concept—a concentrated effort to establish an organization's image in the consciousness of relevant publics—seemed to me just what Northeastern needed. By the fall of that year King and her team had pulled together a three-year plan and contracted with a firm of marketing consultants to begin work on our messaging and graphic look. In parallel, I assembled a team of senior Northeastern administrators to oversee the project. We quickly agreed that we would focus on supporting the effort to recruit strong students, partly by working with our admissions professionals on direct outreach to young people and those who influenced them, and partly by enhancing Northeastern's image among the general public. Building on our Vision of providing the country's premier program of practice-oriented education, we adopted "two sides of Northeastern" as the campaign theme, a reference to the way our curriculum alternated periods of classroom study and full-time, paid employment. To express this notion we crafted the tagline "higher learning, richer experience" and reinforced this message with images of students in both academic and workplace settings.

We employed a wide range of vehicles to broadcast our message, including "advertorials" in major newspapers and periodicals, a redesigned home page for our Web site, and a direct-mail campaign to high school guidance counselors with a follow-up program of invitations to visit campus. The campaign also included billboards on highways leading into Boston and New York, sponsorships on National Public Radio, a partnership with America Online, and a second one with the Boston Red Sox featuring a huge Northeastern banner on the upper deck of left field in Fenway Park. I initially resisted this last idea, but King won me over with data showing that the demographic of attendees at Red Sox games was similar to the audience we were trying to reach in metropolitan Boston. In subsequent years I was amazed at the number of people who expressed delight and surprise at this aspect of our campaign. It—along with other slightly undignified initiatives like highway billboards—helped create a "buzz" about Northeastern, a sense that we were an institution on the move. That atmosphere backstopped our direct outreach to potential students and also fostered an air of excitement within the campus community.[5]

How effective was all this? At the end of three years we were clearly achieving our goals with respect to admissions, as I reported in detail in Chapter 4, but the contributions of the branding campaign to this success were not to be assumed. Happily, a survey of high school students, parents, and guidance counselors in Boston and New York found that Northeastern was being seen as more selective than in the past, was now competing with schools like Boston University, George Washington University, Syracuse University, and Boston College, and was a "hot topic" among potential applicants; the survey concluded that the branding campaign had contributed to these shifts of perception. Our review also found it impossible to determine which elements of the campaign were most important. Trustee Ronald Rossetti, who had a background in retail, reminded me of some common wisdom among business executives: "I know that half my advertising budget is a waste of money; I just don't know which half." Despite the ambiguities, both my leadership team and the Board concluded that the branding campaign was helpful. Our research also revealed, however, that success had changed our marketing challenge. We were now competing for more academically demanding applicants who had choices among competitive colleges.[6]

With King's departure in 2003, the branding campaign continued under Brian Kenny during the final years of my presidency, but with modifications. With our position now well established in the Northeast, we focused greater attention on national markets, including California, Florida, and Chicago. We increased the emphasis on academic excellence to reflect a shift of interest among our applicants from preparing for a job to obtaining a quality education. We began to stress the value of the Northeastern experience as a preparation for graduate school as well as for work. We also shifted away from an exclusive focus on the undergraduate program to a presentation of the whole University, and we expanded our target audiences to include alumni/ae, academic leaders at other national universities, and the local community. We continued to use a similar mix of vehicles as in the first phase of the campaign though with an increased emphasis on digital communications and the internet.

At the end of my presidency I felt our initiatives in marketing and advertising had been far more successful than we had expected when we began them. Our dramatic progress in admissions selectivity was the most explicit evidence of this and was the subject of many admiring comments by academic colleagues around the country. The broader marketing program had also attracted the attention of my fellow presidents. The members of my team who led these efforts, especially Philomena Mantella and Brian Kenny, had acquired star status in their professional communities, richly deserved in my appreciative view. We had not intended to promote a national movement to make aggressive marketing a widespread practice in American higher education, but retrospective articles about this new phenomenon suggested that we had contributed to that development. We were okay with that.[7]

## Reaching Out to Alumni/ae

Connecting more effectively with our graduates was a particularly important part of our communications activities during the final years of my presidency. By that time I had come to see alumni/ae engagement as one of Northeastern's most important long-term challenges. The difficulties we experienced achieving the goals of the Leadership Campaign had demonstrated how far behind other private universities we were in this area. Our alumni/ae giving rate was among our weakest metrics in the *U.S. News* rankings, placing us well below the schools with which we were competing for top-100 status. Even more distressing, this percentage had declined over the ten years of my presidency, especially after 1999, while other measures of Northeastern's performance were improving. Although our decline mirrored a national trend and was not necessarily attributable to anything specific about Northeastern, the pattern was still troubling in ways that went far beyond its impact on our rank. I had learned while writing *Academia's Golden Age* that, for private universities and even for public-sector schools, philanthropic support from alums was often the difference between a first-rate institution and a mediocre one. I had also come to understand that urban, commuter universities face particular challenges in this arena, since they do not provide the kind of undergraduate experience that produces fond memories of alma mater. Despite these realities, I could not help seeing our weak record in financial support from graduates as a failure on my part and that of my team, especially since, though I had done everything our alumni/ae relations staff asked me to do, I had focused more attention on other issues that seemed more urgent. With most key elements of our repositioning strategy well established by 2004, it was time to build a high performing alumni/ae relations organization.[8]

We were aware of several challenges. Many of our most successful alums had been allowed to lose their connection with the school and were focusing their philanthropy elsewhere. Some in this group were not especially proud of their Northeastern degree and were using philanthropy to associate themselves with more prestigious institutions. Many who did support us still viewed Northeastern as the academically modest, low-budget operation it had been when they were students, and were not disposed to make the large gifts the University desperately needed. Some who did understand that Northeastern had changed—including some of our top prospects—were ambivalent about what we were doing, pleased with the increased stature of their University, but fearful we were abandoning our historic mission of serving students from backgrounds like theirs. Our message was also complex: We needed to convey the urgency of strengthening Northeastern academically without appearing to disparage the school our graduates had attended. I don't think I ever found an entirely satisfactory way to express this nuanced idea.

It was also the case that Northeastern had never undertaken the hard work of building strong, broad-based alumni/ae engagement. That kind of program had not been necessary when Northeastern was focused on being the largest private university in the country. Through the early 1980s the combination of large enrollments and low costs had allowed the University to flourish financially, so much so, as I mentioned in Chapter 3, that presidents and governing boards had built an endowment from operating surpluses rather than through philanthropic support. Thus fund-raising based on modest gifts from large numbers of alums had not historically been essential to the University's well-being the way it was for the "smaller but better" university we now were. Fund-raising efforts had tended to focus narrowly on a few loyal supporters who were capable of making major gifts for big projects. Broader alumni/ae relations efforts that would produce annual income and cultivate the large donors of the future had been a matter of secondary importance.

During 2004–2005 we took the first steps toward a makeover. We elevated the position of Director of Alumni Relations to a vice presidency and recruited a gifted and experienced professional, Jack Moynihan, to this role. We made an initial allocation of $250,000 to support additional staffing and promised a further increase the following year. We charged our Office of University Planning and Research to undertake a study of alumni/ae giving patterns and attitudes. We charged our new Vice President for Marketing and Communications to develop an outreach plan to support Moynihan's efforts. We allocated a large piece of unused University space in a prime location for an alumni/ae center. We enlisted the help of the college deans and key leaders among our alums, especially William Fowler and Richard Power. All of this allowed us to strengthen our networks of alumni/ae organizations and volunteers, intensify programming both locally and nationally, and improve our alumni/ae magazine. The Trustees were helpful and supportive. The Chair of the Committee on Student Affairs and Alumni Relations, Carole Shapazian, spent many hours helping us shape our strategies.[9]

All of these efforts were in the early stages as I left the presidency in the summer of 2006. I regretted that I had not done more sooner to connect our alumni/ae with the changes that were occurring at their University. I believed that if they fully understood the necessity of creating a new version of Northeastern, if they knew how much we were doing to preserve their school's traditional values while strengthening the University's societal contributions in new ways, and if they realized how much more valuable their degrees would be as we succeeded, they would share my pride in the progress Northeastern was making and would support our efforts. I hoped, at least, we had made a start in this direction for my successor.

## The Role of the Rankings

While our branding campaign during the last five years of my presidency made an important contribution to the ultimate success of our repositioning strategy, our progress toward top-100 status on the annual *U.S. News* rankings was even more pivotal since it provided concrete evidence—to students and faculty we wanted to recruit and to those who influenced them, and to opinion makers throughout academia—that we were, indeed, becoming a selective and quality-focused national university. Indeed, the rankings probably pushed us to adopt more aggressive goals for improvement than we might otherwise have done, since it was hard to argue against the basic proposition that becoming a top-100 university was essential to our future competitiveness. In addition, the annual pattern of upward movement in the rankings boosted the morale of the campus community, reinforced the claims of our internal marketing program, and energized our efforts for the year ahead. Having a metric to document progress mattered enormously.

From the time I announced the top-100 goal in the spring of 2000 to the summer of 2006 when we achieved our objective, I endeavored to keep the campus community working toward this outcome within the broad framework of the Action and Assessment Plan. Each August, as soon as the rankings were published, I met with my leadership team to review where we had gained or lost ground on each part of the formula, set goals for the year ahead and assigned responsibility for overseeing the necessary work. Over the course of the next academic year, I monitored the relevant activities in regular meetings with members of my leadership team. My annual State of the University addresses included detailed accounts of our progress. I absorbed a fair amount of good-natured ribbing—salted with some serious skepticism—for harping on this matter so insistently, but I believed that, if we succeeded, the impact would be worth it and doubters would be converted.

There were many issues to consider as we set annual goals. For me the central question was always how a concerted effort to improve our position with respect to one or another aspect of the formula might affect pursuit of our Aspiration to achieve excellence as a national research university that was student centered, practice oriented, and urban. Some aspects of the formula corresponded with things we would have emphasized even if the rankings had not existed. Examples included strengthening the academic profile of our freshman class, increasing persistence and graduation rates, hiring more full-time faculty and paying them better salaries, improving our faculty-student ratio, and boosting our reputation. Other aspects of the formula were debatable as indicators of educational quality. Examples here included the frequency of small classes, the percentage of faculty with terminal degrees, and the alumni/ae giving rate. We also considered how aspects of Northeastern that were not rewarded by the formula but were important to us—increasing the diversity of our students and faculty, enrolling students from low-income backgrounds, engaging our urban community—would affect our standing. Overall, I believe it is fair to say that the primary focus of annual goal setting remained the Action and Assessment Plan, that some matters important to the AAP received heightened attention because of the rankings, that we never reduced attention to a significant aspect of the Plan because of the ranking formula, and that, around the edges, we made changes on matters of secondary significance because they affected our overall score.

There were always temptations to "game the system" by submitting misleading data to *U.S. News*. We were aware, for example, that some universities had created technically separate entities for poorly prepared freshmen so that the low SAT scores of these students would not be included in entering class averages even though they were, for all practical purposes, regular degree-seeking students. Other institutions admitted weak students in January, since the formula looked only at the September class in computing average SAT scores. Some institutions went so far as to submit false numbers to the magazine, which was dangerous because if the editors realized what was happening (as they did in a few notorious cases) they exacted a stiff penalty. Under Mark Putnam's scrupulous leadership, our policy was to be honest but smart. The numbers we submitted were an accurate representation of reality, but we sometimes made small adjustments in our presentation that could help our score without being misleading. Senior Vice President Mucciolo was especially creative in dissecting the formula to make the way we arrayed data more effective, such as structuring our budget to highlight investments in the academic program.

The top-100 goal played an important role as we set specific objectives for our performance, such as average SAT scores of entering freshmen or the six-year graduation rate. We established numerical targets based on the average performance of a group of private universities similar to Northeastern that ranked between 50 and 100; we called them the "lucky thirteen." This process led us to set some challenging aspirations—like an average freshman SAT of 1160, 35 points above where we were in 1999–2000 when we announced the top-100 goal, or a 70 percent six-year graduation rate, 14 points above our

1999–2000 number. These goals were adjusted each year as the performance of the lucky thirteen changed, usually by improving. I was not at all confident we could achieve the numbers we sought in the time frame we had given ourselves, so there was an obvious risk of failure. However, when I compared our 1999–2000 numbers to those we were reporting at the beginning of my presidency, our progress made me hopeful. In addition, I believed it was vital to be honest with ourselves about what we needed to do. Our ultimate success in not only achieving but exceeding our goals was testimony to the value of setting our sights high.

In our year-to-year work in pursuit of top-100 status, our Office of University Planning and Research, and particularly its director, Mark Putnam, along with his chief analyst, Neal Fogg, played indispensable roles. Each year OUPR provided an analysis of our results on every aspect of the ranking formula. This work supplied much of the basis for discussions within my leadership team as we set objectives for the coming year. As our work proceeded, OUPR created a model of how the formula worked (*U.S. News* never made that information public) that enabled us to simulate the impact of specific changes in our performance, and this allowed us to determine where additional progress would be most helpful. OUPR also undertook numerous specialized studies of ranking-related aspects of our work—admissions and retention were especially important topics—that helped us plan interventions in areas of performance where improvement was needed.[10]

## Breaking into the Top 100

During the initial phase of our top-100 campaign, we focused on admissions selectivity and student persistence since improvements in those areas were critical to the "smaller but better" strategy and to our financial health, as well as to our ranking. This work was described in Chapter 4. As efforts in these arenas began achieving results, we were able to pay more attention to other matters of substantive importance that also influenced our rank. I was particularly proud of the Academic Investment Plan to improve our tenure track faculty-to-student ratio by adding 100 full-time professors over a five-year period. This was essential to making our faculty resources competitive with those of the institutions with which we were now competing. The AIP was a major focus during the final years of my presidency and was described in Chapters 3 and 6. A related emphasis was bringing faculty salaries into alignment with our new group of competitors, a step that became possible as improving retention rates strengthened our financial position. Though neither adding full-time faculty nor raising salaries was motivated primarily by our focus on the rankings, progress on both was extremely helpful in that context.[11]

Toward the end of my presidency it became clear that the solid year-to-year progress we were making in the rankings was not likely to carry us all the way to our goal. Crossing the finish line was going to require improvements in three elements of the *U.S. News* formula that were particularly challenging for us. Two of these involved technical issues: the way the magazine compared faculty salaries and the way it calculated total enrollments. The third issue related to the heavily weighted "peer rating system" by which *U.S. News* determined the overall quality and reputation of individual universities. It was our success in improving our score on two of these three metrics that finally put us into the top 100 in the summer of 2006.

To address the two technical issues, we sought out the senior staffer at *U.S. News* who presided over the rankings project. This was Robert Morse, an institutional research professional and a modest, thoughtful man who operated out of a surprisingly unpretentious office in Washington, D.C. We were greatly aided in approaching Morse by the fact that he and Mark Putnam had a mutually respectful relationship based on shared professional interests.

The problem with comparisons of faculty salaries was that Morse and his team applied a regional cost-of-living adjustment to the actual compensation numbers so that a salary paid to a faculty member in a high-cost region compared unfavorably to the identical salary paid in a low-cost region. Since Boston had a high cost of living relative to the rest of the country, this calculation seriously damaged our score. To get at this problem Putnam and Fogg produced a scholarly paper on the academic labor market demonstrating that regional cost-of-living variances were far less significant than the *U.S. News* formula assumed, and that, moreover, the data used by the magazine to determine regional living costs lagged behind real economic conditions to a degree that rendered them highly problematic. We reviewed the findings with Morse in an extensive back and forth, which led him, ultimately, to concede the validity of our analysis. In the end, however, he refused to change the formula, arguing that even though the magazine's metric was flawed it measured something important and so represented a kind of rough justice.

We had more luck with the calculation of enrollments. Our specific problem here was that the magazine determined the comparative adequacy of an institution's financial resources by dividing the operating budget by the

number of enrolled students. This seemed to us a crude but reasonable element of the formula, since it indicated the level of investment a particular
university could make in its instructional programs. The issue for Northeastern, however, was that each term nearly 20 percent of our students, while
nominally enrolled, were actually away from the University on co-op assignments and were not taking classes, paying tuition, or exercising significant
claims on our resources. We appealed to Morse to allow us to remove these
co-op students from our enrollment numbers for purposes of this calculation
but found him resistant, not because he disagreed with our argument but
because he feared an adjustment for a specific institution would open the
floodgates for analogous claims by other schools. We responded by bringing other co-op universities into the discussion, ultimately producing a letter
from the National Commission for Cooperative Education arguing that the
change we wanted should be adopted for all co-op institutions. Constantine
(Taki) Papadakis, the president of Drexel University and chair of the National
Commission, joined me for a trip to Washington to argue our case in person,
but we failed to move Morse, who continued to agree with us intellectually
but to insist that changing a formula that applied to every institution in the
country was impractical. This pushed us over the edge. In completing the
magazine's annual questionnaire during the spring of 2006, both Drexel and
Northeastern simply removed our co-op students from our calculations. We
held our breath because the penalty for submitting false data was serious. The
magazine accepted the changes without comment.[12]

Influencing the peer-rating metric was the most daunting of the three
ranking issues on which we focused toward the end of my presidency. As
I noted in Chapter 2, the peer rating, which counted for 25 percent of an
institution's overall score, was the least intellectually defensible component
of the entire *U.S. News* formula, since it purported to determine the overall
quality of individual universities by asking senior administrators at similar
institutions to assign them a value on a five-point scale. Precisely because
it was based on poorly informed opinions, the peer rating was notoriously
hard to change. Over the middle years of my presidency, for example, despite
substantive improvements in selectivity and retention, our score was consistently 2.8 or 2.9, a solid improvement over where we had been in 1996 but
well below universities in the bottom quartile of the top 100, which aver-
aged scores between 3.1 and 3.2. The challenge we faced was changing the
minds of presidents, provosts, and admissions deans scattered around the
country, preoccupied with their own affairs, and lacking any motivation to

help another institution improve its rank. We were tempted to abandon hope of improving our reputational score, but when we realized that improvement was crucial to our ultimate success we decided to try.

We proceeded on two levels. One approach was to reach out to academic colleagues through the *Chronicle of Higher Education*, which was read by virtually all senior administrators in the industry. As part of the branding campaign, we mounted an aggressive program of well-designed, highly visible, full-page "advertorials" documenting various aspects of our progress. I believe we were among the first universities in the country to do this, although the strategy subsequently became quite common. Our pieces were tasteful, factual prose essays written to appeal to thoughtful academic leaders. I know we reached our intended audience because I received many positive comments about these pieces from colleagues around the country. (Some may have privately questioned our approach, but I could see that they got our message: Northeastern was changing.) We also campaigned to persuade the *Chronicle* to do a feature story on Northeastern, a multiyear effort that ultimately produced the splashy and flattering front-page story in 2004 that I mentioned above.

In parallel with the *Chronicle* campaign, we organized a targeted effort to connect with the 747 individuals who ranked us in the *U.S. News* survey: the presidents, provosts, and admissions deans of the 249 institutions designated as "national universities" by the magazine. This idea came from two of our communications and public affairs professionals, Edward Klotzbier and Jeffrey Doggett, who argued that we should adopt the tactics used by political candidates to round up delegates to a convention. Seven hundred and forty-seven was, after all, a manageable number. I was responsible for the presidents. I sent them reports or other publications that showcased our progress with handwritten buck slips to get my mailing past their assistants' desks. I sought them out whenever I visited their cities or attended a conference. I always tried to mention data points where Northeastern's numbers were stronger than their own, especially when talking with presidents whose schools outranked us. Provost Abdelal and Senior Vice President Mantella made parallel efforts with their counterparts. We assigned other members of the senior administration who knew one of the 747, or someone close to one of them, to make a point of connecting with that person. It is, of course, impossible to say how much effect any of these contacts had. But our reputational score did begin to improve. In 2005 we jumped to 3.0 and the following year to 3.1. That final increase was critical in elevating us into the top 100 in the 2006 rankings.[13]

## A Quiet Celebration

The issue of *U.S. News* announcing our new rank was released in August 2006, two weeks after I completed my presidency. Subsequent commentary recognized this as a noteworthy achievement. The *Boston Business Journal* accurately called our ascent—from 162 to 98 in less than ten years—"one of the most dramatic since *U.S. News* began ranking schools." I was vacationing on Martha's Vineyard when Mark Putnam called with the news. The two of us shared a moment of private celebration on attaining a prize we had coveted for the entire period we had worked together. Despite continuing criticism of the whole ranking phenomenon, much of it justified, Putnam and I shared the belief that achieving top-100 status was essential to placing Northeastern on a secure footing. From the privacy of my island retreat, I sent a silent note of thanks to my leadership team and to the University's faculty, staff, and students, so many of whom had worked hard for a long time to achieve this goal.[14]

## CHAPTER 9

# Reflections on the Presidency

> What could be more satisfying than to be engaged in
> work in which every capacity or talent one may have is
> needed, every lesson one may have learned is used, every
> value one cares about is furthered?
> —John Gardner, *No Easy Victories*

For any college or university, at any moment in its history, a vacant presidency is a script waiting to be written. This is why the arrival of a new president is always a charged moment for a campus community. There are many approaches to the job across its multiple dimensions: different styles of participation in the life of the school, different patterns of decision making and managing, different areas of substantive focus, different levels of attention to various constituencies, different ambitions. Inevitably, individual leaders adopt unique mixtures of these possibilities. For this reason histories of academic institutions are typically structured around successive presidencies. But new campus leaders are not unconstrained in approaching their responsibilities. Local circumstances can dictate priorities independent from, even in opposition to, a president's preferences. The culture and capacity of the campus community can limit administrative choices. Ideally, individuals seeking presidencies will look for situations compatible with their abilities and interests, and trustees will be thoughtful about "fit." But knowledge can never be perfect, and the Board's decision as well as the candidate's often involve substantial guesswork. The history of presidential appointments includes many instances in which new leaders proved to be poor matches with their chosen institutions.

In my case there was no question about what kind of president North-eastern needed me to be. Northeastern in 1996 needed a "repositioning pres-ident." The University had stepped back from the edge of disaster under the skillful leadership of my predecessor and the Trustees. But the questions of whether and how the University could create a competitive operating model as a "smaller but better" academic institution remained very real. I needed to lead a university still reeling from the crisis of the early 1990s to a position in the academic marketplace in which it could flourish. I happily embraced this challenge. I had admired Northeastern for many years, and nothing inspired me more than moving an institution I cared about to a higher level of achievement and a strengthened capacity to serve society. Still, this focus gave me less opportunity than I would have liked for participating in the daily life of the campus, working with faculty and students on educational issues, contributing to national debates on educational policy, and connecting with the University's alumni/ae and donors and even with members of its govern-ing boards. In the end, I did some of all of these things. But my priority, from my first day to my last, was what I have referred to throughout this volume as the "repositioning strategy." Everything else, including my own intellectual and policy interests, had to be secondary.

For me and my colleagues in Northeastern's administration between 1996 and 2006, the repositioning strategy had two central components: first, to significantly improve both the perceived and actual quality of a Northeastern education, especially at the undergraduate level, in order to establish the Uni-versity as a high quality institution well worth the tuition we now needed to charge; second, to preserve the qualities that had made Northeastern such a distinctive and socially valuable institution over its first century of existence. The first goal was less a strategic choice than an existential necessity. The second was, to some degree, value driven and discretionary. A retrospective assessment of my presidency must focus on whether we achieved these two goals and whether our choices with respect to the second served the long-term best interests of the University as well as those of the broader society.

## Becoming Competitive as a Selective National University

As I left the presidency in August 2006 I felt confident we had come a long way toward where we needed to be. I knew we were a stronger institution in academic terms than we had been ten years earlier. The full-time faculty had grown by nearly 20 percent and the Academic Investment Plan pointed toward a tenured/tenure-track faculty-to-student ratio competitive with the top 100 universities with which we now compared ourselves. The scholarly quality of the full-time faculty had been enriched by 200 new appointments, including forty-five at the senior level, fifteen to named chairs. The undergraduate curriculum had been completely overhauled and modernized in conjunction with the conversion to a semester calendar. The educational benefits of the co-op program had been enriched through a heightened integration of workplace experiences with classroom studies, an improvement in the quality of co-op jobs, and an expansion of placements within emerging industries. Academic support services had been greatly strengthened along with infrastructure support for teaching and learning, including major investments in information technology and smart classrooms.

Beyond the strictly academic aspects of Northeastern, the University was offering an enriched overall student experience. Over half our undergraduates now lived on campus, providing the basis for a vibrant student community. Student organizations and social events were proliferating, and current students were happily engaged in building new traditions for campus life to fill the empty spaces left by our history as a commuter school. In addition, our nonacademic facilities had been greatly improved, most dramatically with the cluster of attractive residential buildings but also through modernized library spaces and expanded choices for eating and socializing. Our surveys told us we were making solid progress in improving the business services that Northeastern students had historically characterized as the "NU shuffle." The gradual process of greening and beautifying the campus, which had begun under my two predecessors, had matured to the point that our physical setting was now a major advantage as prospective students considered Boston-based schools. Boston itself continued the pattern of robust growth and improvement that was making a city long known as a student mecca an even more attractive place to spend one's college years. Our immediate neighborhood was a major beneficiary of that revival.

The most important metrics all indicated that the changes my team and I had championed were having the intended result. Entering students were far better prepared for university-level work than they had been in previous years and were also more diverse in ethnic and geographic terms. Applications were growing in number and becoming more national and international year after year. Persistence and graduation rates were on a steady upward trajectory. The enhanced scholarly strength of the faculty was apparent in our heightened research productivity, as reflected in a substantial increase in annual research expenditures and the establishment of several new centers of scholarly excellence, some supported by multi-million-dollar federal grants. These indicators of academic progress were mirrored in a striking change in the group of institutions with which we competed for students: our top "overlap" schools now included a set of selective private universities in the Northeast and Mid-Atlantic regions and our "win rate" among applicants who also applied to New England's flagship public universities had shifted dramatically in our favor. Not least, Northeastern was ranked by *U.S. News* among the top 100 "National Universities" in the country.

Against the background of so much improvement in the University's academic stature, I was emboldened to assure our governing Corporation, in my final address to that body in May 2006, that the repositioning goal with which I had been charged ten years earlier had largely been accomplished. Still, there were grounds for caution. I and the Board were aware that our progress had been achieved during a time of steady growth in the number of eighteen-year-olds applying to college, and we knew these helpful conditions would begin to reverse in 2008. Any celebration of our progress prompted an inevitable question: Would Northeastern still be competitive as the admissions markets softened? An analysis of this issue requested by the Trustees toward the end of my presidency was encouraging but was also, of course, speculative. So, we wondered. Fortunately, in the years after I stepped down, applications continued to improve in both number and quality and Northeastern's *U.S. News* ranking continued to rise under the skillful leadership of my successor, Joseph Aoun. A decade after my presidency ended Northeastern had clearly confirmed its place as a competitive institution within the top tier of the nation's universities.[1]

### Enacting the "Aspiration"

Assessing our success in retaining several of Northeastern's traditional characteristics as an "urban university" as we increased the school's academic stature must be, to some extent, a subjective exercise. At the beginning of my presidency there were questions about whether we should continue the University's long-standing commitment to cooperative education as well as the companion emphasis on professional and occupational programs. There were also questions about whether we should maintain the traditional priority on undergraduate teaching and learning and the University's historic pattern of engagement with the city of Boston. As I noted in the Introduction to this book, I regarded all these qualities as important expressions of Northeastern's mission, as did most members of my leadership team and many on the governing boards and in the campus community. I understood, however, that my charge from the Trustees was to secure the institution's future. If maintaining any of these policies had loomed as an impediment to our repositioning, it would have been our job to abandon or at least deemphasize it. We need therefore to ask not only whether we achieved our Aspiration to excellence as a "national research university that is student centered, practice oriented, and urban" but also whether this five-fingered characterization of Northeastern was the best framework to guide the University's transformation.

Co-op raised the most interesting questions. As I noted in Chapter 5, our co-op program was the major reason students traditionally gave for applying to Northeastern, and it was the only thing that made the University visible beyond eastern Massachusetts. It was also true, however, that co-op was widely seen as a compromise with a "real" college experience that made higher education financially possible for students from modest backgrounds and that it was not generally associated with academic quality. None of the nation's top-tier universities had adopted this pedagogy as a defining characteristic, so the question of whether a co-op school could attract the highly qualified, affluent applicants Northeastern now needed to enroll to achieve status as a selective national university was quite real in 1996. So too was the companion question of whether Northeastern's historic emphasis on practical studies and workplace preparation could be competitive in the upper levels of an academic marketplace in which schools devoted to the liberal arts and sciences and a handful of elite technical institutes had long held pride of place.

As this volume has made clear, my colleagues and I concluded that the right course for Northeastern was not to abandon our school's traditional educational characteristics but to transform them in three ways: first, by redefining and rebranding co-op as a powerful learning experience rather than a financial aid program; second, by building the arts and sciences as an equal partner with our professional programs; third, by linking professional education, liberal education, and co-op into a three-dimensional curricular model that we called "practice-oriented education." The success of the repositioning strategy makes a strong argument for the soundness of these judgments. Even as the nature of Northeastern's student body changed dramatically, applicants continued to say that the co-op program and our links to the workplace were differentiating assets.

There was no question that building Northeastern's stature as a "research university" had to be part of our strategy: By the late twentieth century strength in research and doctoral education was a sine qua non of top-tier status as a national university. But the decision to position ourselves as a "student-centered" institution and thus to maintain undergraduate teaching and learning as our top priority even as we invested in research and graduate education was debatable. As I noted in the Introduction, the preeminent value attached by the nation's leading universities to the advanced academic functions was leading many upwardly mobile institutions to emphasize these activities at the expense of undergraduate education. Our decision not to follow the conventional path reflected above all our view of what was best for Northeastern. But it also expressed a desire to demonstrate that a university could elevate itself by focusing on undergraduate studies and that emphasizing research and doctoral programs was not the only way to improve a school's stature.

Our approach also recognized the reality that Northeastern's financial resources, while adequate to support incremental progress in research and graduate education, could not underwrite the level of change needed to make distinction in these functions the basis of our repositioning strategy. Moreover, it was clear that our financial viability was going to depend on revenue from undergraduate tuition for as far into the future as any of us could see. It was therefore a matter of common sense, as well as institutional integrity, to focus on excellence in the undergraduate experience. That was the surest route to attracting highly qualified students in the immediate future and, equally important, to retaining them and making them our advocates after graduation. The subsequent success of the repositioning strategy seems to me to confirm the wisdom of our focus. Perhaps, had the dollars been available, the conventional strategy would also have worked. But such a success would not have been as gratifying as "keeping our promises" to the talented young students we were now enrolling.

Urban engagement was the most debatable of the three distinctive qualities that we celebrated in our Aspiration. Like co-op schools, urban institutions tended historically to be locally oriented commuter schools, and the path of upward mobility often led away from the host city. This had been the trajectory followed by Boston's other two traditional private urban universities, Boston College and Boston University, as they made their way into the upper tier of the nation's academic institutions between 1960 and 1990. Was that the right pattern for Northeastern? Obviously, we could retain the benefits of being located in the country's best college town without making a central point of our urban character. Moreover, unlike the cases of co-op and professional studies, a comprehensive pattern of involvement in the life of the city was not essential to enhancing the quality of our baccalaureate program. Indeed, for many future students and their families, the term "urban" had distinctly negative echoes: not only was it associated with institutions of modest academic quality but also it conjured up the cluster of social ills that had devastated the nation's cities in the decades after World War II: poverty, crime, racial turmoil, dilapidated infrastructure. In truth, the inclusion of "urban" in our triad of Northeastern's special qualities was as much value driven as strategic. This was something I, my colleagues in the leadership group, and many in the campus community believed in. Our efforts, epitomized by the Torch Scholarships, to continue enrolling students from modest backgrounds, including graduates of the Boston public schools, was a source of pride and part of what held us together and motivated us as a campus community. Urban engagement did not play an essential role in the repositioning strategy, although we celebrated it in our effort to achieve national visibility. Doing so probably helped us attract socially conscious students and faculty. In the end, however, it expressed a compelling social purpose more than a means to elevate our status.

Burton Clark, one of the country's foremost scholars of higher education, has written about the difference between "secure" and "precarious" innovations in processes of academic change. Secure changes involve activities that are central to a university's competitive strategy and cannot be abandoned without threatening the institution's market strength. Precarious changes are more reflective of the priorities and values of individual leaders or subunits or moments in time.[2] Looking at the three special qualities of Northeastern that my team and I celebrated in the Aspiration on a spectrum from "secure" to "precarious," I would place the decision to retain and transform co-op at the secure end. Any serious movement away from co-op (or, more broadly, experiential education) would surely have placed the University at risk. I would put the priority we attached to undergraduate teaching and learning in a middle position because that value is always subject to erosion and compromise as an upwardly mobile institution strengthens its emphasis on research and doctoral education. I would place urban engagement as the most precarious of our priorities because, as I have noted, and proud as I was and am of the work we did in this area, it was not essential to the operating model on which Northeastern's future depended.

## Administrative Leadership and Academic Change

The preceding paragraphs, and indeed this entire volume, have stressed the importance of the "strategic formula" for Northeastern that my colleagues and I crafted at the outset of my presidency and rigorously pursued for the next decade. Looking back ten years after stepping down, I continue to think that having a clear statement of priorities and a sustained focus over time played a large role in our success. At the same time, I understand that reviewing the progress of Northeastern through the prism of presidential and leadership priorities taps into an ongoing debate among observers of higher education about how institutional change occurs and how important presidential leadership is in the change process. This debate has played out in recent years within the context of a widely shared sense that the significance of the academic presidency has been severely diminished from what it used to be.

Even casual observers of academic history are aware of the presidential titans generally credited with transforming American universities during the late nineteenth and early twentieth centuries: Charles Eliot of Harvard, William Rainey Harper of Chicago, Daniel Coit Gilman of Johns Hopkins, Andrew White of Cornell, James Angel of Michigan. Historical accounts of the universities led by these men tend to depict institutional change as driven by their leadership, and this perspective on how universities evolve lives on among contemporary scholars, most notably James Fisher, who has written several books stressing presidential leadership as the key to institutional progress and adaptation.

In contrast with what I will call the "presidential" perspective on change, some recent observers have stressed the limited importance of presidential leadership. These accounts reflect the growing administrative complexity of universities in the years since World War II as well as the enhanced power of the faculty so ably chronicled by David Riesman and Christopher Jencks. The most notable early proponent of the diminished presidency was Clark Kerr, who described the position as a highly constrained mediator, buffeted by contending internal interest groups and hemmed in by a variety of external forces to an extent that rendered executive leadership nearly impossible. Kerr's view has been widely adopted and often lamented, as in the 1996 report of the Association of Governing Boards, which worried that colleges and universities could no longer adapt to changing social requirements "because the academic presidency has become weak." The classic scholarly statements of this perspective have been provided by sociologists Karl Weick, who characterized universities as "loosely coupled systems," and Michael Cohen and James March, who labeled them "organized anarchies"—both terms implying entities not susceptible to coordinated action driven by executive authority. Taking this notion one step further, some observers have argued that a strong presidency is not essential to institutional adaptation. Robert Birnbaum, for example, argues that universities are "cybernetic" (self-regulating) systems that "evolve not by one omniscient and rational agent but by the spontaneous corrective action of the college's parts."[3]

It is obvious that my account of change at Northeastern stresses the importance of institutional leadership, not just by the president but by a president-led leadership team, and it is deeply at odds with the view that institutional adaptation occurs through the unprompted initiatives of decentralized organizational components. But I do not at all dismiss the insights of thoughtful observers like Weick, Cohen, March, and Birnbaum; nor do I think that a return to the heroic presidency of an earlier era is either possible or desirable. My experience leads me to endorse the idea that the greatest strength of a university resides at least as much in the quality, creativity, and initiative of its component parts as in the talents of a particular president or presidential team.

I resist the notion that we must choose between the two views of academic change that I have been describing. I would argue that universities are well served by a combination of strong leaders pursuing clearly defined priorities and deep, dispersed organizational strength that produces creative change only weakly—and perhaps not at all—related to the goals of a particular president. I would also argue that the importance of institutional leadership varies with the circumstances. When conditions call for incremental progress within a well-defined educational paradigm and a successful operating model, and when the component parts of the institution are generally strong, the cybernetic version of change can produce satisfactory results, and institutional leaders can focus on fixing units that are weak or broken. When, however, there is a need for transformational change at the institutional level, for a new paradigm and a new operating model, central leadership becomes imperative. I do not believe that the cybernetic model can produce the kind of adaptation that was necessary at Northeastern at the end of the twentieth century.

## Cybernetic Change and Institutional Resilience

My view that the circumstances of my presidency called for coordinated action by a leadership team does not mean that the work described in this volume represents all the important institutional changes at Northeastern during those years. To begin with, as I noted in Chapters 5 and 6, there was the dispersed array of scholarly and professional initiatives by individuals and groups of faculty members—not just books written or grants received but significant organizational developments as well, such as the formation of scholarly centers or the creation of academic programs. Parallel processes of development were occurring within the administrative departments of the University. Changes of this order were happening all the time, some, perhaps, inspired by the Aspiration but many reflecting the professionalism and creativity of individuals or groups independent of the focused process of change my team and I were promoting. Striking examples of initiatives from below were the University-wide general education requirement, which was designed with my knowledge and encouragement but with all the leadership coming from faculty, or our honor code, which was developed by students. My contributions to these and similar programmatic innovations were limited to fostering a supportive administrative infrastructure, a constructive and stable work environment, and a spirit of independent enterprise infused by high academic standards. Awareness that such changes were steadily making Northeastern a better university, even when I had limited knowledge of them, was a source of satisfaction and joy throughout my presidency.

The most important example of cybernetic change at Northeastern during my years involved strengthening our international connections, an element of our Action and Assessment Plan but not a theme singled out for special emphasis in our "strategic formula" and not a focus for me personally. At the time of my appointment the University had established several centers of strength in this arena, including majors in international business and international affairs, modest offerings in international co-op and study abroad, and a limited international focus within admissions. Believing that international awareness had become an essential part of undergraduate education, I was eager to support new initiatives in this area and to expand international enrollments, which reached 3 percent of our undergraduates by the fall of 2006 with the goal of 8 percent by 2008.[4] But the University's overall development of international programming during my presidency went far beyond anything I had envisioned, much of it due to the leadership of Provost Abdelal, a native Egyptian, who viewed international collaboration as significant both for the intellectual strength of the University and the cause of world peace.

Abdelal promoted multiple partnerships with universities around the world, especially in the Middle East; created "virtual" scholarly centers focused on the Middle East, Africa, and Latin America; and encouraged the dramatic expansion of study-abroad opportunities, particularly the "Dialogue of Civilizations" program, initiated some years earlier by Professor Denis Sullivan and Dean Lowndes, through which groups of Northeastern students and faculty spend four to six weeks living and studying in other countries. Equally significant was an initiative that came to Northeastern unsolicited from Kaplan, Inc., whose president I had met during my years at the City University of New York. Kaplan was eager to utilize the international footprint provided by its English-language centers, especially in Asia, to build an admissions pipeline to American universities, and it was looking for a well-established institution to help it pilot the idea. We signed on and began enrolling students Kaplan sent us in a transitional first-year curriculum designed by Dean Hopey and his colleagues in the School of Professional and Continuing Studies. Over subsequent years that initial "pathways" program mushroomed into a major source of international students and an increasingly important element of the University's financial strength.

The importance of initiatives by faculty or members of the administration goes far beyond the specific significance of each. The capacity of the university community to generate initiatives in response to new opportunities or challenges is not only an example of cybernetic change but also a measure of the institution's fundamental strength. Institutional resilience is not about the wisdom of a particular strategy or a particular leader but about a broad, deep organizational quality that reflects the energy, creativity, and commitment of the collectivity. Institutional resilience is what allows an institution to survive a weak or failed presidency. In writing *Academia's Golden Age*, I came to realize that places like Harvard and MIT are resilient in just this way; both experienced comparatively unsuccessful presidencies during the years I reviewed, but both continued to gain strength because of their rich organizational resources. The role of a president in this context is less about providing direction than about building a total organization, fostering a passionate commitment to the institution's mission, and encouraging individual initiative throughout the organization. This was one of the messages of

*Built to Last,* a book my team and I studied with some care at the outset of my presidency, and it was one I sought to follow throughout my period of responsibility, even as I kept my own priorities focused on implementing our strategic formula.

Northeastern seems to me a striking example of institutional resilience. I stressed the University's vulnerability in the first chapter of this book, and there is no question that Northeastern was in a precarious position in the early 1990s—too expensive to compete effectively with New England's growing public-sector universities but too undeveloped academically to compete with its private-sector counterparts. Yet Northeastern did not fail. It marshaled its organizational resources, accepted the need for dramatic change, and, within a remarkably short period of time, emerged as a transformed and competitive national university. As this book makes clear, I want to claim some of the credit for this transformation and assign an equal share to my predecessor, John Curry, but I also want to acknowledge that, despite the organizational weakness that I described in the early pages of this book, Northeastern had remarkable sources of embedded strength.

The University was blessed with intelligent and accomplished leaders on the Board who cared about the institution, contributed to our progress in multiple ways, and put steady pressure on me and my leadership team to perform at a high level. The faculty were remarkably loyal—by far the most institutionally engaged faculty I worked with across forty-five years in academic administration. The staff shared this loyalty and commitment, which in some instances took the form of families with multigenerational histories of association with the school. Without question, there was a downside to all this; loyalty to the institution was not necessarily associated with the pursuit of excellence. But the Northeastern community in 1996 provided a solid foundation on which to build toward excellence, and the readiness of the total community to participate in accomplishing the changes my team and I called upon them to accept was striking. The community's resilience was at least as important as the leadership my team and I provided in achieving the repositioning of which we were all so proud. A comment from a faculty member active in governance in those years, Engineering Professor Stephen McKnight, summed this up for me in describing what happened: "You expressed your admiration for us; you told us that the University was in trouble and that we needed to change; and you asked us to help you accomplish what needed to be done. And we did."

## Institutional Resilience and Academic Adaptability

The story of Northeastern's resilience is, of course, not unique, but rather an instance of a larger phenomenon that evokes one of the great strengths of the American system of higher education, grounded as it is in a large number of individual institutions, legally independent in the case of private colleges and universities, and functionally independent in the case of many public campuses that are nominally part of statewide systems. I refer to the remarkable capacity of these institutions to reinvent themselves again and again over extended periods of time as competitive contexts and social needs evolve. It is commonly said by critics of higher education that colleges and universities are sluggish institutions, conservative in their ways, and often unresponsive to changing conditions. It is just as commonly said by academic insiders that those who make this criticism are missing the constant ferment and change that is ever present within structural and organizational frameworks that give the impression of stability.

The issue of institutional adaptability in academia has taken on a special urgency in recent years as the digital revolution has steadily transformed the ways in which we communicate, store, and utilize information. It is hard to read an article or a book that addresses the future of higher education without encountering the prediction that the university as it has existed historically is on a path to obsolescence and will be replaced by some yet to be fully imagined but clearly digitally based system of learning. I am unpersuaded by such notions. My experience at Northeastern combined with my years of prior experience in academic administration and my work on *Academia's Golden Age* has led me to have great confidence in the resiliency of universities. I believe some version of the university as we now know it, meaning a community of scholars and students living and working in a shared physical setting, will be important social institutions for a long time to come; they will find ways, as they are already doing, to harness the new digital technologies to their continuing pursuit of education, research, and social contribution.

I am reminded of a long-ago conversation with Stephen Joel Trachtenberg, later president of both the University of Hartford and George Washington University, but then a young assistant to the new president of Boston University, John Silber. This was around 1970. Silber had recently been appointed, and BU was trying to chart a viable course within the context of internal disarray and the rapid growth of public higher education in

Massachusetts. Trachtenberg and I discussed the future of private colleges and universities. At one point, he looked at me with the authority of someone a few years older than I and a couple of steps further along professionally and asked: "Do you want to know about the future of private higher education?" He paused and then stated definitively: "It doesn't have one." He was referring, of course, to the fact that states were taking over private campuses all over the country, and he was expecting the same thing to happen in Massachusetts, especially with regard to the three major Boston institutions that had traditionally enrolled large numbers of young people from the city and metropolitan region: BU, BC, and Northeastern. That was a perfectly sensible assessment of academia's competitive environment not only in Boston but also nationally in the late 1960s and early 1970s. And yet, over the course of the next four decades, each of these three Boston institutions, one by one, using different strategies, has turned itself into a thriving national—and still private—university. Today all three are among the top fifty universities, public or private, in the United States.

I write about adaptability and resilience to make a point about my experience of the presidency at Northeastern. Seeing the work that my colleagues and I were doing during the ten years that we were responsible for the institution as part of a historic and continual process of adaptation within higher education, and thereby helping preserve the capacity of one institution, within that larger constellation of institutions, to serve its students, its community, and the larger cause of learning and discovery was a great source of satisfaction and pride.

One of the most striking features of our era is the romantic attraction to entrepreneurship among our most talented and ambitious young people. The iconic dream of many students today is to found the next Google, Facebook, Microsoft, or Amazon or a new nonprofit that addresses an urgent social issue such as poverty or illiteracy or environmental degradation. This pattern is a remarkable change from my own generation, which came of age in the 1950s and 1960s. For us the most common ambition after completing our education was much more likely to be affiliating with an established institution—a corporation, a university, a hospital, a government agency, a law firm—and building a career within that settled framework. So I view the frequent disinterest of young people in working within existing institutional structures with a mixture of curiosity, admiration, and concern. I share the view that the entrepreneurial spirit of our people is one of the great strengths of the United States, and I am not surprised that other countries, from Ireland to Japan, send young people here to study in the hope they will acquire some of whatever it is that fosters our enterprise and creativity. But I also wonder if we haven't lost the romance of managing our established institutions, which today's successful start-ups will inevitably become. After all, it is large, entrenched, heavily bureaucratized and often unionized organizations, sluggish and conservative as they can seem to be, that do most of society's work—keeping us healthy, educating us, and providing us with the goods and services we need to live. I was proud to be one of the many members of my generation of Americans who served as stewards of the great institutions that constitute such a critical part of our country's civil society.

## The Satisfactions of the Presidency

One widely repeated implication of the diminished view of the academic presidency has been that the job is unattractive for individuals who are serious about educational and intellectual matters and attracted to institutional leadership. It is claimed that the responsibilities of fund-raising and political glad-handing have turned the president into a combination of cheerleader and traveling salesperson, leaving little opportunity to work on substantive academic matters. It is also asserted that the processes of academic governance, dominated as they are by the principle of shared authority, especially with respect to the faculty, and constrained, especially in public institutions, by union contracts and legislative fickleness, have rendered the presidency more a broker among competing constituencies than a powerful executive. In this image, the job makes enormous demands on the president's time, renders both a normal family life and serious intellectual engagement impossible, and jeopardizes one's health, while offering limited opportunities for leadership and often bringing more abuse than respect from the institutional community over which one presides. Typical of this view is the comment attributed to the CEO of a major company who, after chairing a commission on higher education and learning how academia works, reported that he began to have nightmares of waking up as a college president.

It should be clear by now to a reader of this volume that I am not among those who believe the academic presidency has ceased to be a compelling professional opportunity for those who care about higher education or the strength and well-being of our country. In the preceding paragraphs, I have discussed the satisfactions I experienced as the steward of an important social institution and as the leader of a dedicated and supportive institutional community. In addition, preceding chapters have stressed the rewards of nurturing the talents of students, supporting the creative capacities of faculty, and engaging the challenges of urban America. As my selection of the quotation from John Gardner at the beginning of this chapter suggests, I loved being president of Northeastern University, and truly felt the job required "every capacity or talent" that I possessed, drew on "every lesson [I had] learned," and advanced "every value [that I] care[d] about." In these final paragraphs of reflections, and in service of addressing young people who might be drawn to the presidential role but repelled by the negativity often associated with it, I would like to comment more directly and personally on the pleasures as well as the frustrations I experienced during the ten years of my presidency.

A good place to start is with Edith Hamilton's classic statement of how the ancient Greeks defined happiness: "the exercise of vital powers along lines of excellence in a life that gives them scope."[5] I loved the experience of the presidency in just this way. I found that the role fully challenged whatever store of "vital powers" I possessed and provided ample "scope" for their exercise. I would stress in the first instance the intellectual challenges of the job, since skeptics so often disparage the work of a president as bureaucratic and political. I found the task of understanding Northeastern in its academic, organizational, and financial dimensions and in its competitive and political contexts; of identifying its most urgent needs as well as its capabilities; and of turning that entire analysis into a strategic formula to guide future action to be a fascinating and difficult exercise, more than worthy of whatever intellectual resources I possessed. I was, of course, powerfully supported in this work by a team of associates and colleagues, but I also believed that, in the end, it was my job to decide what was best for the institution, subject, always, to the support of the Board. Still, if things went wrong, as Chair Finnegan frequently reminded me, I and I alone would bear the responsibility. Thus, although I welcomed multiple opinions on the challenges we faced, modified my own thinking along the way, and worked hard to develop consensus within my leadership team, I never asked for a vote on a major issue unless governance procedures required one.

I have adopted Edith Hamilton's term "vital powers" to mean "capacities," but the term also invites a comment about the exercise of power in an academic setting, especially in a discussion of the intellectual challenges of presidential work. Organizational theorists speak of different kinds of power, the most obvious being bureaucratic authority: the ability to command compliance from subordinates as a result of one's position. Bureaucratic power occurs in its purest form in a military organization but also exists, though significantly tempered by cultural and institutional norms, in business organizations and government agencies. It also occurs within the administrative side of a university, and I confess, after many years as a middle-level administrator, to having enjoyed the exercise of this kind of power—deciding that a particular building would be built, a scholarship endowed, a new program funded, or a job candidate hired. With regard to decisions of this order, I was typically (and properly) granted deference by the Board though I knew I would also (again properly) be held responsible for the consequences. Exercising this kind of power across a wide range of institutional matters was unquestionably one of the attractions of the presidency.

But far more important than bureaucratic power in academia is what I would call intellectual or moral authority. Especially in working with the faculty, but, as a practical matter, in working with the administrative staff as well the Board, the job of the president is more to persuade than to command, and the task of persuasion engages both the brain and the character of the president. The members of the university community need not only to find the president's arguments persuasive but also to respect their leader's motives and commitments. I tried as president to the best of my limited ability to exercise power in this way. I did so because I believed that intellectual and moral authority are far more effective than bureaucratic power in eliciting the best efforts of an organization, even when one has the capacity to command compliance. I have worked for academic bosses who had a command-and-control approach to decision making, sometimes including a readiness to impose severe costs in humiliation if acquiescence was not prompt and absolute. Those experiences taught me that to demand compliance based on rank gets just that, compliance, but it rarely inspires maximum engagement by colleagues and subordinates. It is not for me, of course, to assess my success in providing intellectual and moral leadership for the Northeastern community, but that was how I sought to utilize the powers of my position. I would observe, also, that this view of presidential power significantly dilutes the force of laments about the diminished presidency as articulated by observers like James Fisher. Those concerns are about the loss of bureaucratic power. That loss need not imply the impossibility of leadership.

The intellectual requirements of the presidency quickly spill over into political and organizational challenges: translating strategic ideas into concrete actions, organizing the campus community to implement them, and inspiring individual community members to carry them out to the maximum extent of their abilities and energies. Here, again, a president is aided and supported by competent colleagues and—in my case—an institutional community ready to get behind a credible plan, but I also felt a measure of responsibility to play a role that is somewhat akin to that of a conductor in a symphony orchestra or the playmaker on a basketball team. This is the person who is understood by the community to know how the components of a comprehensive plan fit together and who conveys a passionate belief both in the value of the plan and in the work required to achieve it from which members of the community can draw energy to drive their own pieces of the action. Here, too, I am trying to describe how I sought to function, not to characterize my success in doing so. But I did experience the joy of seeing my team and community pull together and of watching their various contributions coalesce into a coherent whole as our repositioning strategy began to work. This was a source of genuine happiness in exactly the sense that I believe Edith Hamilton intended.

Beyond the satisfactions that can result from the "exercise of vital powers," the day-to-day work of the academic presidency provides many sources of pleasure. It gave me opportunities to interact with and learn from a wide variety of talented and impressive people, both inside and outside the organization, including among our governing Corporation, our alumni/ae, and our donors. Such interactions kept me in touch with developments not only in the intellectual and institutional arenas bounded by academia but also in the worlds of politics and business at all levels from our immediate neighborhood in Boston to the national and even international arenas. The work is almost infinite in its variety. On any given day one might move from meeting with an architect on the design of a building, to talking with the mayor of Boston about an issue in the community, to discussing business strategy with a corporate executive, to learning about the science involved in a major grant application, to cheering on the hockey team before an important game. Such interactions, as Gardner implied, call on the full range of one's intellectual dexterity and emotional intelligence.

The ceremonial duties of a president can be another source of pleasure, whether it is welcoming a new class of students in the fall, honoring a retiring faculty member, or addressing the community on a national holiday. Few professional moments in any field can exceed in pure deliciousness academia's annual commencement ceremony in which the president gets to stand before the graduating seniors and their parents, to hear their thunderous cheers, and to know that one has done something good for all those young lives and families. Through all of these moments there is also the simple, egocentric pleasure of being recognized as "the president" as one moves about campus or about town. One can't deny the gratification that comes with that.

Mixed in with the pleasures, of course, are inevitably frustrations and disappointments. Most presidents, myself included, are attracted to the job, at least in part, because they savor the admiration, affection, and support of an institutional community. I was fortunate to have my share of those satisfactions. But on occasion I was on the receiving end of less welcome sentiments. Some of my initiatives proved ill advised. Some speeches were duds. Some people had doubts about my leadership. These things go with the territory. So too does conflict. There were times I had to say "no" to people, to deny young faculty tenure or promotion, or to fire someone I liked—and to accept the anger that such actions inevitably elicited. I did not enjoy the battle with the Division of Cooperative Education that arose when Provost Hall and I tried to implement our Call to Action. I came to believe, however, that being ready to hurt individuals when the best interest of the institution requires it is part of a president's responsibility and that it would be unethical to accept the job unless one is ready to do so. I didn't always live up to this standard, however. In my final years, probably to avoid conflict with people I liked and admired, I was not sufficiently forceful about resolving a power struggle between two of my senior vice presidents, a source of lingering self-reproach.

Some experiences were acutely painful. In the aftermath of the Super Bowl riot I felt ashamed of our students and found myself being held personally responsible for an event that threatened to undermine years of work building Northeastern's reputation. As part of the controversy over building a new home for the African-American Institute I was subject to charges of racism from both students and community residents. Cutting even more deeply, Northeastern experienced a number of student deaths during my presidency; trying to offer some measure of consolation to grieving families and friends was always a source of anguish. So too was the challenge of helping the community mourn a collective loss, as occurred in the national devastation following the terrorist attack on Manhattan's Twin Towers in September 2001.

Three things allowed me to soldier through the difficult or painful moments. First, such moments were relatively rare. Second, and most important, was the steady support and love I received from my wife, Elsa, who gave large amounts of time to helping me do my job. At the beginning of my presidency, I tried to be home for dinner and to protect some private time for the two of us on weekends. Both of us soon realized, however, that the effort was producing more stress than enjoyment. In the end, Elsa said something like the following: "This isn't forever. Much of it is fun. We are having experiences we never thought we would have. Let's just go with it for as long as it lasts and enjoy it together for what it is." This insight liberated us to savor the many pleasures associated with our roles, and it is why this book is dedicated to her.

The third thing that sustained me was my underlying belief in the work. I recall the comment quoted approvingly by Abram Sachar, the founding president of Brandeis University, reporting the response one of his professors gave to a colleague who noted the president's widespread unpopularity among the faculty: In the future no one would remember whether Sachar was a good guy or a bad guy; all that would matter would be whether Brandeis was a great university. Conviction about the importance of helping Northeastern become strong was the bedrock source of determination that helped me through moments of disappointment and self-doubt.[6]


## Coda

Writing this chapter has reminded me of the many pleasures I experienced as president of Northeastern. It has also reinforced the sense, as the quotation from Abram Sachar suggests, that the deepest satisfaction came from knowing that my team and I played an important role in helping a socially valuable institution find its way back from an existential crisis and emerge as a thriving university, changed in some ways but still distinctively Northeastern. As I prepared to leave the presidency in 2006, and in the years since then, it is recognition of that achievement by members of the Northeastern community and by civic leaders and average citizens of Boston, as well as by colleagues in higher education around the country, that has meant the most to me. Members of our governing boards have repeatedly commented that they can scarcely believe the progress Northeastern has made since the difficult days of the early 1990s. Alums have reported admiring comments from friends and colleagues regarding the changes at Northeastern and have told me how good it feels, after years when they had felt ambivalent about their academic pedigree, to be on the receiving end of such compliments. Equally moving have been similar statements from faculty and staff, many of whom have been associated with Northeastern for many years and remember feeling that their institution was seen by the outside world as a good place but not a university of the first rank. I was especially touched several years ago when a middle-aged faculty member thanked me for helping the institution find new sources of strength following the enrollment crisis that preceded my election; he had had young children at that time and feared the institution might fail and that he would not be able to provide for them. Among the many memories that I treasure, that one ranks high.

# NOTES

The following abbreviations are used in the notes.

## PERIODICALS

| | |
|---|---|
| *BG* | *Boston Globe* |
| *CHE* | *Chronicle of Higher Education* |
| *NYT* | *New York Times* |
| *WP* | *Washington Post* |

## NORTHEASTERN UNIVERSITY DOCUMENTS

CorpAdrs + date: President's Address to the Corporation for a specific year

FBF: Freeland Book File, a collection of cited documents held in the Northeastern Archives

NUA: Northeastern University Archives

NUAD: Digitized document in Northeastern Archives

NUFB + date: Northeastern University Fact Book for a given year

PAR + date: Northeastern President's Annual Report for a given year

PresoFiles: President's Office files in Northeastern Archives

PresoFiles + specific topic: A hanging file in President's Office collection

PresoFiles + specific topic + [title]: A folder within a hanging file.

PresoFiles + specific topic + [title] + "Document Name": A document within a folder.

SoU + date: President's State of the University Address for a specific year

### Introduction

1. My understanding of the AUU, and of the broad context of urban higher education, relies heavily on the work of Steven Diner, whose *Universities and Their Cities* (2017) is the first comprehensive study of this topic; for the AUU see especially, pp. 23-25. Diner reports that the term "urban university" first appeared in the *New York Times* in 1913, which he takes to mean that the term had little or no use prior to that date. For "slavish subservience," see Kolbe, p. 114. For membership of AUU, see Association of Urban Universities, 1930, 1959. For study of off-campus experience, see Kolbe, pp. 210-20. For decline of cities after World War II, see Teaford.

2. Diner, chap. 3, provides an excellent discussion of responses of city-based universities to urban decline, including the specific institutions I mention. For Chicago, see also Webber

in Perry and Wiewel; Nash, chap. 2. For Columbia, see also Nash, chap. 8. For Hopkins, I have relied on two student papers, one by Mirtha Garcia and Laurie Forcier and the other by Brittini Bragg, both available in NUA, FBF, Introduction. For Boston University, see Freeland, 1992, pp. 286–87. For NYU, see Diner, p. 71. For Pittsburgh, see Alberts, Book IV; Deitrick and Soska in Perry and Wiewel, chap. 1; Diner, p. 31. For new public urban universities after World War II, see also Klotsche, p. 14.

3. For debates within AUU, see Diner, pp. 44–48, 72–75. For the status of this debate in early 1980s, see Waetjen and Muffo. For first use of the "in" vs. "of" distinction, see Diner, p. 40. For argument that urban universities must focus on local students, see Elliott, chap. 2. For Elliott's perspective as representing the general view, see Diner, p. 91. For dissolution of AUU see Diner, p. 91.

4. For Penn, see Rodin; Kromer and Kerman; Diner, chap. 3. For Columbia, see Nash, chap. 8; Diner, chap. 3. For Chicago, see Webber in Perry and Wiewel.

5. For argument that academic change occurs because of effective presidents, see Fisher, 1984, 1988, 1991. For argument that change is "cybernetic," see Birnbaum, 1988, 1992. See also below, Chapter 9, n. 3.

## Chapter 1

1. For colleges in colonial and antebellum periods, I have relied on Rudolph's classic history of American higher education and on Thelin's more recent volume, which adds important complexity to Rudolph's account. For "antipathy," see Rudolph, p. 92; Thelin endorses this characterization; see NUA, FBF, chap. 1, e-mail Thelin to Freeland, September 24, 2016, "Re: Draft." For "collegiate way," see Rudolph, pp. 86–96. For early examples of urban universities, see Klotsche, pp. 8–12. For Penn and Columbia as city-based, see Diner, p. 4.

2. My discussion of the development of urban higher education relies on Diner, Klotsche, Berube, Kolbe, and Levine, chap. 4. For founding dates of urban institutions, see Klotsche, pp. 8–12. For the 44 percent statistic, see Kolbe, p. 112. Klotsche, p. 7, reports the number was 50 percent by 1960. For early history of Northeastern, see Marston.

3. For early years of AUU, see above, Introduction this book, n. 1; for Dabney and "of" vs. "in" distinction, see Diner, p. 40. Elliott provides a contemporary view of urban institutions and stresses serving local students. For distinctive characteristics of urban universities and discussion of the AUU, see Kolbe, part. II, chap. I; for "slavish subservience," see part. II, p.114; for list of commitments that characterized AUU members, see part II, p. 50; for field work and cooperative education, see part. II, chap. VII; for adult education, see part. II, chap. VI. I have also relied on Levine, chap. 4; Berube, chap. 1; Klotsche, chap. 1. For 137 schools offering cooperative education in 1920, see Levine, p. 49. Levine is particularly strong on practical and vocational programs. Berube emphasizes local service, arguing that urban universities looked to the land grants for models, not to traditional elite universities. For percentage of commuters, see Levine, p. 75. For Penn's drop in status after enrolling local students, see Levine, p. 72. For research on urban problems at Chicago, see Shils, pp. 220–21.

4. For development of Northeastern between 1900 and 1930, see Marston, chaps. 1–5; Freeland, 1992, pp. 63–65. For Ell quote, see Freeland, 1992, p. 65.

5. For patterns of post–World War II development among American universities, see Freeland, 1992, chap. 2; for pressures to build research and doctoral programs, see pp. 5–7, 357–60. For the post–World War II decline of cities, see Teaford, chaps. 5, 6. For dissolution of AUU, see above, Introduction this book, n. 3.

6. For universities' responses to urban decline, see above, Introduction this book, n. 2. For examples of schools that participated in slum clearance programs during urban renewal, I have relied on Perry and Wiewel. For Temple, see Temple University Library, Special Collections Research Center, oral history "Interview with Millard Gladfelter (10/15/76)"; Diner, pp. 55–56. For Pittsburgh, see Alberts, Book IV, chaps. 26, 27. For state takeovers of private urban universities, see Klotsche, pp. 14–15; for state takeovers of municipal universities, see p. 12. For 73 percent students in publics by 1970, see Freeland, 1992, p. 88. For CUMU, see Diner, p. 128

7. For Northeastern during Knowles, see Frederick, 1982; Freeland, 1992, pp. 260–68, 288–89, 391–92. For decline in student quality under Knowles, see NUA, Corporation and Board of Trustees Records (A12), Box 37, Folder 29, "Report of the Special Committee on Enrollments," April 1991, p. 5; two summaries are in NUA, FBF, chap. 1. For "head table of academic respectability," see Frederick, 1982, p. 45. For Ryder years, see Frederick, 1995. For Carnegie Commission, see Freeland, 1992, p. 289.

8. For growth of public higher education in 1950s and 1960s, see Freeland, 1992, chap. 6. For Boston College and Boston University during the 1950s and 1960s, see Freeland, 1992, chap. 5. For discussion of Northeastern's crisis and related statistics on enrollments, finances, and personnel, see Feldscher, chap. 3; for Curry Fall 1990 State of the University speech, see pp. 31–32. For Northeastern admissions statistics during 1980s, see also NUA, NUFB 1990–91; relevant tables are in NUA, FBF, chap. 1. For Trustee review of enrollments and finances during 1980s, see NUA, Corporation and Board of Trustees Records (A12), Box 37, Folder 29, "Report of the Special Committee on Enrollments," April 1991; for "over the past decade," see p. 15; for "life threatening," see p. 34; for 3,600 as Fall 90 admissions target, see p. 7.

9. For a full review of Curry's presidency, see Feldscher. For improved selectivity by 1995, see NUA, NUFB 1996–97.

10. For discussion of negative impacts of research and doctoral education on undergraduate teaching and learning, see Assembly on University Goals and Governance, pp. 8, 9, 16, Thesis 23; American Council on Education, Special Commission on Campus Tensions, pp. 40, 41; Carnegie Commission on Higher Education, pp. 12, 78, 117, 160; President's Task Force on Higher Education, p. 13; see also Freeland, 1992, pp. 103–7.

11. For a perspective on the role of city-based universities in urban revitalization that I share, see Rodin, chap. 1.

## Chapter 2

1. The President's Office files in NUA contain extensive documentation on the restructuring process, which represented Curry's final effort to put the University on a path to a balanced budget. The conclusion was that the operating budget needed to be further reduced by $15 million (6 percent) over the next three to four years; see NUA, FBF, chap. 2, "Summary of Restructuring Committee Report"; the President's Office files also contain Curry's memos to the University's administrative leaders dated March 25, 1996, calling for a new round of budget cuts, and they also document the back-and-forth that ensued with various departments regarding plans to achieve the assigned reductions. For discussion of the importance that including work experience as part of a college education had acquired by the end of the twentieth century, see Thomas Friedman, "The Internship: Not the Movie," *NYT*, op-ed, June 9, 2013.

2. For Curry-era strategic plan, see NUA, Office of the Provost Records (A24), Box 239, Folder 50, "The Connected Campus." For 1996 SoU speech, see NUA, PresoFiles, RMF, where

there is a complete set of my SoU speeches and annual CorpAdrs's. All these speeches, along with my inaugural address, are available in NUAD.

3. For Conant on "intensification," see Freeland, 1992, p. 54. The PresoFiles in NUA contain three hanging files on the Intensification process labeled "Intensification," "Intensification Initiatives," and "Intensification Funding"; included are memoranda from Freeland to administrative leaders in the academic and student-services areas requesting proposals for initiatives that could produce prompt results in improving performance. The files also contain proposals submitted, responses to proposals, and spring 1997 allocations. See also NUA, PresoFiles, Organizational Structure, "Report on Student-Centered Service Excellence Initiative, Phase I Update," by Hirsh Hills Associates, June 9, 1998, which reviews progress on a multi-unit effort covering Bursar, Career Services, Cooperative Education, Criminal Justice, Lane Health Center, Office of the President, and Residential Life.

4. For faculty Senate discussion of "practice-oriented education" as a defining characteristic of Northeastern in spring 1997, see NUA, FBF, chap. 5, "Notes from Michaela re POE Chronology"; while there was no formal action, the discussion was favorable. For the report of the reaccreditation visiting team noting broad understanding of and support for the Mantra following its campus visit, see NUA, PresoFiles, Accreditation NEASC Site Visit, "Report to the Trustees, Faculty, Administration and Students of Northeastern University by an Evaluation Team Representing the Commission on Institutions of Higher Education, New England Association of Schools and Colleges," based on a site visit on October 25–28, 1988, pp. 8, 10, 13, 26. A key first step in fleshing out the Mantra was involving the University's administrative leadership in this discussion; this process began at a leadership retreat in June 1997; for the remainder of my presidency, the leadership group held twice yearly retreats at which a consistent focus was progress within the five dimensions of the Mantra; for records of these retreats, see NUA, PresoFiles, Leadership Retreats; for a summary, see NUA, FBF, chap. 2, "Summary of Leadership Group Meetings." For 1998 reaccreditation self-study, see NUA, PresoFiles, Accreditation/NEASC, "Northeastern University, Institutional Self Study, Decennial Reaccreditation, 1998, Vols. I & II."

5. For first published version of the Action and Assessment Plan, June 1999, see NUA, Provost Office Records (A24), Box 161, Folder 64; annual updates of the plan are also available in the Provost Office Records. For unit planning, see extensive documentation in NUA, PresoFiles, Unit Plans. For annual reports of progress toward our goals, see SoU's and CorpAdrs's, cited above, n. 2. Copies of annual "report cards" for several years between 1998 and 2006 can be found in NUA, PresoFiles, Report Cards; also in NUA, Office of the Provost collection (A22); as of October 2016, copies for several years were also on file in the Office of Institutional Research. In working with departments to develop unit plans, we were helped by Michael Dolence's and David Norris's planning ideas and especially their ideas about Key Performance Indicators (KPIs).

6. For documentation of our work on marketing, see NUA, PresoFiles, Marketing, organized by year. For early marketing reviews, see annual marketing files, including "A Review of Marketing and Communications Programs at Northeastern University," Dick Jones Communications, July 1997; for discussion of the process that solidified our marketing strategy led by Michael Keeshan of MagiKbox, see memo, Freeland to Leadership Group, January 4, 1999; see above, n. 4, "Summary of Leadership Group Meetings," March 1999.

7. For decision that "practice-oriented education" would be the basis of our Vision Statement, see NUA, PresoFiles, Marketing [1999], "Memorandum, Freeland to Leadership Group, 5/10/1999 with attachment." I should note that Northeastern's official mission statement at this

time included a commitment to the pursuit of "knowledge for its own sake," a standard academic sentiment somewhat at odds with the Mantra's emphasis on being practice oriented; believing a debate on this phrase would not be useful, I simply ignored the mission statement, which most members of the campus community had never read, and focused discussion on the Mantra.

8. For annual leadership retreats, see above, n. 4, "Summary of Leadership Group Meetings."

9. For a typically critical assessment of the rankings, see Robert Kuttner, "College Rankings or Junk Science?" *BG*, February 25, 2006.

10. For SoU's in 1998 and 1999 and CorpAdrs in 2000, see above, n. 2.

11. For Leadership retreats, see above, n. 4, "Summary of Leadership Group Meetings." Our session with Zemsky occurred during June 1998.

## Chapter 3

1. The following statement from one long-term member of the Northeastern community and also an alum, who reviewed this chapter in draft form, conveys a strong sense of the institution at the time I became president: "When I returned to NU in [the 1970s] I was delighted to be back 'home.' My colleagues, many of whom I had known as my teachers, embraced me. The same was true of the many staff people with whom I became acquainted . . . all the people with whom I associated were committed to NU, many were alums. We knew the University as the place that gave us a chance. Perhaps we could not get into (or afford) other places. From day one I knew I was getting a good education but was it as good as BU or Harvard? Probably not, I thought. Our campus was ugly, our sports teams were terrible. Most of us commuted so when the sun went down we left. In many ways this was the place I returned to. . . . It was a culture dominated by alums and long serving staff and faculty who, while realizing our deficiencies, chose to ignore them and instead defended them—'that's who we are.' NU was insular in part because we saw ourselves as different. You [i.e. Freeland] inherited an infrastructure that had been in place for a very long time. There were many good, hardworking, and dedicated people, but some were caught in a time warp. . . . As the first outsider . . . you took a different view. Ironically, since you had practically no power base on campus you were able to act freely (although I suspect you may have discovered some minefields), unburdened by decades old campus entanglements. All of this is simply to say that your candid (I suspect you have held back!!!) comments are accurate, and presented in a way that is respectful to NU and to those who worked here."

2. For discussions of becoming a "high performance organization," see Leadership retreat files, Chapter 2 this book, n. 4. For *Built to Last,* see Collins and Porras; Leadership retreat discussion of this book occurred in June 1999. See also NUA, PresoFiles, Excellence Awards, which include extensive documentation of this process for FY2001-FY2004. For Aspiration Awards, see NUAD, http://wayback.archive-it.org/1746/20101117052311/http://northeastern.edu/voice/pdfs/2003/030429.pdf.

3. For discussion of Trustee Professors Program, see Chapter 6. Members of my Leadership Team who became presidents were David Hall, University of the Virgin Islands; Christopher Hopey, Merrimack College (Massachusetts); Mark Putnam, Central College (Iowa); Patricia Meservey, Salem State University (Massachusetts).

4. Weick.

5. For organizational tensions at end of Knowles presidency, see Freeland, 1992, pp. 281-282, 392. For Ryder's approach to governance, see Frederick, 1995, chap. 3. For Curry's efforts to enhance faculty role, see Feldscher, esp. chap. 4.

6. For president's annual reports (PAR), see NUA, PresoFiles, Annual Reports for the appropriate year. For SoU's and CorpAdrs's, see above, this book, Chapter 2, n. 2. For annual report cards, see above, this book, Chapter 2, n. 5.

7. For unit planning, see above, this book, Chapter 2, n. 5. For Excellence Awards, see above, n. 2. As the unit planning process moved from planning to implementation, the Excellence Awards evolved into a program of annual "unit plan achievement awards," which provided budget increments to units that made outstanding progress on their approved plans; see above, this book Chapter 2, n. 2 SoU 2002; see also NUA, PresoFiles, UPC, [SVP]. For shift of responsibility for annual updates of the Action and Assessment Plan to the University Planning Council (UPC), see NUA, PresoFiles, UPC; these files document the work of the UPC on this matter over several years.

8. For number 1 ranking by *U.S. News* in 2002, see Chapter 2, this book, n.2, SOU 2002. "Palpable Sense of Accomplishment" based on numerous comments to author by members of Northeastern community.

9. An extended discussion of efforts to create a student-centered research university can be found in Chapter 4. An extended discussion of changes in the co-op program can be found in Chapter 5. Extensive material on the semester conversion process can be found in NUA, PresoFiles, Calendar [1998-2004] and [Semester Conversion].

10. For decision to rename University Relations "Marketing and Communications" and for discussion of related organizational issues, see NUA, PresoFiles, Organizational Structure, "Memorandum, Freeland to Senior Vice Presidents, 'Organizational Issues in University Relations,' 1/28/2004"; an extended discussion of our work in Marketing can be found in Chapter 7. The January 28, 2004, memorandum also explains my reasons for not combining marketing and university relations with community relations. An extended discussion of our work in Community Relations can be found in Chapter 7. For the Office of Corporate Partnerships, see NUA, FBF, chap. 3, "Corporate Partnerships."

11. For fund-raising during Curry years, see Feldscher, chap. 11. For $153 million endowment in 1989, see NUA, NUFB, 1989-90, p. 122.

12. A useful summary of fund-raising during my presidency can be found in NUA, FBF, chap. 3, "Chronology of Advancement at Northeastern University." For Leadership Campaign, see NUA, PresoFiles, Advancement, organized by years; the files include the study by Ketchum consultants validating the $200 million campaign goal but also noting significant caveats, including the comment that the giving capacity of key prospects is not matched by giving readiness; I should have read this report more carefully before launching the campaign. For a list of top donors and other Leadership Campaign records, see NUA, Office of Institutional Advancement, A90.b4. For Gordon gift, see NUAD: https://web.archive.org/web/20060831221045/http://www.voice.neu.edu:80/060815/1-6-7.pdf. The following individuals made gifts of $1 million or more to the campaign: Irving Levine, Charles and Josephine Hoff, Frederick and Darla Brodsky, Irving and Betty Brudnick, Nonnie and Richard Burnes, Neal Finnegan, Francis and Joan Gicca, John and Patricia Hatsopoulas, Douglas Lockwood, Anthony and Michelle Manganaro, Ronald and Linda Rossetti, Morton and Marcia Ruderman, the Estate of Marguerite Parker, Willard Reuther, and Russell Stearns.

13. For more than 80 percent dependency on student payments, see NUA, FBF, chap. 3, email (plus attachments), Solomon to Freeland, November 7, 2016, "A Question." A copy of "Enrollment and Resource Plan: 1998-2002 and Beyond," March 24, 1998, can be found in NUA, PresoFiles, Retention/Enrollment [1998].

14. For enrollment declines in University College, see NUA, NUFBs, which show evening enrollments falling steadily from 10,423 in 1986 to 6,811 by 1997. A brief history of the

evolution of University College into the School of Professional and Continuing Studies and later the College of Professional Studies, along with information on programming changes, can be found in College of Professional Studies, Academic Council for Lifelong Learning: "Overview," October 14, 2015; a partial copy is in NUA, FBF, chap. 3. An extended treatment of the growing role of the School of Professional and Continuing Studies (SPCS) in graduate studies can be found in Chapter 6.

15. For operating surpluses achieved during my presidency, see NUA, FBF, chap. 3, email, Kneeland (Northeastern's Controller) to Freeland, July 10, 2008. For Academic Investment Plan, see NUA, PresoFiles, Academic Investment Plan. For details regarding construction of new facilities, see NUA, FBF, chap. 4, email, May to Freeland, June 22, 2016; an extended discussion of new facilities can be found in Chapter 4.

## Chapter 4

1. For Shaw on concept of "student-centered research university," see Shaw; information about relevant initiatives can also be found on the Syracuse Web site. My annual report for 2000–2001 was devoted to explaining what Northeastern meant by this concept, see PAR 2000–2001, chap. 3 this book, n. 6; see also vol. I, chap. 5, of our 1997–98 reaccreditation self-study, chap. 2 this book, n. 4; and SoU 1997, Chapter 2 this book, n. 2.

2. For Curry's work on "student centeredness," see Feldscher, esp. chap. 7. For graduation rate data in 1996, 2006, and 2012, see NUA, NUFBs for those years; see also "A Decade of Progress, Northeastern University, 1996–2006," p. 7, Chapter 3 this book, n. 6. Regarding reliance on part-time faculty, see NUA, FBF, chap. 4, table headed "Faculty and Staff Five Year Summary." A study completed in 2002, well into my presidency but prior to implementation of the Academic Investment Plan, revealed the following percentages of sections taught by part-timers in various divisions: Arts, 48 percent; Humanities, 59 percent; Sciences, 41 percent; Social Sciences, 46 percent; Business, 41 percent; Engineering, 51 percent; see NUA, FBF, chap. 4, "Enrollment and Resource Plan Analysis." The study we did of faculty-to-student ratios for the AIP showed that Northeastern had a ratio of Full-time-Equivalent (FTE) Students-to-Tenure/Tenure Track faculty of 26 to 1, compared to 22 to 1 at the schools to which we compared ourselves; similarly, Northeastern had a ratio of FTE Students-to-FTE Faculty of 19 to 1 compared to 17.5 to 1 at the schools to which we compared ourselves. These numbers were the basis for the AIP goal of adding 100 full-time faculty; see NUA, PresoFiles, AIP 2003, "Proposal for a Significant Academic Initiative, Office of the Provost, 12/5/2003." For a well-researched journalistic report on our retention efforts, see BG; "NU tackles student departures," December 21, 2002, by Jenna Russell; a copy can be found in NUA, FBF, chap. 4. For low scores on surveys of student satisfaction, see below, n. 4.

3. For importance of graduation rates, including their financial significance, see SoU 2001, chap. 2 this book. n. 2. For Finkelstein/Eddy Task Force and Mantella Retention Task Force and work on unit-level goals, see NUA, FBF, chap. 4, "Retention Summary."

4. For NUPULSE surveys, see the digital files of the Northeastern University Archives, http://www.northeastern.edu/pdfs + "NUPULSE Surveys." In addition to department-specific surveys and the NUPULSE questionnaires, we regularly administered standardized surveys to measure student satisfaction with a wide range of non-academic services, facilities, and experiences, including the Noel Levitz Student Satisfaction Inventory, the ACUHO/EBI Resident Survey, and the ACUI Student Center Survey. Extensive summaries of findings can be found in NUA, FBF, chap. 4. In general, these surveys revealed two things: first, that student satisfaction was generally improving with regard to most of the issues monitored, although we continued to

struggle in some areas; second, that in most areas of non-academic student life we were starting from a low level of student satisfaction compared with peer institutions. For growth of full-time faculty, see NUA, NUFBs, 1996 and 2007; for continuing reliance on part-timers, see NUA, "Northeastern University Reaccreditation Self Study, 2008," pp. 45–46. For work of Pascarella and Terenzini on student retention, see *How College Affects Students.*

5. Data on changes in applications to Northeastern and the academic profile and geographic diversity of entering students is from NUFBs for 1997–98 and 2006–07. A memo summarizing ongoing work by our enrollment management consultants, Maguire Associates, regarding our admissions work can be found in NUA, FBF, chap. 4, "Box of Maguire Materials #2." For a summary of Maguire's analysis of the over-enrollment problem in 2000, see NUA, FBF, chap. 4, "Northeastern University: Initial Assessment of Freshman Enrollment, 10/20/2000" with attached table of admissions statistics; see also in NUA, FBF, memo, Meservey to President's Cabinet, "Analysis of Acceptance Process for the Current Freshman Class," November 15, 2000; also in NUA, FBF chap. 4, see memo on over enrollment problem "Bulge Year," including quotes from *BG* article on this situation. For a summary of admissions-related studies by OUPR, see NUA, FBF, chap. 4, "Admissions Studies." For fourth ranking in total applications in 2006, see CorpAdrs 2006, Chapter 2 this book, n. 2. For seventy-fifth ranking in overall selectivity, see above n. 2, "A Decade of Progress," p. 3.

6. A list of retention-related studies completed by OUPR can be found in NUA, FBF, chap. 4. For efforts to increase the percentage of full-pay students, see NUA, FBF, chap. 4, documents grouped together under title "Discussion of Pell, Financial Aid," especially the table titled "Estimated Family Income" from the PowerPoint presentation "Outline of Enrollment Management and Student Affairs Five-Year Plan," and also Goal 2.5 of the Enrollment Management and Student Affairs (EMSA) "Unit Plan, 2003–2008." On role of co-op salaries in covering college costs, see "Jean Eddy Co-op Earnings Memo" and "Financial Aid Equalization" in NUA, FBF, chap. 4. For Presidential Scholars Program in Inaugural Address, see NUAD, Chapter 2 this book, n. 2; for development of program, see NUA, FBF, chap. 4, "Presidential Scholars"; for success of program, see also NUA, FBF, chap. 4, memo, Mantella to Freeland, January 4, 2010, reporting that of 108 student recipients all but three had graduated or were still enrolled; key donors were Arthur Pappas, Donald Kramer, Roy and Leora Beaton, Ronald and Lynn Rossetti, Alan and Judith Tobin, Edward Galante, Irving Levine, Anthony and Michelle Manganaro, and Michael Zamkow; at the time I stepped down, the Trustees organized a campaign to support two additional Presidential Scholars in my name, a gift to the school in my honor that I very much appreciated.

7. For OUPR studies of relationship of residential status to retention, see above, n. 6.

8. For campus improvements under Curry, see Feldscher, chap. 10. For Ryder, see Frederick, 1995, chap. 14. For a summary of the building program's impact on the University's residential capacity, see NUA, Office of the Physical Planning and Design records (212-042), Box 1, "Institutional Master Plan Notification Form, Third Amendments to the Institutional Master Plan," July 10, 2006; helpful details were also provided in a private email from Nancy May, dated June 22, 2016, in NUA, FBF, chap. 4. For summaries of press reviews of West Village buildings, see NUA, FBF, chap. 4, "Campbell Articles." A complete list of the fourteen design awards won by Rawn Associates for Northeastern work can be found in NUA, FBF, chap. 4, "Northeastern University-AIA Awards."

9. Data on growth of student organizations in Northeastern's records appears to be quite inexact, so any statement on this matter is an approximation. The NUFB 1996–97 puts the

number at 190; the Student Handbook for 2006 reports 240. For honor code proposal, see NUA, FBF, chap. 4, "Background Information on Honor Code Proposal at NU, 10/2009."

10. For leadership retreat discussions, see summaries of 2003 and 2004 retreats in NUA, FBF, chap. 4, "Managing Student Expectations: Leadership Retreat 2003 and 2004" and "We Care Campaign." For surveys of student satisfaction, see above, n. 4. For statement that our student satisfaction scores exceeded those of our peers by 2006, see NUA, FBF, chap. 4, "Report Card Slide #43," page 42 of "Assessing Our Strategic Position, OUPR, Fall 2006."

11. For percentages on Pell grants, see above, n. 6, documents grouped together under "Discussion of Pell, Financial Aid," especially Goal 2.6 from "Enrollment Management and Student Affairs Division Unit Plan, 2003–2008," and memoranda from Philomena Mantella and Anthony Erwin on this topic. For work on non-traditional admissions, see NUA, FBF, chap. 4, group of documents titled "nontraditional admissions."

## Chapter 5

1. Regarding importance of co-op to Northeastern's visibility: In 2002, the editors of *U.S. News* ranked Northeastern first in the country for institutions that linked practical experience with classroom study; see SoU 2002, Chapter 2 this book, n. 2. For 2,300 alums at Raytheon, see Frederick, 1995, p. 267.

2. The idea of "practice-oriented education" was a major theme of my inaugural address in January 1997; see above, Chapter 2, n. 2.

3. For efforts to strengthen co-op during the Curry years, see Feldscher, chap. 6; the report of the University-wide committee is summarized on p. 125. The 1991 report of the Trustees' Special Committee on Enrollments also stressed the importance of co-op and the need for the program to be "rethought and updated"; see Report of Special Committee, section on "Standing Committee Work," Chapter 1 this book, n. 7; a copy of relevant pages is in NUA, FBF, chap. 5. For activities integrating co-op and classroom at end of Curry's presidency, see NUA, FBF, chap. 5, "Vozzella Report on Integration of Co-op and Classroom"; see also "The Integration of Co-op and Academics—Where We Are," September 19, 1996, NUA, PresoFiles, POE [1996].

4. For Intensification Program and co-op, see NUA, PresoFiles, Intensification, memo, Freeland to Vozzella, January 29, 1997; see also NUA, PresoFiles, Intensification Initiatives, memo, Freeland to Pantalone, May 29, 1998, "Proposed Intensification Initiatives," and memo Woolever to Scranton, February 19, 1998, "Integration Initiative." For research program on co-op by OUPR, see NUA, PresoFiles, POE, "Assessing the Impact of Cooperative Education at Northeastern," October 2000; for a summary of this report, see NUA, FBF, chap. 5, "Report on Co-op by Office of University Planning and Research." For results of OUPR research, see several documents in NUA, FBF, and chap. 5, "Summary of Co-op Metrics for 2005 Board Briefing"; "Co-op Metrics" (undated PowerPoint presentation); "Practice Oriented" (undated PowerPoint presentation); see also NUA, PresoFiles, Co-op [2002].

5. For skepticism among faculty about value of co-op, I have relied chiefly on my own impressions. But this concern was reinforced in a private communication from Curry's Vice President for Co-op, Jane Scarborough; see also Feldscher, p. 129. It was also the finding of Professor Raelin as a result of interviews he conducted as the first Director of the Center for the Study of Practice-Oriented Education, see below, n. 13. Former Dean of Arts and Sciences Lowndes offers a somewhat different view, namely that many faculty recognized the value of co-op but were structurally isolated from it and uncomfortable with the fact that coordinators were eligible for tenure. My comment that co-op coordinators came to regard co-op as a

separate academic discipline is based on their presentation to the Trustee Special Committee on Cooperative Education in 1998; for a summary see NUA, FBF chap. 5, "Summary of DCE [Division of Cooperative Education] Presentation." In addition, the DCE letter to the Trustee Special Committee on Cooperative Education, see below, n. 7, accuses me of failing "to recognize cooperative education as an academic discipline with its own body of knowledge and principles to guide its practice"; see also "Co-op as a Separate Discipline" in NUA, FBF, chap. 5, "Notes by Colleen, 1/15/09."

6. For "Call to Action," see NUA, PresoFiles, Co-op [1999] and [2000], "Call to Action on Cooperative Education," Richard M. Freeland, David Hall, September 1998.

7. For initial response of DCE to the Call to Action, see memo from Call to Action Divisional Committee to Freeland et al., September 14, 1999, in NUA (A22), Box 149, Folder 17; the cover memo and table of contents is in NUA, FBF, chap. 5. For summary of college responses to the Call to Action, see "Call to Action Response Submissions by College/Department" in NUA, FBF, chap 5. For more detailed responses of colleges to the Call to Action, see NUA, PresoFiles, POE; the annual co-op files also contain several documents related to the implementation of the Call to Action. For DCE's meeting with Trustees' Special Committee, see NUA, FBF, chap. 5, "DCE Letter to Michael Cronin." For my response to the DCE letter, see NUA, A22. B149.F17.002.pdf; a copy is in NUA, FBF, chap. 5. For DCE presentation to Cronin Committee, see NUA, FBF, chap. 5, "Report of 1/13/2000 from the Division of Cooperative Education to Michael Cronin and the Co-op Subcommittee." For final report of Special Committee, see NUA, PresoFiles, POE, "Report to the Academic Affairs Committee, 1/17/2000"; a summary can be found in NUA, FBF, chap. 5, "Notes by Colleen, 1/15/09."

8. For strict oversight arrangements, see draft memo from Porter to DCE coordinators, January 27, 2000, in NUA A22.B149.F17.001.pdf. For Provost's efforts to move forward with implementation of the Call to Action in early 2000, see NUA, A22.B211.F03.001.pdf, "Memo from Provost David Hall to Vice President Porter," 2/29/2000; copies of both documents are also in NUA, FBF, chap. 5. For a general review of progress on the Call to Action and research on co-op, see PowerPoint presentation, "Co-op and Top 100," Abdelal, Lyford, Putnam, Freeland, in NUA, PresoFiles, Board of Trustees Board Briefings, [material for October 20, 2005, briefing].

9. For summary of ILM status as of 2001, see "ILM Response Submissions by College/ Department, 2001" in NUA, FBF, chap. 5. For summary of progress on ILMs in each college as of 2005, see two-page report titled "Integrated Learning Model" in NUA, FBF, chap. 5. For the ILM in Computer and Information Science, see former Dean Finkelstein's marginal comment on draft p. 9 in NUA, FBF, chap 5. For a report on progress on ILMs, see Memorandum from Malcolm Hill, Vice Provost for Undergraduate Education, "Integrated Learning Model Update, 9/2003," in NUA, PresoFiles, Co-op [2003]. A summary of approved unit plans for the colleges of Engineering, Business, Arts and Sciences, Health Sciences, Computer Science, and Criminal Justice with respect to integrating co-op experiences into the academic curriculum can be found in NUA, FBF, chap. 5. See also, generally, POE folders and ILM folders in NUA, PresoFiles.

10. For recording co-ops on transcripts, see NUA, FBF, chap. 5, memo, Allen to Freeland, May 26, 2017, "Questions." One reason to weed out co-ops that were not intellectually challenging came from the research of Paul Harrington's Center for Labor Market Studies, which showed that co-op experiences strongly linked to a student's field of study resulted in significant first-job salary benefits but that co-ops with little relation to a student's field of study had little or no first-job salary benefit. See two studies in NUA, FBF, chap. 5, "The Contributions of Cooperative Education to the Early Labor Market Success of College Graduates" and "The Influence of Co-op

Program Participation on Post Graduation Earnings of Northeastern University Graduates." For research showing that co-op enhanced classroom learning, see two PowerPoint presentations in NUA, FBF, chap. 5, "co-op metrics" and "practice oriented."

11. Individuals who held deanships for limited periods of time during my presidency were Roger Abrams (Law), James Fox (Criminal Justice), Daniel Givelber (Law), James Gozzo (Bouvé College of Health Sciences), Paul King (Engineering), Robert Lowndes (Arts and Sciences), Patrick Plunkett (Bouvé College of Health Sciences), and Eileen Zungolo (Nursing). A partial list of new academic programs, undergraduate and graduate, established during my presidency can be found in NUA, FBF, chap. 5, "New Academic Programs, 2001–2006."

12. A review of college-level plans for ILMs reports commitments to develop cross-collegiate minors in the plans of Engineering, Business, Criminal Justice, Computer Science, and Health Sciences, see NUA, FBF chap. 5, "Minors and Dual Degree Programs." For a thoughtful comment on the value of cross-college programming, see NUA, FBF, chap. 5, email, Finkelstein to Freeland, June 14, 2016, "Reviews." For the new general education requirements, see NUA, FBF, chap. 5, "General Education at Northeastern University, Final Report and Recommendations." For the unified calendar, see above, n. 9, memo, Allen to Freeland, May 26, 2017. For minors on transcripts, see NUA, FBF, chap. 5, memo, Allen to Freeland, July 21, 2016, "Manuscript Pages."

13. For "The Institutionalization of Practice-Oriented Education at Northeastern University," see NUA, PresoFiles, Provost [1998]. This folder also includes material on the work of the Provost's Advisory Committee on POE. For white paper on promotion and tenure policies, see "Summary of POE Faculty Advisory Group White Paper" and also "White Paper on Impact of Practice-Oriented Education on the Promotion and Tenure of Faculty" in NUA, FBF, chap. 5. For Center for the Study of Practice-Oriented Education, see Joseph Raelin, "Status Report on POE," November 15, 2003, in NUA, PresoFiles, Provost [2003]; this document summarizes Raelin's view that many faculty members continue to view co-op and POE with skepticism; a summary can be found in NUA, FBF, chap. 5. For Fraser role, see NUA, FBF, chap. 5, memo, Freeland to Abdelal and Fraser, "Jim's Role in Promoting POE," May 2, 2005; see also "Summary of Discussion between Jim Fraser, President Freeland, Ahmed Abdelal" in FBF, chap. 5. For POE awards program, see NUA, FBF, chap. 5, "Summary of POE Awards Presentations." National POE conferences were held in 2001, 2003, and 2005; see NUA, FBF, chap. 5, "Bi-annual Conference on POE"; a complete set of materials for the 2001 conference can be found in NUA, PresoFiles, Provost [2001]. For Vice Provost Hill's records regarding implementation of POE, see NUA, PresoFiles, Provost [1996 and beyond].

14. As examples, here are two comments from members of the Northeastern community written in 2016 about the continuing importance of practice-oriented education: (1) "Co-op evolved upward to meet expectations of an improving student body and new faculty were arriving who saw co-op in a new light. It took a generation to happen. Also must factor in international experiences as well as much better internships. The tide lifted all boats." (2) "Although new terminology might replace the old, the core ideas [of POE] are still pretty much intact . . . but for most students it's still co-op and quality jobs. When you have great co-op positions, everything seems to work so much better, especially the contributions to the student's personal and intellectual development. And interestingly enough the high-quality students we are now attracting are the most excited about co-op. The combined major programs . . . have grown enormously in popularity." See notes from Finkelstein and Fowler in FBF, chap. 5.

15. For *CHE* pieces, see February 19, 1999, "How Practical Experience Can Help Revitalize our Tired Model of Undergraduate Education," and January 15, 2000, "The Practical Path,

Too, Can Be High Minded." For *Atlantic* piece, see October 2004, "The Third Way." Information about the LEAP initiative can be found on the AAC&U website at www.aacu.org.

## Chapter 6

1. My concerns about the negative impacts of the emphasis on research and advanced graduate education as institutions across the United States expanded during the 1960s and 1970s were widely shared by thoughtful observers of higher education. For an extended discussion of these critiques, see Freeland, 1992, pp. 401 ff; see also Chapter 1 this book, n. 10.

2. For research and graduate development under Ell and Knowles, see Frederick, 1982, chaps. 9 and 10; see also Freeland, 1992, pp. 249, 264–65. For Ryder, see Frederick, 1995, chap. 5. For Curry, see Feldscher, chaps. 4 and 5. For a brief review of doctoral development under Knowles, Ryder, and Curry, see NUA, FBF, chap. 6, memo, Romero to Freeland, February 3, 2017, "Research Expenditures." For summary information on doctoral programming and NRC rankings in 1995, see NUA, PresoFiles, Graduate Program Evaluation Process, Graduate Review Working Group, Report, 1997; see also NUA, PresoFiles, Graduate Program Review, memo, Hedlund to Graduate Program Coordinators, December 6, 1996.

3. For Curry-era strategic plan on graduate programs, see "The Connected University," Chapter 2 this book, n. 2, section on "integrating research and graduate education."

4. For a summary of the approach to graduate education in the Action and Assessment Plan, see NUA, FBF, chap. 6, "Action and Assessment Plan: Graduate Program Goals." For Lowndes report, see NUAD, A.22.B259.F12; for a summary, see NUA, PresoFiles, Hedlund Mat. Research, "Building on the Lowndes Report," March 1, 2000; for a complete summary of the report, see NUA, FBF, chap. 6.

5. A list of the thirty-one endowed professorships in existence at the time of my appointment can be found in Feldscher, pp. 289–90; a copy also can be found in NUA, FBF, chap. 6, along with documents summarizing endowment amounts for various professorships. A detailed chronology of Bluestone's appointment and achievements can be found in NUA, FBF, chap. 6, "Center for Urban and Regional Policy"; an article describing his work on housing can be found in the 2005 edition of *Synthesis*, a magazine highlighting Northeastern's interdisciplinary research, available online at https://web.archive.org/web/20060828124042/http://www.research .neu.edu/synthesis_ research_magazine/documents/synthesis05fall.pdf; a comprehensive summary of CURP work can be found in NUA, FBF, chap. 6, "Northeastern University, Dukakis Center for Urban and Regional Policy." A detailed summary of Lane's appointment and work on establishing the Institute for Global Innovation Management can be found in NUA, FBF, chap. 6, "International Business and Global Marketing." A set of documents covering the full development of the Trustee Professors program during my presidency can be found in NUA, FBF, chap. 6, labeled "Trustee Professors."

6. Documents summarizing appointments to additional named chairs and to unnamed appointments at the senior level can be found in NUA, FBF, chap. 6, "Named Chairs and Senior Appointments"; see also NUA, "A Decade of Progress," p. 3, "leading national scholars," Chapter 4 this book, n. 2.

7. For new guidelines for Research Centers and Institutes, see NUA, PresoFiles, Research Centers, Institutes, Proposals, memo, Baer to University Faculty, June 8, 1998, "Reorganization of Research Administration"; a summary of the approval process for this new policy can be found in NUA, FBF, chap. 6, "Establishing Research Centers and Institutes at Northeastern." For Office of Technology Transfer, see summary memo in NUA, FBF, chap. 6, "Technology

Transfer." For summary of successive restatements of research goals in the Action and Assessment Plan, see NUA, FBF, chap. 6, "Action and Assessment Plan: Research." For Hedlund work on restructuring research support bureaucracy, see NUA, PresoFiles, Hedlund Mat. Research; see also above, n. 7, memo, Hedlund to University Community, June 8, 1998; see also summary of this work in NUA, FBF, chap. 6, "Hedlund Materials." For doubling of investment in research support, see NUA, "A Decade of Progress," p. 9, Chapter 4 this book, n. 2. For Hall initiative requesting proposals for new research centers in 2000 and 2001, see NUA, PresoFiles, Research Institutes 2000–2001 and Research Institutes 2001–2002; see also NUA, FBF, chap. 6, "Establishing Research Centers and Institutes at Northeastern." For a list of new research centers established during my presidency, see NUA, FBF, chap. 6, "Research Centers and Institutes founded 1996–2006"; see also NUA, "A Decade of Progress," p. 9, Chapter 4 this book, n. 2. For ten-year increase in Research Expenditures from external sources, see National Science Foundation, "Survey of Research and Development Expenditures at Universities and Colleges," FY1996 and FY2006; I am indebted to Professor Robert Lowndes for help in tracking down this information; a summary of Dr. Lowndes's calculations can be found in NUA, FBF, chap. 6, "1996–2006 Research Expenditures by Source."

8. Silevitch's early work in electromagnetic research is described in Frederick, 1995, pp. 79, 141, 254. A chronology of the development of CenSSIS can be found in NUA, FBF, chap. 6, "Center for Subsurface Imaging and Sensing"; a brief account can also be found in Johnson, pp. 95–98. A chronology of the Biotech initiative can be found in NUA, FBF, chap. 6, "Biotech initiative Summary"; see also NUA, *Synthesis*, Fall 2004, above, n. 5. A chronology of the Nanotech initiative can be found in NUA, FBF, chpt. 6, "Nanotechnology at Northeastern;" see also, NUA, *Synthesis*, Fall 2004, above, n. 5.

9. For a summary of research projects exhibited at the Research Expo between 2007 and 2009, see NUA, FBF, chap. 6. For research productivity in Engineering, Pharmacy, and International Business, see NUA, "A Decade of Progress," p. 8, Chapter 4 this book, n. 2. For undergraduate research program, see NUA, *Synthesis*, Fall 2006, p. 18, above n. 5. The Office of Technology Transfer did not ultimately bring in enough revenue to justify itself and was closed after my departure; a successor organization, however, the Center for Research Innovation, was soon created to take up the core function of the Office of Technology Transfer, which was to promote the commercialization of Northeastern's research.

10. A complete file of the records of the graduate-program review can be found in NUA, PresoFiles, Graduate Program; this file contains Vice Provost Hedlund's memo to Graduate Program Directors calling for program-level self-studies, December 6, 1996; the 1997 "Report of the Graduate Review Working Group;" and a summary of the group's recommendations in a memo from Hedlund to Freeland and Hall dated October 26, 1998, "Summary of All Program Graduate Evaluation"; a summary of this process can be found in NUA, FBF, chap. 6, "Graduate Program Review Summary." It should be noted that College of Engineering Dean Allen Soyster argued strongly against closing the two "high concern" PhD programs (chemical and industrial) in the College because doing so would not save much money in the short run and, in the long run, would rob the College of programs that, with new faculty appointments, could become strong contributors to the University. I trusted Soyster and accepted his recommendation, which proved over time to have been wise.

11. A partial list of new academic programs, including new doctoral programs, established during my presidency can be found in NUA, FBF, chap. 5, "New Academic Programs 2001–2006."

12. A summary of graduate-program development in the School of Professional and Continuing Studies (the new name for University College) can be found in College of Professional Studies Academic Council for Lifelong Learning, "Overview," Chapter 3 this book, n. 13.

13. Graphs summarizing graduate enrollments during my presidency at the University and College levels can be found in NUA, FBF, chap. 6, "Graduate Enrollments, 1985–2008." See also "Sam Solomon comments on grad. enrollments" in NUA, FBF, chap. 6.

14. A chronological summary of the work of the Special Committee, including a summary of its final report, can be found in NUA, FBF, chap. 6, "Special Committee on Graduate Education." A file on the staff work supporting the Special Committee is in NUA, PresoFiles, Graduate Programs. The Committee's report was presented to the Trustees in a PowerPoint presentation on December 5, 2005. A document summarizing the targeting of resources under the Academic Investment Plan to strengthen specific graduate programs can be found in NUA, FBF, chap. 6, "AIP and Graduate Education."

## Chapter 7

1. For Special Committee, see Chapter 1 this book, n. 7; for a brief summary of the Committee's references to Northeastern's urban character, see NUA, FBF, chap. 7, "Colleen's Summary of Finnegan Report re Urban." For Strategic Planning report, see Chapter 2 this book, n. 2; see also a summary in NUA, FBF, chap. 7, "Colleen Review of Baer Report." For Curry's promise to local elementary school (Tobin Scholars Program), see Feldscher, pp. 169–70. For "best nonprofit," see Feldscher, p. 175.

2. For Penn's evolving relationship to West Philadelphia from the 1950s to 1990s, see Strom. For the Rodin years at Penn, see Rodin; for Penn's evolving attitudes under her predecessors, see Rodin, Chapter 3; see also Kromer and Kerman; and see memo, Adams to Freeland, March 7, 2005, "UPenn," in NUA, FBF, chap. 7. For Chicago, see Nash, chap. 2, and Webber. For Columbia, see Price; see also Marcuse and Potter. For Pittsburgh, see Deitrick and Soska. For St. Louis University, see Cummings, Rosentraub, Domahidy, and Coffin. For Ohio State, see Dixon and Roche. All the preceding case studies (except Price and Nash) are chapters in Perry and Weiwel, which is a rich source of case studies on the evolution of university-community relations between the 1950s and the 1990s; the book explores the full spectrum of possibilities regarding a university's path to active cooperation with a troubled urban neighborhood, from initial efforts to erect barriers to community encroachments, to major conflict triggered by demolition and relocation, to reasonable levels of cooperation from the beginning. For Yale and Trinity, see Grunwald, p. A03; a copy is in NUA, FBF, chap. 7. For Urban 13 and Great Cities Universities, see Diner, p. 128. An additional organization of urban public universities that emerged in these years in close association with APLU and promoted engagement between universities and host cities was the Coalition of Urban Serving Universities (CUSU). For broad trends in university-community partnerships and renewed interest in urban research, see Diner, chap. 6.

3. There is a rich literature on this pattern; see Maurrasse; Campbell; Fisher, 2006; Levenson; Diner, chap. 6.

4. For high level of interest in urban issues among Northeastern faculty, including results of faculty survey, see NUA, 1998 reaccreditation, vol. 1., p. 85, Chapter 2 this book, n. 4; see also "Northeastern as an Urban University, Findings and Recommendations, NEASC Urban Task Force Report," NUA, FBF, chap. 7. For Urban Outreach Council, see NUA, PresoFiles, Urban Outreach Council. For AAP "urban" section, see Chapter 2 this book, n. 5.

5. For popularity of urban campuses in the 1990s, see statement by Robert Franek, publisher of the *Princeton Review* and vice president of admissions services, quoted in "New York

University Tops Harvard as Students' Dream College," Bloomberg.com, March 24, 2005: "Over the last five to eight years, urban schools have had an incredible renaissance with college students"; a copy is in NUA, FBF, chap. 7. For Boston's economic revitalization, see Bluestone and Stevenson.

6. For Center for Community Service, see NUA, FBF, chap. 7, "Center for Community Service." For School of Social Science, Public Policy and Urban Affairs, see NUA, FBF, chap. 7, "School of Social Science, Public Policy and Urban Affairs."

7. For family income of entering freshman and Pell students, see documents grouped together under the title "Discussion of Pell, Financial Aid," including table "Estimated Family Income," Chapter 4 this book, n. 6; the twenty-fifth percentile of students applying for financial aid rose from $27,000 in 2001 to $51,500 in 2006. For data on minority enrollments, see NUA, NUFB 1996 and 2006. For our goals with respect to student diversity, see "Enrollment Management and Student Affairs Division Unit Plan, 2003-2008," Goal 2.2, Chapter 4 this book, n. 11; a brief summary is in NUA, FBF, chap. 7, "Notes on Diversity of Freshman Class." For data on diversity of Northeastern's faculty in 1996 and 2006, see NUAD, A22.B177.F035, "Diversity Overview, Fall 1996," Office of Institutional Research, October 1997, and NUAD, Institutional Self Study for NEASC Reaccreditation, September 2008, p. 44. The University's records of persistence and graduation for various student groups are incomplete; the statement on improving persistence of students of color is based on freshman-to-sophomore retention data for 1996 to 2002; see tables in NUA, FBF, chap. 7.

8. For Boston Public High School Scholarship Program, see NUA, FBF, chap. 7, memo, Mantella to Freeland, March 10, 2016; NUA, FBF, chap. 7, memo, Mantella to Freeland, March 9, 2004, "Notes for Mayor's Meeting"; NUA, FBF, chap. 7, "Boston Area Scholarships." For Northeastern providing more scholarship support for Boston Public School students than other institutions, see NUA, FBF, chap.7, memo, Turner to Freeland, March 11, 2016; see also NUAD, "Northeastern and Our Neighbors: A Partnership for Vibrant Communities," Northeastern University, c. 2006; a copy is in NUA, FBF, chap. 7; see also CorpAdrs. 2006, Chapter 2 this book, n. 2. For material on Mantella's work to increase enrollments from Boston Public Schools, see NUA, PresoFiles, Mantella self-evaluation reports in folders for 2004 and 2005; see also, in same file, "Enrollment Management and Student Affairs Unit Plan, 2004." For a comprehensive summary of outreach efforts to Boston Public Schools, including Case work and $34.5 million figure, see NUA, FBF, chap. 7, "Work with BPS."

9. A comprehensive list of Northeastern's urban-oriented research activities can be found in NUA, PAR 2004-2005. A list of centers founded during my presidency is in NUA, FBF, chap. 7, "Research Centers and Institutes founded 1996-2006." For significance of distinction between being "in" a city and "of" a city, see Chapter. 1 this book, n. 3. For close working relationship between the School of Social Science Public Policy and Urban Affairs and city hall, see NUA, FBF, chap. 7, memo, Bluestone to Freeland, March 15, 2016.

10. For brief summaries of the Renaissance Park and Davenport Commons projects, see NUA, FBF, chap. 7, "Renaissance Park Timeline" and "Davenport Commons." For Davenport, see Calder, Grant, and Muson.

11. For inventory of community-service activities, see NUA, FBF, chap. 7; see also above, n. 8, "Northeastern and Our Neighbors." For growing student presence in community and tensions with neighbors, see Watson as well as Bombardieri; summaries of both articles can be found in NUA, FBF, chap. 7, "Student Residential Patterns." For continuing significance of this issue, see BG editorial, "Avoid Town-Gown Disputes: Get Moving on New Dorms," January 17, 2010; a copy is in NUA, FBF, chap. 7.

12. For events surrounding the Super Bowl riot, see the following articles in *BG*, "Antici-pation, Preparation for Super Bowl Battle," Michael Rosenwald and Jenna Russell, January 31, 2004; "Driver Plows into Revelers Near NU," Scott Greenberger, February 2, 2004; "Boston Lowlife," editorial, February 3, 2004; "No More Riots," editorial, February 5, 2004; "Colleges Say Their Officers Doing All They Can," Marcella Bombardieri, February 6, 2004; "Northeast-ern to Give Police Names of 12," Heather Allen, February 13, 2004; "Quiet Riot," editorial, Feb-ruary 15, 2004; "Winning, and Losing It," Carla Reidy, *Boston Globe Magazine*, February 22, 2004; "Ivy League Scandal to Hit Newsstands," Campus Insider, February 22, 2004; "NU Can-cels Rap Show in Response to Rioting," Marcella Bombardieri, February 26, 2004; "Canceled NU Concert Stirs Anger and Debate," Ralph Ranalli and Heather Allen, February 27, 2004; "A Lesson at Northeastern," editorial, February 28, 2004; "Lack of Community Spirit" and "Hard Lesson for NU students," letters to the editor by Stephen Redding and Chris Lohmann, March 1, 2004; "Charges Sought Against 6 after Super Bowl," Marcella Bombardieri, March 13, 2004; "Drinking Games," Donovan Slack, *Boston Globe Magazine*, March 24, 2004; "Few Hours Get Focus in Death of Student," John Ellement and Marcella Bombardieri, March 20, 2004; "NU's Growing Pains," Marcella Bombardieri, undated; a complete collection of these articles is in NUA, FBF, chap. 7.

13. Freeland, 2005. The four coauthored pieces were published in the "Campus Viewpoints" feature of *CHE* in the summer of 2006; copies of three of them—May 5, June 19, and July 8—are available in digital form from NUA. For Boston Foundation Report, see, The Boston Foundation (TBF) Web site, Reports, "A New Era for Higher Education-Community Partnerships," October 11, 2005.

## Chapter 8

1. For consultant reports, see NUA, PresoFiles, Marketing [1997], "A Review of the Mar-keting and Communications Programs, Northeastern University," Dick Jones Communications, July 1997; NUA, PresoFiles, Marketing [1999], "Northeastern Competitive Terrain," MagiKbox (Keeshan), April 26, 1999; also NUA, PresoFiles, Marketing [1999] "Strategic Marketing Plan Final Report," June 22, 1999, MagiKbox. For outcomes of initial marketing discussions, see NUA, PresoFiles, Marketing [1999], memo Freeland to Hall, Meyer, and Mucciolo, "Next Steps in Marketing Efforts," September 1, 1999; see also NUA, PresoFiles, Marketing [1999], memo Freeland to Senior Vice Presidents, "Strategic Communication Planning, 1999-2000," Septem-ber 10, 1999. For a summary chronology of marketing work from 1997 to 2005, see NUA, FBF, chap. 8, "Chronology of Branding/Marketing at Northeastern University."

2. Charge to University Relations to develop initial plan included in September 10, 1999, memo from Freeland to Senior Vice Presidents et al., see above, n. 1; see also NUA, FBF, chap. 8 "Chronology of Branding/Marketing at Northeastern University. For University Relations plan, see NUA, PresoFiles, Marketing [2001], "Northeastern University Strategic Marketing Plan: 1/2001"; a summary can be found in NUA, FBF, chap. 8. For investments under King and Kenny, see NUA, FBF, chap. 8, "Branding Campaign Summary"; see also NUA, FBF, chap. 8, memo, Solomon to Freeland, January 18, 2017, "one other thing." For Northeastern as marketing leader, see NUA, FBF, chap. 8, National Center for Public Policy and Higher Education, *Crosstalk*, sum-mer 2006. Brian Kenny believes Northeastern was the first university to have a vice president for marketing reporting directly to the president.

3. For sample quotations from my speeches to the campus community promoting a heightened appreciation of Northeastern's quality and status, see NUA, PresoFiles, FBF, chap.

8, "Speeches: Enhancing Public Perceptions of NU." My claim about Northeastern's preeminence in entrepreneurship is based on Roberts, p. 63; for relevant quote, see NUA, FBF, chap. 8, "Edward Baer Roberts."

4. A summary of my board memberships, speeches, opinion pieces, and other writings over the course of my presidency can be found in NUA, FBF, chap. 8, "Presidential Speeches." The flurry of Boston-area stories about Northeastern's progress in 2004–2005 included pieces in the *Boston Business Journal* and *Boston Magazine* as well as a feature TV segment on WCVB's "Evening Chronicle"; see CorpAdrs 2005, Chapter 2 this book, n. 2. One amusing result of my efforts to become visible in the Boston community was being named one of the fifty most powerful people in the city by *Boston Magazine* in its April 2012 issue. For *Chronicle* story, see *CHE*, "No Longer a Safety School," April 23, 2004; excerpts can be found in NUA, FBF, chap. 8, "*Chronicle* Article on NU."

5. A summary of the branding campaign, including budget allocations, can be found in NUA, FBF, chap. 8, "Branding Campaign Summary."

6. For research on effectiveness of branding campaign, see NUA, PresoFiles, Marketing [2003], "Northeastern University, Branding Discussion," December 15, 2003. For Northeastern' s becoming more competitive, see study by Kane Parsons and Associates in spring 2003 comparing our "win rate" against the major New England public universities with respect to students accepted by both between 2000 and 2003; the numbers were striking; Northeastern went from enrolling 40 percent of shared acceptances to 73 percent vs. UMass Amherst; from 34 percent to 71 percent vs. UConn; from 50 percent to 78 percent vs UNH; and from 65 percent to 75 percent vs URI; see also NUA, PresoFiles, Leadership Retreat [September 2003], PowerPoint presentation "Leadership Retreat, 9/18/2003," p. 9. For leadership team assessments, see NUA, PresoFiles, Marketing [2004], "Memo to Senior Vice Presidents, 'Review of Branding Campaign, 2-02-04,'" January 29, 2004.

7. For revisions in branding campaign under Kenny, see NUA, PresoFiles, Marketing [2003], "Northeastern University, Branding Discussion," December 15, 2003; NUA, PresoFiles, Marketing [2004], email, Monsen to Patrick et al., May 14, 2004, "headline creative from yesterday's branding meeting" with attached PowerPoint presentation titled "fall planning" NUA, PresoFiles, Marketing [2005], "Northeastern University Integrated Marketing and Branding," PowerPoint presentation for President's Cabinet, November 17, 2005. For national recognition of our efforts, see *Crosstalk* article, above, n. 2. Interestingly, although we thought our entering freshmen were becoming more focused on continuing their education after college, in reality the percentage going to graduate school was generally stable between 1998 and 2006, fluctuating between 13 percent and 18 percent; see NUA, FBF, chap. 8, "NU Students Going to Graduate School."

8. For declining alumni/ae support, see NUA, PresoFiles, Alumni Relations, "Trends and Patterns in the Alumni Giving Rate at Northeastern," Office of University Planning and Research, July 14, 2005. For new funding to support Moynihan initiatives, see NUA, FBF, chap. 8, memo, Solomon to Freeland, "one other thing," January 18, 2017.

9. For a summary of efforts to strengthen alumni/ae relations work, see NUA, FBF, chap. 8, "Alumni Relations"; see also NUA, PresoFiles, Alumni Relations, "Richard M. Freeland, President, Alumni Relations Assessment, 11/2/2005." For Kenny plan, see NUA, PresoFiles, Alumni Relations, "Alumni Relations and Advancement Marketing Plan," June 2005, with cover note from Kenny dated June 27, 2005. For a summary of alumni/ae relations initiatives, see CorpAdrs 2005, Chapter 2 this book, n. 2. I am indebted to former Senior Vice President for Development

Eugene Reppucci Jr. for his thoughtful and confirming review of my characterization of Northeastern's traditional efforts with respect to alumni/ae relations.

10. In September 2014, *Boston Magazine* ran a story on Northeastern titled "How to Game the College Rankings." While the piece was generally accurate in portraying the way my team and I approached rankings (and actually contrasted our honest but tactical efforts to the readiness of other institutions to submit false or misleading information), we were not happy in the title's implication that we were less than scrupulous in advancing our cause. The piece also mistakenly attributed to our focus on the rankings decisions that were taken for quite different and more substantively important reasons, such as launching a major program of residential construction or accepting the Common Application for Freshman Admissions. One case in point is slightly ambiguous and worth noting: Northeastern regularly admitted students in January because of attrition during the fall semester; this was a revenue-driven decision that preceded and was unrelated to our work on the rankings. Our goal was to keep our seat count as close to capacity as possible. Early in my presidency we focused on admitting transfer students for January admissions but later switched to admitting freshmen who were not as well qualified as those we admitted for the fall. We did this because these freshman applicants were academically stronger than the transfers we had been admitting. In both cases—transfers and freshmen—the goal was revenue. A comprehensive list of relevant OUPR studies, together with other examples of OUPR work on the rankings, can be found in NUA, FBF, chap. 8, "OUPR Work on Rankings"; see also NUA, FBF, chap. 8, memo Putnam to Freeland, March 20, 2017, "A Question." For how we set goals based on comparisons with the "lucky 13," see CorpAdrs 2000, Chapter 2 this book, n. 2, including slides.

11. For role of Academic Investment Plan in Top-100 strategy, see NUA, FBF, chap. 8, "The Top 100 and AIP." Regarding faculty salary increases, we allocated $2.5 million for this purpose between FY2004 and FY2007; see also NUA, FBF, chap. 8, memo, Solomon to Freeland, "a question," January 18, 2017, with attachment "operating budget increases" for FY2004 to FY2007; see also NUA, FBF, chap. 8, PowerPoint presentation by the Financial Affairs Committee of the Faculty Senate, 2004, "Improving Faculty Compensation and Becoming a Top 100 University."

12. For discussion of co-op enrollments and cost-of-living adjustments in *U.S. News* formula, see NUA, FBF, chap. 8, letter, Freeland to Morse, January 11, 2005. OUPR's work on the cost-of-living issue was presented to the Association of Institutional Research at its Boston Forum in 2004; a brief summary is in NUA, FBF, chap. 8, "Faculty Salary/Cost of Living." Our efforts to subtract co-op enrollments from the computation of "financial resources" was inspired by a suggestion from a Moody's analyst during a regular bond-rating review; see NUA, FBF, chap. 8, memo, Richman to Bak, "FTE enrollment," January 4, 2005, and attached "Northeastern University, Strategic Financial Assessment."

13. A document summarizing the 747 project can be found in NUA, FBF, chap. 8, "474 [sic] Project." See also, in NUA, FBF, chap. 8, a table displaying Northeastern's peer assessment rating from 1998 to 2013.

14. A table displaying Northeastern's overall rank from 1997 to 2007 can be found in NUA, FBF, chap. 8, "Northeastern' s Overall Rank, *U.S. News* 1997–2007 Editions." For recognition of Northeastern's success in improving its ranking, see Max Kutner, "How to Game the College Rankings," *Boston Magazine*, September 20, 2014; *Boston Business Journal* quote is on p. 158; Robert Oakes, "How Northeastern Cracked the Code to the *U.S. News* College Ranking System," *WBUR*, September 9, 2014 (online edition); *Legally Sociable* (online newsletter), February 12, 2016. As a postscript, Northeastern continued to climb steadily in the *U.S. News* rankings under

my successor, reaching forty by 2018, an outcome that was beyond my wildest dreams when we started work on the rankings in 2000; see http://www.usnews.com/rankings/best-colleges /national-universities.

## Chapter 9

1. Data on improved student selectivity, academic preparation, geographic diversity, persistence, and graduation rates, as well as the expansion of the full-time faculty are presented in Chapter 4; that chapter also includes information on facilities improvements, including growth of the residential population, as well as on student satisfaction surveys. Information on improvements in the co-op program is presented in Chapter 5. Data on the growth of the faculty, the appointment of senior faculty and named chairs, the overall increase in research expenditures, and the establishment of centers of scholarly excellence can be found in Chapter 6. Changes in the ethnic and racial diversity of Northeastern students and faculty are presented in Chapter 7, along with data on the socioeconomic diversity of students. Changes in Northeastern's "overlap schools" are discussed in Chapter 8, including note 6. The number of applications to Northeastern continued to grow steadily during the years after my presidency. By the fall of 2016, total freshman applications had roughly doubled (to 51,000) since 2006 when I stepped down. The average freshman SAT score was now 1426, having increased by nearly 200 points, from 1230 over the same years. The acceptance rate had tightened from 49 percent to 29 percent. Geographic diversity had also continued to grow, with enrollment of students from Massachusetts and New England declining from 56 percent to 35 percent of the class, while numbers from the Southeast, Midwest, and West had grown, as had international enrollments; see NUA, NUFB 2016–17; copies of key tables are in NUA, FBF, chap. 9, "NU Freshman Profile Data, 2016." Also Northeastern continued to climb steadily on the *U.S News* rankings, reaching fortieth by 2018, Chapter 8 this book, n. 14.

2. Clark, pp. 327–33.

3. Fisher, 1984, 1991; Fisher, Tack, and Wheeler; Jencks and Riesman; Kerr; Association of Governing Boards, 1984, 1996; Cohen and March; Birnbaum, R. 1988, 1991; Weick. For a more extended discussion of these issues, see Freeland, 2001.

4. International enrollment goals can be found in Enrollment Management and Student Affairs unit plan for 2003–2008, Chapter 4 this book, n. 6.

5. Hamilton, p. 21.

6. Sachar, p. 207.

# BIBLIOGRAPHY

Alberts, Robert C. *Pitt: The Story of the University of Pittsburgh, 1787–1987*. Pittsburgh: University of Pittsburgh Press, 1986.

American Council on Education, Special Commission on Campus Tensions. *Campus Tensions: Analysis and Recommendations*. Washington, DC, 1970.

Assembly on University Goals and Governance. *A First Report*. Cambridge, MA: American Academy of Arts and Sciences, 1971.

Association of Governing Boards of Universities and Colleges, Report of the Commission on the Academic Presidency. *Presidents Will Lead—If We Let Them*. Washington DC, 1984.

———. Report of the Commission on the Academic Presidency. *Renewing the Academic Presidency: Stronger Leadership for Tougher Times*. Washington DC, 1996.

Association of Urban Universities. Proceedings of the Annual Meeting: 1930, 1959.

Berube, Maurice R. *The Urban University in America*. Westport, CT: Greenwood, 1978.

Birnbaum, Robert. *How Colleges Work: the Cybernetics of Academic Organization and Leadership*. San Francisco: Jossey-Bass, 1988.

———. *How Academic Leadership Works: Understanding Success and Failure in the College Presidency*. San Francisco: Jossey-Bass, 1992.

Bluestone, Barry, and Mary Huff Stevenson. *The Boston Renaissance*. New York: Russell Sage, 2000.

Bombardieri, Marcella. "NU's Growing Pains: School Struggles to Reshape Itself as a Good Neighbor." *Boston Globe*, April 6, 2004.

Calder, Allegra, Gabriel Grant, Holly Hart Muson. "No Such Thing as Vacant Land: Northeastern University and Davenport Commons," chap. 14. In David C. Perry and Wim Wiewel, eds., *The University as Urban Developer*. Armonk, NY: M. E. Sharpe, 2005.

Campbell, Robert. "Universities Are the New City Planners." *Boston Globe*, March 20, 2005.

Carnegie Commission on Higher Education. *A Digest of Reports of the Carnegie Commission on Higher Education*. New York: McGraw-Hill, 1974.

Chandler, Alfred D. *Strategy and Structure: Chapters in the History of American Industrial Enterprise*. Cambridge, MA: MIT Press, 1962.

Clark, Burton. "Organizational Adaptation and Precarious Values: A Case Study." *American Sociological Review* (June 1956): 327–33.

Cohen, Michael D., and James G. March. *Leadership and Ambiguity: The American College President*. New York: McGraw-Hill, 1974.

Collins, Jim, and Jerry Porras. *Built to Last: Successful Habits of Visionary Companies*. New York: Harper Collins, 1994.

Cummings, Scott, Mark Rosentraub, Mary Domahidy, and Sarah Coffin. "University Involve-
    ment in Downtown Revitalization," chap. 9. In David C. Perry and Wim Wiewel, eds., *The
    University as Urban Developer*. Armonk, NY: M. E. Sharpe, 2005.
Deitrick, Sabina, and Tracy Soska. "The University of Pittsburgh and the Oakland Neighbor-
    hood," chap. 2. In David C. Perry and Wim Wiewel, eds., *The University as Urban Developer*.
    Armonk, NY: M. E. Sharpe, 2005.
Diner, Steven J. *Universities and Their Cities*. Baltimore: Johns Hopkins University Press, 2017.
Dixon, David, and Peter J. Roche. "Campus Partners and the Ohio State University," chap. 15.
    In David C. Perry and Wim Wiewel, eds., *The University as Urban Developer*. Armonk, NY:
    M. E. Sharpe, 2005.
Dolence, Michael G., and David M. Norris. "Using Key Performance Indictors to Drive Strategic
    Decision Making," *New Directions in Institutional Research*, No. 82. San Francisco: Jossey-
    Bass, Summer 1994.
Elliott, Peggy G. *The Urban Campus*. Phoenix, AZ: American Council on Education, Oryx Press,
    1994.
Feldscher, Karen. *The Curry Years: Smaller but Better, Northeastern University, 1989-1996*. Bos-
    ton: Northeastern University, 2000.
Fisher, James L. *The Power of the Presidency*. New York: Macmillan, 1984.
———. *The Board and the President*. New York: Macmillan, 1991
Fisher, James L., Martha W. Tack, and Karen J. Wheeler. *The Effective College President*. Phoenix,
    AZ: American Council on Education, Oryx Press, 1988.
Fisher, Karen. "The University as Economic Savior." *Chronicle of Higher Education*, July 14, 2006.
Frederick, Antoinette. *Northeastern University, Coming of Age: The Ryder Years*. Boston: North-
    eastern University, 1995.
———. *Northeastern University: An Emerging Giant: 1959–1975*. Boston: Northeastern Univer-
    sity, 1982.
Freeland, Richard M. *Academia's Golden Age: Universities in Massachusetts, 1945–1970*. New
    York: Oxford, 1992.
———. "Academic Change and Presidential Leadership." In Philip G. Altbach, Patricia J. Gum-
    port, and D. Bruce Johnstone, eds., *In Defense of American Higher Education*. Baltimore:
    Johns Hopkins University Press, 2001.
———. "Universities and Cities Need to Rethink Their Relationships." *Chronicle of Higher Edu-
    cation*, Point of View, May 13, 2005.
Gardner, John W. *No Easy Victories*. New York: Harper and Row, 1968.
Grunwald, Michael. "Colleges Embracing Towns They Once Held at Arm's Length." *Washington
    Post*, June 6, 1999.
Hamilton, Edith. *The Greek Way to Western Civilization*. New York: New American Library,
    Mentor Book, 1948.
Jencks, Christopher, and David Riesman. *The Academic Revolution*. Garden City, NY: Double-
    day, 1968.
Johnson, Wayne C. "Industry as a Catalyst for Innovation." In Luc E. Weber and James J. Duder-
    stadt, eds., *University Research for Innovation*. London: Economica, 2010.
Kerr, Clark. *The Uses of the University*. Cambridge, MA: Harvard University Press, 1963.
Klotsche, J. Martin. *The Urban University*. New York: Harper and Row, 1966.
Kolbe, Parke R. *Urban Influences on Higher Education in England and the United States*. New
    York: Macmillan, 1928.

Kromer, John, and Lucy Kerman. "West Philadelphia Initiatives: A Case Study in Urban Revitalization." Philadelphia: University of Pennsylvania, 2004.

Levenson, Michael. "Nonprofit Groups Found to Add to Job Market." *Boston Globe*, March 6, 2005.

Levine, David O. *The American College and the Culture of Aspiration.* Ithaca, NY: Cornell University Press, 1986.

Marcuse, Peter, and Cuz Potter. "Columbia University's Heights: An Ivory Tower and Its Communities," chap. 3. In David C. Perry and Wim Wiewel, eds., *The University as Urban Developer.* Armonk, NY: M. E. Sharpe, 2005.

Marston, Everett C. *Origin and Development of Northeastern University.* Boston: Northeastern University, 1961.

Maurrasse, David J. *Beyond the Campus: How Colleges and Universities Form Partnerships with Their Communities.* New York: Routledge, 2001.

Nash, George. *The University and the City.* New York: McGraw-Hill, 1973.

Pascarella, Ernest T., and Patrick T. Terenzini. *How College Affects Students.* San Francisco: Jossey-Bass, 2005.

Perry, David C., and Wim Wiewel, eds. *The University as Urban Developer.* Armonk, NY: M. E. Sharpe, 2005.

President's Task Force on Higher Education. *Priorities in Higher Education.* Washington, DC: GPO, August 1970.

Price, Robert. "Turning Columbia Around," chap. 9. In George Nash, ed., *The University and the City.* New York: McGraw-Hill, 1973.

Roberts, Edward B. *Entrepreneurs in High Technology: Lessons from MIT and Beyond.* New York: Oxford University Press, 1991.

Rodin, Judith. *The University and Urban Revival.* Philadelphia: University of Pennsylvania Press, 2007.

Rudolph, Frederick. *The American College and University.* New York: Alfred Knopf, 1962.

Sachar, Abram. *A Host at Last.* Boston: Atlantic Monthly Press, 1976.

Shaw, Kenneth. *The Intentional Leader.* Syracuse, NY: Syracuse University Press, 2005.

Shils, Edward. "The University, the City, and the World." In Thomas Bender, ed., *The University and the City.* New York: Oxford, 1988.

Strom, Elizabeth. "The Political Strategies Behind University Based Development," chap. 7, In David C. Perry and Wim Wiewel, eds., *The University as Urban Developer.* Armonk, NY: M. E. Sharpe, 2005.

Teaford, Jon C. *The Twentieth Century American City.* Baltimore: Johns Hopkins University Press, 1986.

Thelin, John R. *A History of American Higher Education.* Baltimore: Johns Hopkins University Press, 2004.

Waetjen, Walter B., and John A. Muffo. "The Urban University: Model for Actualization." *Review of Higher Education* 6, no. 3 (Spring 1983).

Watson, Jamal. "Students Head for the Hill." *Boston Globe*, March 5, 2001.

Webber, Henry. "The University of Chicago and Its Neighbors," chap. 4. In David C. Perry and Wim Wiewel, eds., *The University as Urban Developer.* Armonk, NY: M. E. Sharpe, 2005.

Weick, Karl. "Educational Organizations as Loosely Coupled Systems." *Administrative Science Quarterly* 21 (1976).

# INDEX

AAP. *See* Action and Assessment Plan

Abdelal, Ahmed, 107, 110, 121, 122, 124, 128–29, 171, 183

academic calendar. *See* semester calendar

academic freedom, 56

Academic Investment Plan (Northeastern), 70, 78, 107, 121, 122, 130, 168, 175

accreditation, of universities, 40–41

Action and Assessment Plan (AAP), 42, 44–45, 49, 58–60, 117, 120, 137–38, 166–67, 182

admissions process, at Northeastern: criteria in, 91; demographic figures pertinent to, 36; diversity as factor in, 140–43, 213n1; finances in relation to, 68; for graduate programs, 128–29; international students, 183; January admissions, 212n10; marketing in relation to, 159, 161; numbers of applicants, 213n1; strengthening of, 29, 75, 79–81, 90–91; urban engagement as influence on, 2, 3, 138–43. *See also* selectivity, in Northeastern admissions process

admissions process, in universities: of BU and BC, 27; of urban universities, 2, 3, 27; adult and continuing education, 8, 19, 68–69. *See also* selectivity, in university admissions process

advertising. *See* branding campaign; marketing

advertorials, 162, 171

African Americans, 2, 22, 141. *See also* diversity

alignment, difficulty of achieving in universities, 56–60

Allen, Linda, 105

alumni/ae, of Northeastern: co-op valued by, 93; financial gifts from, 53, 66–67, 89, 123, 164; professorships funded by, 118–19;

programming for, 53; their perceptions of Northeastern, 164; university relations with, 159, 163–65

American Council on Education, 161

American Institute of Architects, 87

America Online, 162

Amherst College, 45

anchor institutions, urban universities as, 137

Angel, James, 180

annual reports, of Northeastern President, 71, 92, 96, 106, 113, 153, 159

Antioch College, 93

Aoun, Joseph, *xv*, 176

Arizona State University, 73

Asian-American students, 141. *See also* diversity

Aspiration, 43–44, 49, 50, 51, 54, 58–59, 137, 156, 158, 166–72, 177, 182. *See also* Mantra; strategic formula; Vision Statement

Association for Computing Machinery, 119

Association of American Colleges and Universities, 111

Association of Governing Boards, 180

Association of Public and Land-grant Universities, 135

Association of Urban Universities (AUU): dissolution of, 4, 8, 13, 24; history of, 1–3, 13, 16–17; membership of, 1, 25; principles of, 1, 3–4, 12, 13, 16; responses of, to urban decline, 2–3, 22–24; urban commitment of, 19–20

athletics, at Northeastern, 160

athletic stadium, at Northeastern, 89

*Atlantic*, Freeland article in, 111

authority, university presidents' establishment of, 188–90

autonomy, as academic value, 56, 98, 157–58

AUU. *See* Association of Urban Universities